Time Molecules

The Business Intelligence Side of Process Mining and Systems Thinking

Eugene Asahara

Technics Publications
SEDONA, ARIZONA

115 Linda Vista
Sedona, AZ 86336 USA

https://www.TechnicsPub.com

Edited by Steve Hoberman

Cover design by Lorena Molinari

First Printing 2025

ISBN, print ed.	9781634627481
ISBN, Kindle ed.	9781634627498
ISBN, PDF ed.	9781634627504

Library of Congress Control Number: 2025935833

Contents at a Glance

Contents

Figures

Tables

Code

Prologue

We must train ourselves to think at the level of integrated processes and systems, not at the fragmented level of "things". The world in which we're immersed is not made up of isolated, static objects but of interconnected, evolving processes—nested, linked, and parallel. Yet, we're usually conditioned to isolate our understanding of systems to reductionist, discrete, specialized tasks—sub-components of a system.

This book will show you how to apply the principles of process mining and systems thinking to business intelligence (BI), pushing Markov models beyond their traditional utilization, and integrating event logs to uncover the hidden patterns driving your organization. That is, beyond providing fragments of insights, leaving the heavy connecting of the dots to our weary intellect, that actually learned to dislike seeing the forest for the trees.

By rethinking how we process and analyze events, Time Molecules empowers readers to go beyond traditional BI metrics like sums and counts, integrating the dynamic nature of processes into analytical insights.

Though efficient in the short term, the mindset of "thing-based analysis" robs us of something deeper: the skill to readily see the emergent nature of systems, the way small interactions cascade into larger effects, and the wonder inherent in how processes evolve over time. By focusing primarily on the speed and efficiency of our mechanistic processes (workflows), we risk missing the insights and opportunities that come from truly understanding the relationships between events, the interplay of systems, and the hidden patterns they reveal.

Time Molecules is about reclaiming this insight. By thinking in terms of interacting processes rather than the qualities of isolated things, we gain a clearer understanding of how systems work, how they interact, how they change, and how we can shape them. This shift in perspective isn't just about improving efficiency; it's about embracing the complexity and beauty of the systems we inhabit. It's about moving beyond merely solving problems to uncovering the deeper truths that emerge when we see the world for what it is: a tapestry of evolving, interconnected processes.

Every business is a set of processes. Even if the processes are well understood, it's imperative to be cognizant of how these systems and their interaction with other systems are evolving. When our view into the innards of an enterprise is primarily through traditional BI, it's easy to lose sight of the complexity and richness of the real world. The data captured in our databases is not a mirror of reality but a selective shadow—a distillation of what we believe is important enough to measure and track. Most would say that's a good thing since we've filtered out the noise of the messy world. But that noise isn't separate from our processes.

Despite such a fragmented view of the enterprise, businesses, like living organisms or intricate machines, do exist and thrive in the real world, adapting to unpredictable and dynamic forces. They do not simply follow static plans; they metabolize, react, and evolve to their environments. This dynamic nature of businesses, teeming with interactions and dependencies, reveals a complexity that our BI systems often reduce (flatten) into simplified abstractions. But through the heroics of the human workers, each an intelligent agent scattered through the enterprise like our T cells, the business' life continues.

Further, businesses don't exist in a vacuum. They are a system of processes, intricately linked to other systems of processes, both within and beyond the enterprise and within taxonomies of levels. Each process is not just an isolated mechanism, but part of a dynamic ecosystem where interactions evolve and influence one another. The compact form of these interacting, evolving processes is what we model as Markov models—capturing the essence of how systems behave, adapt, and transform over time. Embracing this perspective not only enhances how we design and interpret these systems, but also reminds us that beneath the abstractions lies a living, interconnected reality, constantly in motion.

Intuition for Time Molecules

I like to start my live presentations with a little meditation—a fun angle at the topic to ease our minds into the subject at hand. In this case, I'd like to share an analogy of time molecules to a core concept of life on Earth. These thoughts were inspired over many days of hiking through the mesas and canyons of Capitol Reef over the past few Springs.

I struggled with whether to include this topic in the book. I decided to leave it in because it vividly illustrates the root of what this book is about. As sentient creatures living in a time when AI has taken a massive leap forward, we ought to reflect on what makes our own intelligence special. As we move through the world, we often recognize two or more things happening together—or we sense faint echoes between something we see now and something we've seen before. Our curiosity instinctively kicks in. We wonder how they're connected, or whether they might be manifestations of a common pattern. We follow these analogies, tracing their lower-level similarities, exploring correlations—stretching the analogy until it finally breaks. But from that playful exercise, we're usually rewarded with insights we wouldn't have discovered otherwise.

With that said, let's examine a system of what we normally think of as molecules, proteins, to what I'm calling time molecules. Obviously, the analogy isn't perfect—biology is very complex, but so are the processes we all deal with in our businesses and daily lives.

I've long thought of a compelling analogy between the business concepts in this book and the very essence of life on Earth—our DNA. Although I'm not a microbiologist, the parallels are intriguing, especially when thinking about BI and event processing. DNA, chains comprised of four types of building blocks, "ACGT" molecules, serve as a kind of recipe or playbook—a foundational plan. But the ACGT molecules are not the same as the 20 amino acids that make up proteins, which are the actual building blocks of life.

Of course, it's important to clarify that while the analogy to DNA is helpful for framing these ideas, it's not a one-to-one comparison. DNA operates differently than business processes; it's not inherently sequential in its use, and biological systems often function in parallel rather than the stepwise manner seen in workflows modeled by tools like Markov models. This limitation doesn't detract from the inspiration DNA provides, but it does remind us to appreciate the distinct nature of the systems we're discussing.

Recipes, for example, are nothing like the objects created from them. The recipe for a dish is a bunch of paper and ink, while the dish it describes is fabricated and assembled from real ingredients. DNA is the design, while proteins are the building blocks of the physical realization of that design.

In a similar way, in the world of business, we have plans, models, and documentation—things like UML diagrams, design documents, and even PowerPoint decks. Collectively, these form the "DNA" of our enterprise, the recipes for complex systems. The artifacts are studied by armies of knowledge workers, who, like RNA, translate those plans into action. The events these systems produce—transactions, processes, decisions—are like the amino acids, forming sequences that drive the system forward.

Just as amino acids combine to form peptides, events of a business combine into sequences, following patterns that can be captured and analyzed. And much like proteins, these sequences of events can be modeled and understood through Markov models, providing insight into how systems evolve and interact. Figure 1 shows a set of Markov models that are distillations of various business processes. It does look like a soup of molecules.

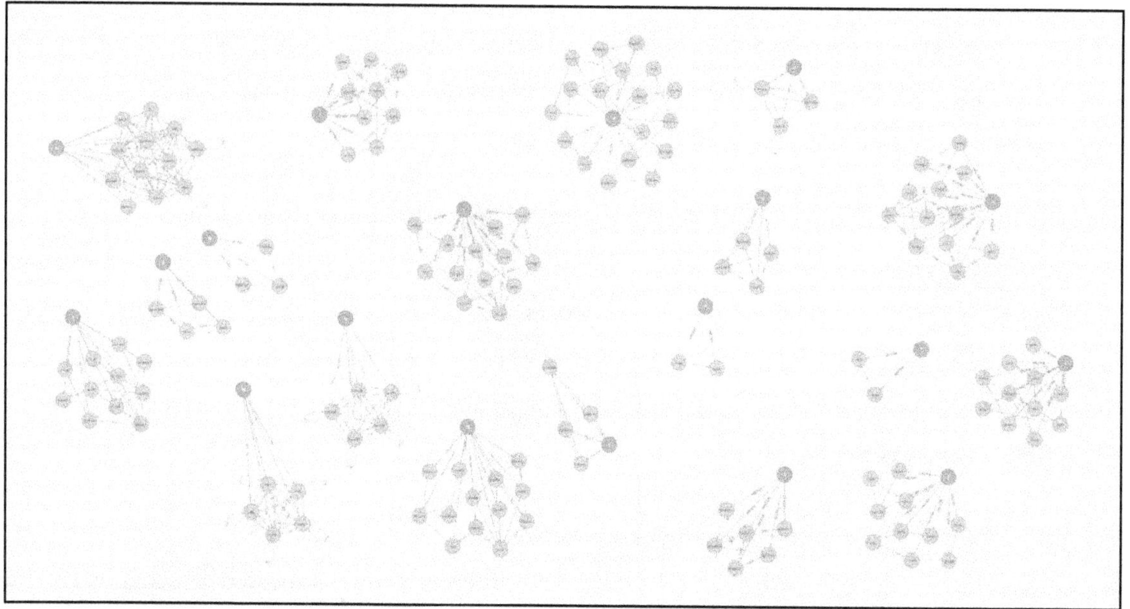

Figure 1: Markov models resemble molecules. They are compressions of processes.

Table 1 maps the biological concepts to BI concepts.

Biological Concept	Business Intelligence Concept	Context Explanation
Amino Acids	Events	**Biological:** A set of 20 types of molecules which are the "Lego-level" element of life. **Business:** Individual events (transactions, interactions) are the fundamental units.
DNA	Recipe, playbooks, Documents (UML, CAD, etc.)	These are the plans that guide the development of an organism or business systems. In both cases, the plans are physically nothing like the real-world phenomenon they describe.
RNA – mRNA and tRNA	System Facilitators (Human and Robots)	**Biological:** Translate what is encoded in DNA into the functioning systems, like mRNA directing ribosomes. **Business:** The people or machines/robots working in an assembly plant.
Ribosomes	Execution Engines / Workflow Systems	**Biological:** Build a product. In this case, peptides, chains of amino acids. **Business:** Carry out the actual manufacture of things.
Peptides	Event Sequences	**Biological:** Chains of amino acids. **Business:** Chains of events that generate business processes.
Proteins	*Markov Models*	***Biological:*** *A "folded" version of a long chain of amino acids.* ***Business:*** *A structure describing a data set of events.*

Table 1: Comparison of biological concepts to business concepts.

Playbook to Reality: DNA and System Design

Just as DNA encases the encodings necessary to build an organism, our initial business models and system designs—captured in UML diagrams, CAD designs, articles of incorporation, performance plans, etc.—serve as the foundational recipes or playbooks of our business. These documents are more than mere plans; they are the genetic code awaiting transcription to create something functional and interactive.

Similarly, just as proteins translate DNA into the functional structures of life, Markov models are a transformation of raw event data into a structure conducive to analytical insights. They reveal the hidden dynamics of business processes, enabling organizations to analyze evolving patterns, predict future states, and enhance decision-making. In *Time Molecules*, we'll explore how this transformation bridges the gap between static abstractions and living, evolving systems, offering a roadmap for embedding process thinking into mainstream BI.

RNA: The Builder of Systems

In biological terms, RNA reads and interprets DNA to build proteins. Similarly, in business environments, developers, analysts, and automated systems act as the RNA, translating static designs into the components of dynamic, functioning systems. Each line of code, each integration, brings the recipe/playbook to life, much like RNA translates genetic code into forms that form proteins.

Peptides to Proteins: Events and Markov Models

In the bustling ecosystem of a fully operational business system, every transaction, every user interaction, and every automated response generates events. These events are the amino acids of our system—complex molecules that bind together to form structures with specific functions. As amino acids form peptides, events chain into sequences, often repetitive, that we can track and analyze.

Here, the Markov model serves as the protein of our analogy. It isn't merely a mathematical construct; it represents the dynamic, ongoing processes of a business system. Markov models capture the transitions between states in our event sequences, offering a structured yet flexible representation of processes over time.

Peptides to Proteins: From Logs to Models

The transition from extensive logs of events to cohesive Markov models mirrors the biological process of peptide folding into functional proteins. Each model we build, much like each protein synthesized, is a testament to the complexity and adaptability of our systems. These models allow us to predict future states, understand potential system failures, and enhance overall efficiency—effectively allowing the system to "learn" from past behaviors.

The Living System of Business Intelligence

Embracing the analogy between biological processes and business system operations provides a profound insight into our approaches to data analysis and system design. By understanding business systems as living entities—where documents are DNA, systems builders act as RNA, events function as amino acids, and Markov models embody proteins—we can foster environments that are as resilient and adaptive as entities of the natural world.

> *This holistic view bridges the gap between the static and the dynamic, theoretical and the practical, encouraging us to see beyond the code to the living system it supports. Just as the study of life extends beyond DNA to the proteins and processes that define existence, our study of business systems extends beyond their creation to their operational life and the intelligence they manifest.*

Evolution

The processes of life on Earth evolve through a ceaseless dance of interaction, changes, and adaptation. It's a web of systems of cause and effect that comprise the ecosystems. These interactions form what might best be described as a *system of processes*—a heterogeneous network of interdependent dynamics that touch at key points, whether through competition, cooperation, shared resources, and other known and unknown forces. Just as DNA evolves under pressures experienced by the organisms it codes for, influenced by the shifting balance of prey, predators, and environment, business processes evolve under the pressures of their own ecosystems: competitors, technological advancements, and shifting market demands.

This system of processes reflects more than isolated changes; it captures the interplay of interconnected forces. Taxonomies and ontologies are the starting framework for understanding these connections. They categorize and map the relationships between the variety of things involved with a process. They help us to see how seemingly disparate systems—like sales and logistics, or customer satisfaction and operational efficiency—touch and influence each other in often surprising ways.

In this context, Markov models become more than a snapshot of transactions; they embody the adaptability of a business system, encoding not just the state of the system—as most databases do—but also its capacity to evolve. Much like DNA is a foundation of the taxonomy of organisms, Markov models contribute to a business taxonomy, allowing processes to be classified, studied, and enhanced. They capture not just where processes are but how they might evolve, enabling businesses to navigate their ecosystems with the same resilience and adaptability as life itself.

Models of How the World Works

In the course of our daily normal lives, we make many subconscious or "intuitive" decisions almost every instant—from steps as we walk to whether we've had enough work for the day. What usually goes unnoticed are the models of the world in each of our heads. We don't usually think of how we came up with a thought or decision until it seems inconsistent with reality, and our curiosity is engaged to investigate and correct. The models are different for each of us based on our unique experiences. Most of these models in our heads are indirectly trained—not programmed. They are statistical knowledge bases of what we experience, observe, or are repetitively told. Those models predict what will happen next. More interestingly, through the exploration of the webs of these predictive models in our heads, we figure out how to make something happen that we desire. That's a much more powerful, proactive mode.

When we learn a subject such as physics or programming, we consciously *train* those models in our heads. To be a great physicist or programmer, we need to replicate the knowledge outside our heads to perform tasks masterfully and/or contribute towards the evolution of those models. Analogous models have traditionally existed in our enterprise software systems. They are reflected in the software code. Software, which until recently was programmed almost entirely by people, is an encoding of models invented by people. When we teach other people what we know, we train them, not program them like we explicitly program computers.

For the most part, the model we encode in software is a black box to other software or even those who don't have access to the code. We give software some kind of input and it gives us an output.

We also don't have direct access to the way other people think—theory of mind. We generally don't have direct access to most of the processes within corporations or governments. For the most part, I know I don't give much thought to how I make decisions unless I sense outrageous consequences for being wrong until my decision blows up in my face or someone asks me. The point is intelligence goes beyond mapping causes to effects, symptoms to diagnoses. Our intelligence is about taking in data, subconsciously or semi-consciously running through the models of the world in our heads, and coming up with constrained solutions. That is, solutions that solve our problems without creating more problems. This book is about a focus on process models, providing AI with elements of how things work in the world.

Introduction

The goal of this book is to provide practical guidance on incorporating process mining and systems thinking into the BI process, while equipping BI practitioners and BI consumers with the intuition needed to apply core constructs, like Markov models, at scale. By developing a deeper understanding of processes over time and subsets of the BI dimensional space, readers will be able to move beyond snapshot insights of BI dashboards and unlock the more fluid potential of BI and AI systems.

One of the key outcomes of this book is the removal of what is sometimes referred to as *process blindness*—the inability to recognize or understand the underlying processes that drive complex systems. Many practitioners get stuck focusing on the qualities of things and events without fully grasping the interconnected processes that shape outcomes. Without a system-level awareness, those outcomes can include unintended consequences and fall into traps—often much worse than simply making the less optimal decision.

I intend this book to help BI professionals overcome that deficiency by providing both foundational knowledge and advanced techniques for process mining and Markov modeling, enabling them to see the entire probabilistic flow of events in a single structure rather than reacting to isolated moments. By cultivating this process-oriented thinking, BI practitioners can better anticipate changes, make wiser decisions, and ultimately master the complexities of today's hopelessly dynamic business environment.

Since AI entered the public spotlight with the release of ChatGPT two years ago (Nov 2022), we've seen the beginning of a profound shift in how we interact with and understand data and processes. Of course, as AI continues to grow in capability, it will play a correspondingly growing role in decision-making, automation, and process optimization across industries.

The primary audience for this book is BI practitioners and consumers—analysts, data engineers, knowledge workers—and executives, such as CIOs and CDOs, who are responsible for guiding their organizations through technological shifts. If we wish to preserve and enhance our personal relevance in this new AI-powered landscape, we each need to develop a deeper, more powerful understanding of the world—one that sees processes as fluid, evolving over time, and driven by curiosity—that proactive force of the mind that continually seeks better ways of doing things.

Cycles

Life and business are made of interacting processes. Iterations of these processes are cycles and each cycle is observed as a specific case, which is a defined context or sequence of events. Without cycles, processes don't reset back to square 1 to begin again, and there would be only chaos. That's much messier than the complexity of life that already feels tough enough to manage.

In business, we're familiar with many cycles, such as sales cycles, where each case represents a journey composed of fairly familiar sequences of events—from initial outreach to customer engagement to final purchase. These cycles do not exist in isolation. While they have structural integrity within their cases, they interact with other cycles, leading to subtle or drastic changes. Ideally, these effects are gradual and manageable, but internal events or interactions between systems can lead to transformations that ripple through and redefine the cases involved.

Every process has phases, like the troughs and crests of a wave, and these phases manifest similarly across a wide range of contexts. In nature, we observe the seasons as a perfect embodiment of cyclical processes. Winter gives way to spring, followed by summer and fall, each season marked by distinct events—new growth, harvest, dormancy, and the eventual return to winter. Each cycle builds on the last and influences the next, creating a continuous loop of transformation, much like individual cases that collectively shape a larger system.

In the world of business, cases and their cycles are readily apparent:

- **Product development cycles:** Concept, design, testing, and launch, followed by updates and iterations.
- **Supply chain cycles:** Procurement, production, distribution, and restocking, repeated to ensure consistent availability of products.
- **Hiring cycles:** Identifying talent, interviewing, hiring, training, and evaluation.

Even in our daily lives, cycles within cases are ever-present:

- **Morning routines:** Each day begins with waking up, preparing, commuting, working, and resting, only to restart.
- **Health and fitness cycles:** Alternating periods of intense activity, recovery, and progress toward fitness goals.

These processes often interact. For instance, a company's sales cycle may overlap with its product lifecycle, as a new product launch can impact sales trends, requiring adjustments to the cycle. These interactions are akin to collisions between cases, where the cycles of one system influence another—sometimes subtly, sometimes profoundly.

Whether in financial markets, with their cyclical trends of booms and busts, or in nature, where even ocean tides follow regular cycles of rise and fall, the principles of processes and cycles govern pretty much everything we observe. In both simple and complex systems, understanding these cycles and the cases they form helps us navigate uncertainties and plan for future events.

In Time Molecules, we aim to capture and model these processes using Markov models, enabling us to study how cases evolve over time and how their interactions shape larger cycles in business, life, and nature.

Why a Book Founded on Markov Models?

This book is about predicting the probabilities of what will happen next. That ability is fundamental to our intelligence. We can't strategize and plan without the ability to predict what will happen at every step.

In this current AI era dominated by LLMs, where "predicting the next word" is often used to describe their functionality, and that LLMs being these unprecedentedly powerful human-made structures, Markov models (MM) seem archaic by comparison. Why not just use LLMs? The simplicity of MMs and transparency provide a counterpoint to the troubling black-box nature of LLMs, making MMs an enduring and essential tool in modeling time-based processes.

It's worth observing that while MMs and LLMs significantly differ in appearance and utilization, they share a surprising conceptual similarity: both are forms of compression over vast amounts of sequences. MMs are a compression of event sequences into a probabilistic structure that summarizes how processes tend to unfold across many cases. Likewise, LLMs compress the structure of language across massive corpora—encoding how word sequences (for simplicity, think phrases, sentences, paragraphs) typically follow one another. In both cases, a richer form of information emerges from capturing commonalities across massive numbers of examples. One compresses transitions between events and the other compresses transitions between tokens, but both ultimately model how the next step flows from the current state.

Recurrent Neural Networks (RNNs) also deserve a mention. They live in the gap between the deterministic simplicity of MMs and the complex contextual power of LLMs, serving as the direct predecessors to the Transformer architecture of today's LLMs. RNNs introduced the idea of sequential memory and step-by-step processing, paving the way for advances in modeling time-dependent data.

MMs, RNNs, and Transformers (used in LLMs) all have overlapping purposes: modeling and predicting sequences. However, their approaches and strengths differ significantly. MMs focus on direct probabilistic transitions between events, LLMs predict the next word in a sequence using attention mechanisms, and RNNs model sequences step by step with memory. Table 2 highlights these differences, while Appendix I provides a deeper dive.

Aspect	Markov Models	RNNs	Transformers (LLMs)
Core Idea	Probabilistic transitions	Step-by-step memory-based	Attention-based relationships
Strengths	***Simple, efficient, interpretable***	Handles short to medium sequences	Context-rich, long-range understanding
Weaknesses	Limited memory, simplistic	Struggles with long sequences	***Computationally expensive, black box***
Applications	Time-series analysis, predictions	Speech recognition, forecasting	Text generation, reasoning

Table 2: Comparison of MM, RNN, and LLM.

MMs excel at lightweight, interpretable predictions, while RNNs and Transformers handle more complex scenarios with higher computational requirements. Yet, MM's simplicity, transparency, and efficiency make them indispensable, especially in contexts where interpretability, traceability, and resource constraints matter.

MMs continue to hold a place in the landscape of Machine Learning (ML) and probabilistic modeling, and their foundational role in understanding time-based processes makes them an ideal subject for a comprehensive exploration. Their combination of fundamental simplicity, computational ease, and their intrinsic focus on time are qualities that make them both unique and universally applicable across a wide range of domains.

MMs are among the most fundamental algorithms when it comes to modeling sequences of events. They distill the complexity of temporal processes into a compact and intellectually manageable (for humans or computationally manageable for computers) form by focusing on transitions between events, guided by the principle that the future depends only on the present.

This "memoryless" property, known as the Markov property, captures the essence of how many real-world processes operate, where the next step is influenced directly (at least predominantly) by the current state rather than the full history of prior events. This makes Markov models not just another tool in the ML toolbox, but a foundational idea for modeling sequential behavior—central to probabilistic frameworks like Hidden Markov Models (HMMs), and conceptually related to time-series methods such as ARIMA, state-space models, and Kalman filters, which each deal with evolving state across time.

One of the standout features of MMs is their computational simplicity. They are mathematically grounded and straightforward to implement and scale. The calculations involved in MMs are easily computed, making them accessible even in resource-constrained environments. Despite the ease of computation, they are still powerful. MMs are capable of handling complex temporal dynamics with surprising effectiveness, all while remaining interpretable and transparent. This balance of simplicity and power is a gift and makes MMs a practical choice for both beginners and seasoned professionals looking to model time-based phenomena.

Compare the creation of MMs to highly iterative, sort of trial-and-error processing of ML algorithms such as decision trees, clusters, support vector machines, Fourier transforms, and especially neural networks. Like the sum and count aggregations of our old friends, the OLAP cubes, the simplicity lends itself to at-scale deployment and on-the-fly creation. Markov models and sum and count aggregations are single iteration and *mostly* additive (more on "additive" later).

OLAP cube aggregations and Markov models require a sorting operation in the same manner as a SQL GROUP BY.

At their core, MMs are time-centric, designed to model processes where the sequence and timing of events matter. In many real-world scenarios—from predicting customer behavior to understanding biological processes—time is the critical factor. MMs excel in these situations because they inherently account for the order of events, providing a structured way to predict future events based on current observations. This time-centric nature makes MMs particularly relevant in today's data-driven world, where understanding how things evolve over time is key to insights and making informed decisions. By building this book on MMs, we are diving into a concept that is theoretically rich and practically indispensable. These models provide a lens through which we can view and understand a wide array of time-based processes, from the simplest sequences to the most complex systems. Whether you are new to the concept or looking to deepen your understanding, a focus on at-scale MMs offers both a robust foundation and a versatile toolset for exploring the temporal dynamics that shape our world.

What can we see with MMs at scale? One of the most annoying aspects of solutions of all types is that the "physics" changes at different scales. What works great at small scale falls apart at large scales. On the other hand, profound phenomena can be revealed at large scales, just as LLMs have demonstrated these past few years. MMs are fundamental, easily computed, and intrinsically tied to time—the very elements that make them worthy of being the cornerstone of a book.

With such qualities, their consistent structure across applications makes it easier to analyze processes and compare dimensions, even when deployed in parallel with different time-based algorithms or machine learning models.

Time Molecules are to decision forests as Markov models are to Decision Trees, but operate in a probabilistic, time-centric framework. Whereas decision forests aggregate thousands of decision trees to improve predictive accuracy, Time Molecules scale up to millions—or even billions—of interconnected MMs, each capturing sequential event transitions. Instead of static branching decisions like in decision trees, Markov models assign probabilistic weights to event sequences, making them better suited for process mining, dynamic decision-making, and real-time intelligence. This approach decentralizes intelligence across a vast network of time-aware models, much like how decision forests distribute decision-making across many trees.

A Quick and Simple Example

If we jotted down the day-to-day weather across a period of time, we could compute the table shown in Table 3—a transition matrix. It's a table of probabilities between an event following an event. For example, the top-left cell indicates that given sunny weather on a day, there is a 0.60 probability the next day will be sunny as well.

Current Day	Next Day - Sunny	Next Day - Cloudy	Next Day - Rainy
Sunny	0.60	0.30	0.10
Cloudy	0.20	0.50	0.30
Rainy	0.10	0.40	0.50

Table 3: Compression of daily weather.

The weather probabilities above are close to that of San Francisco from October through March, which experiences fluctuating weather between sunny, cloudy, and rainy days, especially during transitional seasons like spring and fall. This is a Markov model. Let's say we have daily data points from the last ten years—about 3,650 days. That long list is compressed into a succinct description of the weather. The model itself loses the specific weather for each day, but it presents something that is usually much more useful in compact form.

Keep in mind that those are not probabilities for weather on a given day. For example, San Francisco is certainly not sunny 60% of days from October through March. That is something we do with a stationary distribution, which we'll cover soon. Figure 2 is what Table 3 looks like in a graph form. It kind of looks like a depiction of a molecule.

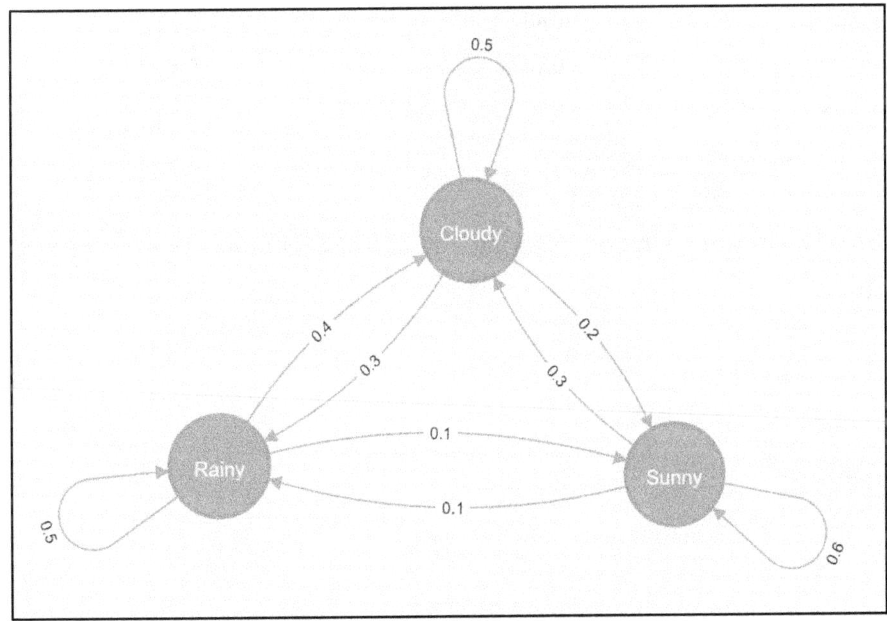

Figure 2: Sample Markov model of the weather of San Francisco.

Another city that might show similar weather patterns but differs from San Francisco is Seattle. Seattle has more frequent rainy days but still experiences transitions predominantly between sunny, cloudy, and rainy conditions, especially in spring and fall. Table 4 is an example transition table that could resemble Seattle's weather.

Current Day	Next Day - Sunny	Next Day - Cloudy	Next Day - Rainy
Sunny	0.50	0.40	0.10
Cloudy	0.30	0.40	0.30
Rainy	0.10	0.30	0.60

Table 4: Example of day-to-day weather transitions in Seattle.

Seattle tends to have more frequent transitions to rainy weather compared to San Francisco, but still cycles through periods of sunny, cloudy, and rainy days.

San Francisco and Seattle are relatively temperate cities with seasonal variations that are not as harsh as Chicago. But what about a city with a clear distinction between seasons? For example, for Boise in the winter, we need to adjust the probabilities to reflect the likelihood of snow, with occasional rain and fewer sunny days. Table 5 shows how the new table might look, isolated to winter in Boise.

Current Day	Next Day - Sunny	Next Day - Cloudy	Next Day - Rainy	Next Day - Snowy
Sunny	0.50	0.20	0.10	0.20
Cloudy	0.15	0.40	0.15	0.30
Rainy	0.10	0.20	0.30	0.40
Snowy	0.15	0.20	0.10	0.55

Table 5: Example of day-to-day winter weather transitions in Boise.

The MMs for each city are a kind of "painting," an abstract representation of the weather for the respective city.

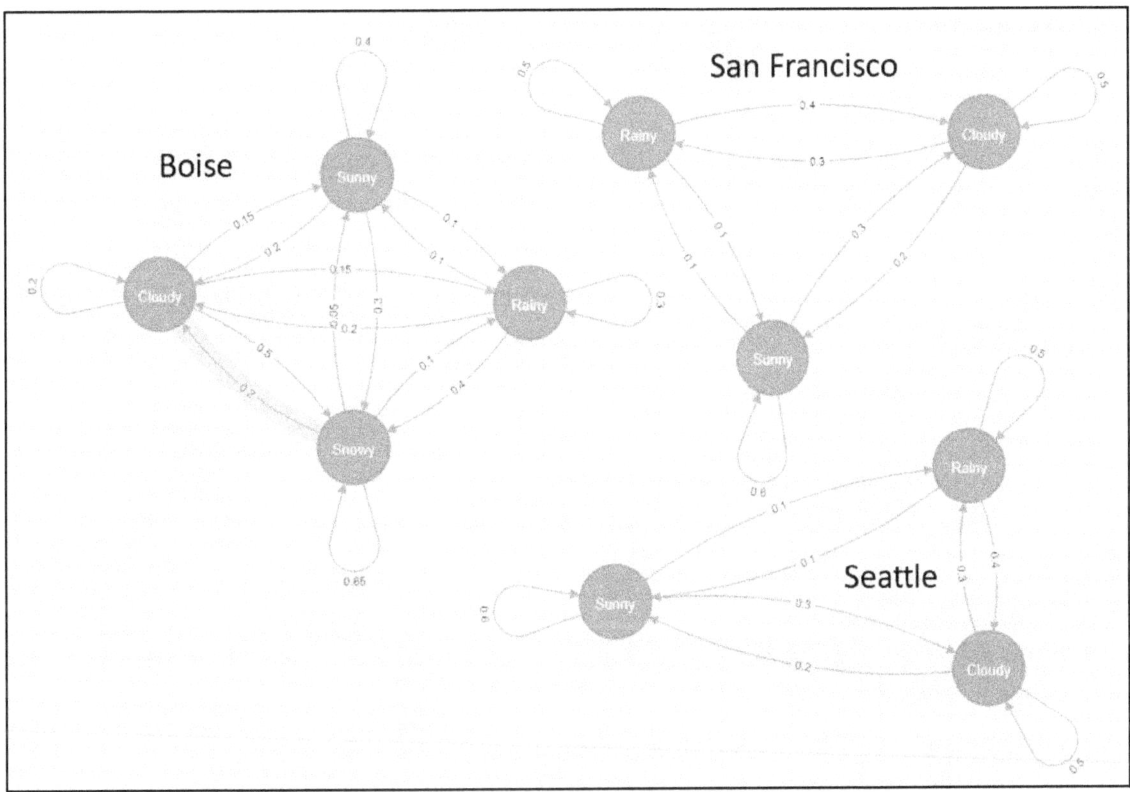

Figure 3: Markov models depicting weather for three cities.

Throw the Ball to Where the Receiver Will Be

Many tend to operate frustratingly under the assumption that conditions remain as they are. It's inconvenient to consider that the world is constantly changing and that our plans always come with some level of blind faith. While this approach can lead to short-term success through sheer will and cunning, it has limitations. In sports, like throwing a ball where the receiver will be, we must play to where we predict future changes will place us rather than fixating on the conditions of the present. This mentality of operating several steps ahead is crucial in dynamic environments—which is everything.

In business, the same principle applies: if we only react in the realm of current conditions, we miss opportunities to adapt and innovate. Strategic thinking allows us to find paths forward, not just by optimizing what we see now but by anticipating where conditions will shift. Relying only on brute force eventually leads to diminishing returns, but by planning for future possibilities, we maximize our chances for sustainable success.

We've been trained to see the world in what are really unnatural ways. In our efforts to optimize, control, and improve systems, we often break them down into fragments, isolating each into simpler bite-sized chunks so that we can make each one more efficient. This works well for machines, where conformance is key and predictable and reliable performance is crucial. But this reductionist mindset falters when applied to the complex, interconnected systems that define our world.

In complex systems, interactions are as important—if not more so—than the individual components themselves. Optimizing each part in isolation won't give you the full picture of how a system behaves over time. The interconnectedness, the constant flow of events, is lost when we only focus on static snapshots of data.

This idea is deeply resonant in Zen philosophy. The Zen master Takuan Soho[1] tells the story of the sword: when you see your opponent's sword, it's already too late—the strike has already happened—the milliseconds after you see his sword. What you perceive at any instant is the past, not where the sword actually is by the time you begin to react—in large part because it's thought that humans take about 200 ms for the brain to process and react. In the same way, reacting only to what we see in front of us means we are always a step behind, eating the crumbs left behind by the innovators.

This applies to how we approach systems in business, life, and technology. In sports, business, or AI, mastery results in the ability to see multiple steps ahead, much like a chess grandmaster aware of moves several turns into the future. It's not enough to react to what's present—we must anticipate and plan for what's coming.

This thinking forms the basis of my work in *Time Molecules*. We live in a time where AI is increasingly integral to decision-making and process optimization. But for AI to truly realize its potential, it needs to rise above the way we've been trained to think in this industrial, reductionist era. AI must think in systems and processes—the flows of actions over time—and anticipate the transitions from one state to the next. This is where systems-oriented data and Markov models come

---

[1] Takuan Soho: https://en.wikipedia.org/wiki/Takuan_S%C5%8Dh%C5%8D.

into play, offering an easily computable probabilistic framework that helps AI look ahead, predict, and adapt.

We've been conditioned to think in single steps, but the path to true mastery lies in seeing the entire system, understanding the forces of its evolution, and predicting the future events that drive meaningful outcomes. In this era where AI will be handling more complex tasks continuously, humans must cultivate a deeper understanding than the shallow level sufficient for the short attention we're grown into—a systems intuition that allows us to see the entire process, the interconnected whole.

As we move into the future, this approach—rooted in systems thinking—will be our edge in keeping up with the increasingly complex world we inhabit.

The TL;DR of the Book for the BI Data Engineer

Time Molecules is a system of dimensional analysis of processes. We can quickly build Markov models sliced and diced in many ways and compare the characteristics of the different models.

It is inspired by OLAP cubes of the BI world, built by products such as Kyvos Insights and SQL Server Analysis Services (SSAS). The data warehouse counterpart is called the Event Ensemble—an abstracted data warehouse of events across all sources and domains. The centerpiece of the Event Ensemble is the EventsFact table (like a data warehouse fact table), a log of all events.

The Model Ensemble is centered around the real-time creation, caching, and analysis of Markov models—which I call Time Molecules—that are calculated from the data of the Events Ensemble.

The primary properties of an event are the date/time, the event name, and a case. A case represents a specific cycle of a process. In some cases, there may not be a clear case identifier (case ID). For such cases, process mining is used to sort and extract case IDs as well as the event types valid for a particular case type. Secondary properties are anything else further qualifying the case and/or event. For example, an employee ID or location ID.

Markov models are easily computed with just one pass through a subset of the EventsFact table. An MM is the product of simple computation, in the same way that a sum and count aggregation is the product of OLAP cube processing. Similarly, both MMs and aggregations can be saved as a kind of cache to preserve the compute used to create them. The computed MMs are stored in the Model Ensemble, where they can be referenced for subsequent analysis.

A Few Notes About this Book

Time Molecules vs TimeSolution vs Markov Models

Although these three terms might appear interchangeable, here's how I use them:

- **Time Molecules:** Refers to the concept as introduced in this book or referring to the book itself. The name is inspired by Markov models but emphasizes the *visual and conceptual* framework of time-based transitions.

- **TimeSolution:** The *specific, sample database* implementation (using SQL Server) for the walkthroughs. This database contains the actual tables, procedures, and data structures that exemplify the principles of Time Molecules and Markov-based reasoning. There is no space since TimeSolution is the name of the database.

- **Markov Models:** The *core mathematical structures* underlying the entire solution. Markov models capture the probabilities of moving from one state to another over time, and they are the foundational concept behind "Time Molecules."

Vendor Agnostic

I attempted to be as vendor-agnostic as I could be. My experience happens to lean very much in the Microsoft direction, so the examples and tools tend to be MSFT products such as SQL Server and Visual Studio. But that's not an indication of products I favor. It's what I know. But more importantly, I believe it to be a very solid platform.

Sequel to Enterprise Intelligence

Although this book is designed to stand on its own, it really is the first sequel to my previous book, *Enterprise Intelligence.* It would help to have read Enterprise Intelligence first, where I cover a wide breadth of background topics. However, with at least some level of BI experience as a BI consumer or developer, I don't believe that will be necessary.

Markov models I describe in this book tie into the BI structures I describe in *Enterprise Intelligence*—the Insight Space Graph (ISG) and the Tuple Correlation Web (TCW). We'll explore this integration in the "Enterprise Intelligence" chapter.

Minimum Math and Code

I limit the coding presented in this book primarily to SQL. The SQL syntax is designed to be simple. Much of that simplicity is due to its specialized scope of dealing with relational databases—unlike Python or Java, which must express a wide computation scope. It abstracts querying a relational database into three major parts: The data source (FROM), data we want (SELECT), and filters (WHERE). Of course, SQL can become much more complicated, but the degree of difficulty is kept to a low level.

A good portion of this book is a walkthrough of the TimeSolution database, implemented with Microsoft SQL Server. Following along with the code isn't necessary at all, but the walkthrough is the mechanism by which I introduce important concepts.

Markov models are directed graphs. However, in their transition matrix form, linear algebra can come into play. So, although I may mention linear algebra, it's not necessary to understand how it works—mostly what we can do with it.

Most of the SQL presented isn't really "SQL" either. It mostly uses custom functions and stored procedures that encapsulate (hide the messy innards of the function from you) the concepts of Time Molecules. The functions are primarily in the FROM clause.

I would like to offer a thought, though. I only speak English. But if I were just starting out in life, at least in the U.S., the ability to speak Spanish would be a great asset. Similarly, with the state of AI and where it will soon be, mastering hard-core coding wouldn't be my first choice if I were starting my career. However, understanding simple coding languages like SQL is a relatively easy and useful step in understanding how machines process data. So for the non-codey readers, think of this as a gentle introduction to coding.

In an era dominated by machine learning and AI, we (humans) must move closer to how we've historically communicated with data systems—through coding. Although SQL and relational databases are among the simplest forms of coding, they remain enduringly useful as a simple but powerful form of human-to-machine communication "for the masses."

Supplementary Material

This book focuses on providing a relatively high-level overview of the Time Molecules concepts, aiming towards keeping it concise and readable. While some code examples are included throughout the book, they are limited to SQL and the focus is on explanatory text of what the SQL does, not an analysis of the code itself, to ensure accessibility for readers. To avoid overwhelming technical details and appendices, I have provided supplemental information through additional resources.

Given the rapid evolution of the AI field, supplementary and updated materials are available in the accompanying GitHub repository and on my blog site.

GitHub Repository

The book has an accompanying GitHub repository: https://github.com/MapRock/TimeMolecules

The repository contains:

- **Code, sample data, and new tutorials** related to the concepts in this book. SQL, Python, Cypher, OWL/RDF/SPARQL.
- **Figures** in this book that are rather busy and easier to view in full size and full color.
- **CSV files of tutorial queries**, allowing readers to explore the data without requiring software installation.
- **Appendices** decoupled from the book, available as a live document: *Time_Molecules_Book_Eugene_Asahara_Appendices.pdf*. Any reference to an appendix in the book points to this document.

For those seeking further exploration, the GitHub repository offers additional code examples and in-depth technical material.

My Blog Site

For ongoing updates and my latest thoughts on technical issues, visit my blog at: https://eugeneasahara.com. Specifically, follow-ups to this book will be posted here: https://eugeneasahara.com/category/time-molecules/.

Intent of Supplementary Materials

This book intends to provide a conceptual overview of Time Molecules without the messiness of delving deeply into code or exhaustive technical details. While the book includes SQL code to illustrate concepts, the focus remains on textual explanations to ensure clarity. Supplementary resources like the GitHub repository and my blog allow for deeper exploration of code, data, and evolving ideas, ensuring the book remains accessible while enabling readers to explore further as desired.

Lastly, whenever I refer to "future works," it could mean a future book, blog posts, or new material on the GitHub repository, depending on the scope of the topic.

CHAPTER 1

Background Concepts

The initial inspiration for Time Molecules came from my experience as a long-time BI architect and developer, particularly with SSAS OLAP cubes. I saw an opportunity to introduce a new form of aggregation—one focused on processes instead of tuples—that could complement the traditional tuple-qualified sum and count methods of pre-aggregated OLAP. This new aggregation method, based on Markov models, enables dynamic analysis of event sequences, capturing transitions between events over time—a concept that moves beyond static facts to incorporate process-based insights.

While traditional BI focuses on analyzing entities—customers, products, or locations—by slicing and dicing through dimensions for various perspectives of these "things," it often treats the processes linking these entities as secondary or incidental. For example, BI might summarize coffee sales by region or product category but do not consider the sequence of events to be a first-class structure.

This "thing-focused" approach excels at measuring outcomes but leaves a gap in understanding the dynamics that drive those outcomes.

Sorting out those dynamics was left to intelligent humans. All BI did was compute and present the values we requested. But the business environment only becomes more complex with more moving parts and through information technologies and AI, it runs faster and faster. We humans require more profound systems-thinking support from our BI systems.

While the approach I'm suggesting might sound redundant to systems thinking and process mining, my goal here is not to provide a technical guide or cookbook on these topics, but rather to build a solid intuition for the dimension of time that process mining adds to our traditionally "thing-focused" BI analysis.

To illustrate these ideas, I developed the TimeSolution database, which plays a prominent role in this book, showcasing how Markov models at scale can provide deeper, time-centric aggregations to better support human and AI analysts at this special time when AI is accelerating the dynamics of our activities to crazy levels.

In this chapter, I will lay out the background concepts that underpin *Time Molecules*. These include:

- **Systems Thinking**: Understanding interconnected systems and their behavior over time.
- **Process Mining**: The exploration, organization, and analysis of business processes through event data.
- **Pre-Aggregated OLAP**: The traditional foundation that inspired this work.
- **Markov Models**: A probabilistic approach to modeling transitions and processes.
- **Business Intelligence (BI)**: The larger context where these techniques are applied to enhance insight and decision-making.
- **LLMs and the Semantic Web**: Exploring how Large Language Models can work with structured knowledge from the Semantic Web to enhance AI's understanding of processes and relationships between entities.

Please keep in mind that I'm just introducing concepts in this chapter. The walkthroughs will dig deeper into the concepts.

Systems Thinking

Sometime in the 2000s, my contact at a large manufacturer made an insightful comment: they could optimize isolated parts of their system, but they couldn't optimize the entire system. While individual components could be optimized to high levels of performance, unforeseen circumstances usually emerged with the system as a whole—sometimes much later. Most of us in software development know this is common during both integrated testing and production releases—a simplified or slimmed-down model of the world isn't quite the same as the real world. What's trickier is understanding how the smallest oversight can ripple and magnify through a complex system, leading to unexpected slowdowns or failures.

In reality, our business processes aren't intended to be complex systems. They are intended to be simple—at best, complicated, not complex machines. However, as they unavoidably interact with other processes, their parts wear down, and the world around them changes in unexpected ways. This forces our processes from manageably complicated to the messiness of complex. This interaction forces processes to maintain themselves and evolve, requiring the input of resources from others and introducing risks to sustain such transformations.

When I worked as a SQL Server performance tuning expert, optimization of novel problems (couldn't find a solution through a Google search) started with understanding how the system worked holistically, which enabled spotting bottlenecks that slow everything down and friction that wastes resources. Often, the waste products of one process serve as the fuel for another, like silage from grain crops becoming the food for cattle. These inefficiencies and interactions reveal how even the smallest imbalance in a system can have far-reaching effects—just as in the interconnected world of our business processes.

All that unfolds in the world is fundamentally an interaction of systems. Systems have integrity, otherwise they would just be chaos. They possess a certain resilience that allows them to withstand and influence the forces of other systems. This interplay of resilience is what shapes how systems affect and transform one another over time. Some of these systems are the ones we've purposefully built—like the systems comprising a car, for example. A car is a marvel of engineering, with every part designed to function in harmony with the others. What is the most important part of a car? Engine? Tires? Chassis? Gasoline? A car doesn't function as a whole, as a system, without any of those parts.

But a car is a special type of system. It is a machine, deterministic in its dynamics. Humans, through their expertise, can learn everything about how components of a machine work together, tuning and optimizing each part to fit within the predictable, well-defined boundaries of the machine. But cars also interact with other systems—the road, bad drivers, the weather—all of which reduce it to a moving part in a complex system.

The Mysteries of Natural Systems

But then, there are systems we didn't create—natural systems that emerged and evolved without a designer's recipe or a user's guide. Take, for example, humans themselves. We didn't invent ourselves, nor do we come with a manual that explains every process within our bodies. Our understanding of any of these natural systems that we didn't design began with the simplest of observations. We noticed cause and effect and building knowledge upon knowledge over time—building a cascading web of cause and effect.

Yet, beyond the systems we recognize, there are countless others we haven't fully grasped, and haven't even noticed. These could be spontaneously arising systems, emerging out of interactions with other systems, born from complexity itself. These systems evolve as they continuously interact with their environment and exert influence on other systems around them. Some of these naturally arising systems may blend seamlessly into others, disappearing or transforming into something new entirely.

Systems Evolving in a Chaotic World

Our understanding of the vast majority of these systems is superficial at best. They are constantly evolving, complex beyond measure, and what we think of as a single system is usually a system of systems, each interconnected with blurred boundaries with countless others. In reality, no system exists in a vacuum; each one is embedded in a network of dependencies and influences, shaped by the continuous flow of its interactions.

Markov models serve as a system's "elevator pitch"—a simple way to analyze and make sense of a system's behavior when we know almost nothing about it. MMs are constructed out of logging of observations (emissions of events) from the system. They are a condensed, abstract model from which we can predict and understand how a system might evolve over time based solely on the current state, without needing to delve into its entire history.

Designed Systems vs Emergent Systems

One of the most important distinctions for this book is recognizing the difference between designed systems (those we intentionally impose on the world) and emergent systems (those that arise spontaneously). But it's not a clear-cut line; it's a spectrum. Even when we design a system, that doesn't guarantee that it will function the way we imagined in real life. Consider inventory management: in theory, everything that comes in and goes out is meticulously recorded, yet we still need to conduct full physical inventories because things happen that escape the notice of the inventory system.

Or take, for instance, a small roadside restaurant—one of those unbranded places along an interstate. There appears to be a consistent process for serving customers, yet the process is likely undocumented. Instead, it exists as tacit knowledge passed down from one generation of waitstaff and cooks to the next, carried forward through observation and experience rather than official documentation.

Why Systems Thinking Matters for Time Molecules

Given that all we observe are interactions of systems within systems, a goal of this book is to help train ourselves to see the difference between the systems we deliberately design and deploy and those that simply emerge on their own, or sometimes it is a form that evolved from what we deployed.

We must understand that even the most rigorously planned systems will diverge from our expectations as they interact with the real world—like our friend, the Coronavirus. This is where systems thinking comes in—it teaches us to see the broader context, to appreciate that no single system stands alone, and to use this insight to develop deeper, more intuitive models of how the world operates.

The essence of systems thinking in this context isn't just about knowing what a system is—it's about understanding how that system changes, adapts, and blends with other systems over time. And it's this foundational perspective that will allow us to see the true power of process mining, systems thinking, and Markov models in capturing the dynamic complexity of the real world.

Process Mining: Bridging the Gap Between Theory and Reality

Process mining is an application of systems thinking. It bridges the gap between theory and practice, enabling organizations to see their operations clearly and adapt to the complexities of the real world. Businesses can uncover hidden inefficiencies, align operations with strategy, and prepare for the challenges of an ever-changing environment.

All entities—whether creatures, enterprises, or machines (including Earth)—operate as systems of interconnected processes. For businesses, these processes should ideally be well understood.

However, in practice, knowledge is often fragmented, confined to departments or even individuals. Most organizations quickly outgrow the capacity for any single person to fully comprehend their operations. And as things change and challenges arise in the midst of an organization just trying to keep things going, ad-hoc workarounds are introduced without systemic alignment.

The Challenge of Misalignment

During my time at a corporation managing the collection and processing of specialized materials from sites across the U.S., I witnessed firsthand the challenges of misalignment between theoretical processes and on-the-ground realities. Handling these materials is a highly regulated activity, with processes varying based on the type of material, its origin, and evolving federal and state regulations.

At HQ, managers attempted to maintain a theoretical understanding of how things were "supposed" to work, but in the field, teams scattered across the entire U.S. faced unexpected challenges—from evolving laws to procedural changes to unforeseen circumstances. These often necessitated improvised solutions—workarounds that were rarely reported back into the central system—leading to growing disconnects, much like a game of telephone where each iteration introduced distortions.

The situation reminded me of physical inventories: no matter how sophisticated the tracking system, periodic checks are needed because the real world is always more fluid and unpredictable than the relatively static systems in place (esp. true for implemented software to support operations). This is precisely where process mining shines—it digs into the messy reality to reveal how processes actually operate versus how they are imagined to operate.

Why Process Mining Matters

The primary goal of process mining is to uncover gaps between intended processes and actual execution. That gap could range from "there's obviously some process in play, but no one has documented it" to "what's happening in the field isn't quite what we thought". Analyzing event logs and process flows identifies deviations from expectations, providing insights crucial for high-stakes operations, such as healthcare or handling hazardous materials, where minor deviations can lead to serious consequences.

Process mining helps combat process blindness, a phenomenon where HQ's theoretical view of a process, the software's representation of it, and the field team's practical execution diverge significantly.

By providing a clear lens into real-world adaptations, process mining builds a feedback loop to bridge these gaps.

Systems Thinking in Process Mining

Systems thinking underpins process mining by emphasizing the interactions and interdependencies across processes. It's not enough to understand each step in isolation. Process mining enables a holistic view of how steps interact, how changes in one area ripple and snowball across the system, and how unintended consequences emerge. Combining process mining with systems thinking provides organizations with the tools to intentionally manage complexity, adapting to evolving regulations, market demands, or unforeseen challenges.

Process Mining in Today's Business Environment

In a data-rich world, process mining is becoming an essential tool for uncovering inefficiencies, optimizing workflows, and aligning operations with real-world behaviors. However, in recent informal conversations with some of my data colleagues, I was shocked to find that none had even heard of process mining. I hadn't either when I first began compiling material for this book three years ago. But since then, process mining seems to have grown substantially, although it has yet to hit the sharp spike of the hockey stick curve.

Transforming event logs from enterprise systems (such as ERP, SCM, or CRM) into sets of informative models reveals the flow of processes, detects inefficiencies, and checks for conformance with predefined workflows.

Process mining doesn't stop at discovery. It analyzes root causes of inefficiencies—like bottlenecks or rework—and provides actionable recommendations for improvement. Integration with modern technologies like Robotic Process Automation (RPA) and AI/ML amplifies its impact by identifying inefficiencies, automating their resolution, and forecasting future performance.

Process mining offers a critical layer of insight for BI professionals and Chief Data Officers (CDOs). While BI tools focus on trends and metrics, process mining explains why these trends occur by mapping the flow of events through systems. It provides:

- **Granular Transparency:** Showing how processes are executed, not just what outcomes they produce.
- **Efficiency Gains:** Enabling continuous optimization based on real-time event logs.
- **Data-Driven Decision Making:** Highlighting deviations from workflows and pinpointing areas for improvement.

Leaks and Friction

"Leaks" and "friction" refer to inefficiencies or losses that occur during a process. Leaks represent unintended losses—such as revenue leakage from unbilled services, inventory shrinkage due to theft or damage, or customer churn during onboarding processes. Friction refers to resistance or inefficiencies that slow down or waste resources in the system, such as delays in order processing, excessive approval steps in workflows, or bottlenecks in supply chains. Identifying and addressing these issues is crucial for optimizing complex systems, whether in logistics, manufacturing, or business processes.

Figure 4 illustrates a truck route with actual and expected values for key metrics—fuel, weight, and miles—at different points in the journey. The expected values (shown in parentheses and italics) serve as benchmarks for evaluating performance. For instance:

1. At "Arrive StoreA," the weight is 5 tons (actual) compared to the expected 4.99, showing relatively good alignment.

2. At "Arrive Home Base," the actual fuel in the tank is at 57% compared to the expected 55%. While the discrepancy is small, chronic discrepancies could indicate a potential inefficiency or leak in fuel management.

3. At "Arrive StoreB," miles traveled between points are also compared to ensure the route is being executed as planned, helping to identify any unnecessary detours or inefficiencies.

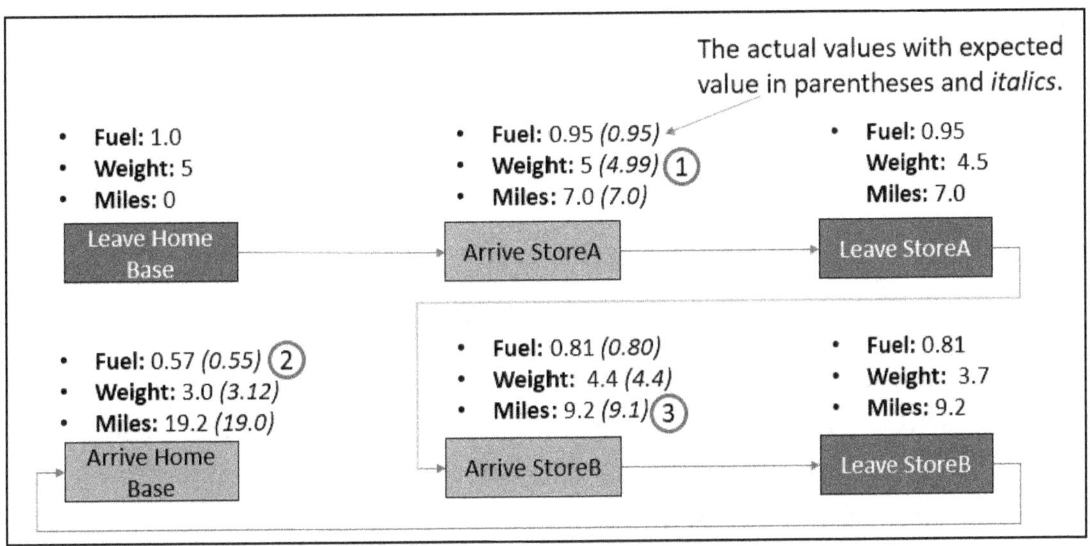

Figure 4: System optimization is about reducing leaks and friction.

This approach highlights areas where processes deviate from expectations, enabling precise identification of bottlenecks, inefficiencies, or waste. By tracking these deviations across time, businesses can uncover patterns, make data-driven adjustments, and optimize their operations for improved performance. This concept ties directly into process mining by providing the tools to analyze and refine processes, ensuring that resources are utilized effectively while minimizing leaks and friction.

Building Hypotheses and Markov Models

Once events are organized into processes, we can begin building Markov models that capture the transition probabilities and metric statistics between events. For instance:

- **In poker**, transitions could represent rounds of dealt cards, play actions, and ante and collection.
- **In logistics**, transitions might track the movement of inventory through supply chains.

Markov models act as hypotheses of a system, providing insights into how processes flow and where bottlenecks or inefficiencies might occur. These models not only help identify patterns, but also serve as tools to validate and refine workflow models—the "theories" that define how systems or workflows should operate.

In the end, this process mining approach enables us to move beyond raw data ingestion of events into a clear, grounded system-wide understanding of how events within processes interact dynamically.

Why This Book Doesn't Cover Petri Nets

Readers familiar with process modeling might wonder why I haven't included Petri nets—particularly stochastic Petri nets—in this book. Petri nets are well-known in academic and systems engineering circles for modeling concurrent processes and resource flows. They excel at simulating how tokens (representing resources or items) move through a system, handling parallelism, queues, and complex dependencies. In fields like manufacturing systems, distributed computing, or workflow engines, they are a powerful formalism.

However, this book is focused on the BI side of process mining and systems thinking. My background is rooted in BI, where the challenges center less on simulating detailed process logic and more on uncovering and analyzing real-world processes from vast amounts of messy, fragmented event data. This is why I've framed Time Molecules as the process-oriented counterpart to OLAP's sum and count aggregations. Rather than modeling process rules from scratch, we're looking to aggregate massive event logs into interpretable Markov models that summarize actual behaviors across the enterprise.

Petri nets are fundamentally about simulating predefined processes. Time Molecules, on the other hand, are about discovering how processes actually unfold—comparing patterns, identifying deviations, and quantifying inefficiencies, all in a form familiar and actionable to BI professionals and executives. For organizations dealing with millions or billions of process instances, the scalability, interpretability, and integration offered by Markov models align better with BI objectives.

Petri Nets are invaluable in domains that require detailed system simulation. However, this book aims to bridge process mining and systems thinking into the analytical BI side, emphasizing process discovery over simulation. Readers interested in simulating detailed system behavior may wish to explore Petri nets separately. Here, the focus remains on leveraging data-driven models that reveal how systems actually operate in practice and provide actionable insights at scale.

Business Intelligence

As with my previous book, *Enterprise Intelligence*, Business Intelligence is the spearhead of my discussion. BI is a highly disciplined craft. It has been honed for decades in enterprises, providing trustworthy, cleansed, relevant, and secured data to decision-makers in a user-friendly and highly-performant manner. It makes sense that we should implement advanced techniques on top of a proven methodology and implementations.

In *Time Molecules*, we will explore how we can analyze and process events across a range of business scenarios. The bread-and-butter query pattern of slicing and dicing are essential techniques in this kind of analysis.

The concepts of slicing and dicing are about examining data from different angles, much like how we break down time molecules in event-driven systems.

Slicing and Dicing of Sets of Tuples

If you're new to BI, that title sounds awful. In a nutshell, think of having a large number of ingredients in your kitchen and wish to sort them into groups to count how many you have (e.g., ten Fuji apples, five cans of various brands of sardines) and the sum of how much they weigh (e.g., four pounds of Fuji apples and one pound of sardines). It doesn't make sense to go shopping unless you know what you have and how much of it.

Slicing and dicing is such a prevalent pattern of analytics queries that it led to the creation of dimensional modeling along with OLAP cubes to optimize multi-dimensional analysis. At its core, slicing and dicing answers the fundamental question: "What is the [metric] by [something], [something else], and [something else]?" Whether it's analyzing sales by region, product category, and time period, or customer behavior by location, age group, and purchase frequency, this multidimensional analysis is foundational to decision-making in BI.

Slicing is about filtering data across a number of entity attributes to focus on a specific subset. For example, in a customer service process, slicing might mean looking at only the complaints that occurred during some timeframe for Product A sold in some city. By applying this filter, we isolate a smaller, more relevant portion of the data, isolating data points of interest and setting aside the rest as noise.

In the Time Molecules context, slicing could involve filtering event data to focus on particular events under specific contexts. For instance, you could slice the data to examine only cases where customers received a refund after a complaint or focus on interactions within San Francisco during a specific timeframe.

Dicing takes this further by breaking down values by specific combinations of attributes in the sliced (filtered) data set. For example, in a sales process, dicing could mean breaking down sales by region, product category, and month--each unique combination, a row in a data set.

Those combinations of attributes are the structure of tuples—which are the fundamental "things" of multi-dimensional analysis. A tuple represents a specific combination of attributes that defines what we are talking about, such as [electronics, Midwest, Q3 2024]—a thing.

Traditional BI, founded on data warehouses, ETL, OLAP cubes, and visualization tools such as Power BI and Tableau, focuses on analyzing the value of these "things." Yes, traditional BI does involve work processes and sequences, but it's not the focus. Every point (which is a point in multi-dimensional space) on virtually any visualized chart/graph is a tuple. This flip from thing-centric (tuple) to process-centric highlights the shift in perspective that Time Molecules aims to address.

Applying These Concepts in Time Molecules

When applying slicing and dicing to Time Molecules, the focus shifts from analyzing metrics of things to exploring the probabilities of transitions between events within processes running in a complex environment. In traditional dimensional models or OLAP cubes, metrics describe attributes of entities ("things") in a relatively fixed, deterministic way.

Time Molecules recognize that real-world processes are shaped by complexity, and probabilities serve as a way to collapse and quantify the uncertainty that's due to this complexity.

Focusing on time-based models provides a better view from which we can move quicker through the gathering of correlations to understand cause and effect.

In an idealized world, processes would be as deterministic as machines, with transitions between steps having probabilities of 1.0—certainty. For example, if every customer interaction followed a perfectly predictable script, there would be no variability to account for, so we always know what will happen. That's why we go through so much trouble creating more rules—in the hope that someday, things will always happen in a predictable and desirable way. But in the real world, countless interactions affect cycles of a process in avoidable or at least unintended ways. A delay in shipping, a miscommunication with a customer, or an unexpected system error will alter how a process unfolds—most likely in an inconvenient way. Probabilities measure these disruptions, giving us a lens through which we study processes as they actually occur, rather than how they are intended to function. For instance, slicing by date within Time Molecules lets us examine how the probabilities of event transitions change over time for a specific process. Has the likelihood of transitioning from Event A to Event B increased or decreased between 2019 and 2024? Are there periods where certain transitions become less likely, indicating disruptions or inefficiencies? This ability to track probabilities over time helps us mitigate uncertainty by identifying emerging processes in the evolution of the known processes—new processes emerge at the intersection of existing processes.

In a financial context, dicing could uncover how the probability of fraud detection leading to action varies across regions, customer types, or transaction categories. By analyzing probabilities across multiple dimensions, we can uncover hidden patterns that explain why certain transitions are more likely in some contexts than others.

Time Molecules fundamentally differ from traditional OLAP cubes by focusing on processes and events rather than static attributes. In an OLAP cube, metrics describe values at fixed intersections in a multidimensional space, like sales revenue by region and time. Time is often treated as just another dimension—albeit the most used. Time Molecules flip this perspective, treating time as the backbone and probabilities as the primary metric. Instead of asking, "What are the metrics at this intersection (point) of the multi-dimensional space?" we ask:

What is the probability of transitioning between specific events?
How do these probabilities vary over time and across dimensions?
What disruptions or anomalies are shifting these probabilities?

By slicing and dicing event transitions, Time Molecules enables us to examine the true impact of complexity on processes. They reveal how disruptions—whether small or systemic—affect the likelihood of transitions, helping us identify where processes are stable, where and why they might be breaking down, and how they adapt. In this way, probabilities become the key to understanding processes in a dynamic, unpredictable world.

Time Molecules are Another Fact Aggregation

The notion of Time Molecules is a progression of my 26 years of experience with pre-aggregated OLAP cube systems—primarily SQL Server Analysis Services (SSAS) and more recently, Kyvos Insights. So, I've noticed compelling parallels between OLAP cubes and Time Molecules.

Time Molecules are Like OLAP Aggregations

Time Molecules are a compression of a collection of cycles (iterations, cases) of a process. This is similar to the more familiar concept of the compression of a log of facts into sum and count aggregations of OLAP cubes.

In the context of AI structures, Time Molecules isn't even in the ballpark of LLM sophistication. Time Molecules are very simple structures to calculate and are discrete structures—which are among its primary advantages. But in a somewhat analogous way to LLMs, scaled out across a very large number of combinations of attributes, the breadth of simple models could be formidable.

At-Scale Analysis and the Role of Time Molecules

The concept of at-scale analysis lies at the heart of Time Molecules. It draws inspiration from the aggregation techniques of OLAP systems like SSAS and Kyvos Insights, which compress vast datasets into condensed, manageable forms. Just as OLAP enables the slicing and dicing of data in massive data warehouses (DW), Time Molecules enable the aggregation and study of countless permutations of event sequences across wide-ranging dimensions. That is, by at-scale, I mean the creation, caching, and analysis of a great number of unique MMs built from sliced and diced subsets of a DW of events.

In traditional BI, sum and count aggregations are a compressed view of data—a practical form that is an easier structure for helping decision-makers identify trends and patterns. Time Molecules extend this paradigm to processes. They are a compression of cycles of events into MMs, which reveal the underlying probabilities and metrics like the time between events, variance, or other attributes.

This process-centric compression allows for a detailed exploration of the more dynamic "how" and "why" questions. At scale, Time Molecules offer:

- **Broad Dimensional Coverage**: Analyze processes across hundreds or thousands of combinations of attributes, like different product lines, regions, or customer types.
- **Dynamic Insights**: Study how probabilities, durations, or variabilities evolve across time and space. For instance, how does the process of fraud detection differ between urban and rural regions?
- **Emergent Patterns**: Identify new steps (events) or pathways in a process as they arise, revealing shifts in behavior or strategy requirements.

On-the-Fly Computation of Time Molecules

Even though the MM algorithm is light on computation, it still can involve massive numbers of rows. So it can still take a few seconds for tens of thousands of rows to a few hours for trillions of rows to compute. It's the same for OLAP cubes. Most queries to OLAP cubes are often sub-second because of pre-computation—selected values are pre-computed. However, similar to OLAP cubes, not all possible MMs can be precomputed and stored. The sheer number of combinations across multiple dimensions makes it impractical—the proverbial "more than the atoms in the universe." Instead, a hybrid approach is necessary:

1. **Precomputed Molecules**: Store the most frequently accessed or strategically significant attributes. The tricky part for OLAP cube systems is to automatically figure out what those "most significant" attributes are.
2. **On-the-Fly Calculation**: Compute less frequently used or ad-hoc combinations of attributes as needed, then save them for future reference. Computing in real time is much slower, but Markov models are "relatively" quick computations, and they will be faster, almost instant, if cached for the next time.

This approach substantially promotes flexibility and efficiency, enabling enterprises to leverage the full power of Time Molecules without being constrained by storage or computation limits. By applying these principles, Time Molecules employ Markov models as a practical, scalable framework for process analysis, extending the legacy of OLAP systems into the realm of process-driven BI and AI.

Digital Twins: The Other Side of the Process Mining Coin

While process mining uncovers how processes actually operate versus how they are imagined to operate, digital twins take this a step further by creating a virtual representation of a real-world system that continuously updates in real time. A digital twin mirrors processes, assets, or even entire enterprises, integrating live data streams from IoT devices, enterprise applications, and sensor networks to simulate, predict, and optimize performance.

Where digital twins differ from process mining is their real-time, forward-looking nature. Instead of analyzing historical event logs to reconstruct process flows, digital twins provide live system simulations, often powered by AI and machine learning, allowing for predictive insights and scenario testing. However, they share a common goal with process mining—understanding and improving system efficiency.

This is how Time Molecules could enhance digital twins. While digital twins track live data, Time Molecules model the probabilities and transition behaviors of historical event sequences, uncovering hidden patterns in how processes evolve over time. However, Time Molecules go beyond standard Markov models by working with them at scale in a BI-friendly, slice-and-dice manner—allowing businesses to analyze transition patterns across different dimensions just like they would with traditional dimensional BI data.

By integrating BI-structured, at-scale MMs from Time Molecules, a digital twin could move beyond just mirroring reality into anticipating future states with probabilistic precision, dynamically adjusting predictions based on process variations across time, location, and business segments.

Together, process mining, digital twins, and Time Molecules represent a layered approach to understanding operations:

- Process mining reveals how processes actually run, detecting inefficiencies and deviations.
- Digital twins provide real-time simulations, often enhanced by AI and machine learning, to enable predictive insights and scenario testing.
- Time Molecules add a scalable, BI-sliceable Markov modeling approach, enabling probabilistic insights that can be dynamically segmented across different business dimensions.

CHAPTER 2

Markov Models

Markov models (MMs) are an old (early 1900s) and easily computable kind of ML model. They compress sequences of events into a statistical abstraction, summarizing many cycles of a process into a simple and efficient representation. They are an amalgamation of many cycles over time.

To understand this intuitively, imagine starting a new job where no one mentors you. You'd pick up a few rules just by observing what happens every day—when meetings occur, when people take breaks, or when emails get sent. Over time, you'd form an implicit understanding of these patterns without anyone having explicitly explained them to you. Even my cat has this kind of learning: she knows there's a high probability that I'm about to leave my work area because she hears my chair sliding back from my desk. I didn't teach her that; she learned it simply by observing repeated sequences, day after day.

MMs operate similarly. They aren't focused on processes we've deliberately designed—like workflows or protocols we explicitly designed. Instead, they uncover emergent processes, the ones we weren't consciously aware of or didn't consciously plan. These are the processes shaped by external factors like customer trends, government regulations, or environmental changes.

Like most ML models, what makes MMs especially valuable is that they reveal patterns in the chaos. Studying related MMs can reveal unknown processes, which feels like discovering a new "force" that might explain quirks we observe within the known processes.

For many readers, MMs might be unfamiliar or familiar but arcane—an ML algorithm we outgrew long ago. If I hadn't worked with them, I might have thought the same thing. But at their core, they're a compact representation of a large, messy set of events. Archaic or not, they're an elegant and powerful tool for making sense of the hidden patterns in our world.

Don't worry if these concepts still feel a bit abstract right now. The walkthroughs through TimeSolution are designed to solidify and clarify the ideas explained here.

A Non-Traditional Perspective: Nodes as Events, Not States

MMs traditionally use the term "state" to refer to the nodes. In this book, however, the nodes are events. States describe the current situation, a snapshot of a system, such as being in the state of eating dinner, being classified as a bad loan risk, or being in the state of feeling hungry.

> *Events are indicators of change, the effect of change, and change is what requires intelligent responses. Whenever something changes—whether the status or characteristic of something—events are generated and observed.*

In the mathematical context, state or event doesn't matter—the nodes are just some symbol. For example, A has a 0.35 probability of moving to B and a 0.65 probability of moving to C. It doesn't matter what A, B, and C are. But in our logical minds, as we perceive the world around us, there is a dichotomy. There is a sense of cause and effect, which can be thought of as an event (cause) leading to a new state (effect).

It can be challenging to differentiate between events and states because the same concept can often be rephrased from either perspective. For example, a typical MM might represent weather states like sunny, rainy, or cloudy. In this context, "sunny" is a state that describes the condition of the weather on a given day. To shift the perspective to events, we might phrase it as, "Jan 1, 2024, became a sunny day in Phoenix." Here, the focus is on the transition or occurrence—the change to a sunny state—rather than the static condition itself. This transformation highlights the core distinction: states represent "what is," while events represent "what changed" and drive the dynamic processes that require intelligent responses.

Typically, when viewing a log of events—such as one generated by software running a process—we observe a mix of events and states. For example, updating a database might produce log entries, such as processing (state), error (event), notified DBA (event), rolling back (state), and finished (event). The last event implies a state of being back online (but without the update) or offline (awaiting a remedy by that poor DBA).

Our OLTP (Online Transactional Processing) databases generally consist of collections of things categorized by entities (tables). For example, a customer table describes collections of customers and their attributes, and usually the current state of each customer. The state of a thing (customer in this example) takes two forms:

1. **Their qualities:** Reading a customer row is like looking at a customer and noting their present condition. How would I categorize them? What attributes do I note?

2. **What they are doing:** OLTP databases often include flag columns like active or credit risk, but these typically represent only the current state and do not keep a history of state changes.

The problem with these current state values is that things change. Some things, such as birth dates, don't change (unless it was a mistake). Some things change relatively slowly over months through decades, like current employer, address, or marital status. Some things change quickly, such as the balances of your 401K, checking, and frequent flyer accounts—these are transactional.

Until the advent of data warehousing, the notion of recording the history of state changes wasn't feasible. Before the scalability and ease of cloud technology, storing historical data was a luxury. Data warehousing changed this paradigm, promoting the storage of years of transactional history and the less storage-intense recording of dimensional changes through slowly changing dimensions (SCD).

A data warehouse fact table, transactional history, represents a mix of both things and events. For example, a particular sale is both a thing and an event. What makes a sale a thing is that it can be referred to as a noun—for instance, "the Taylor 314ce guitar I purchased from Rodney on Dec 10, 2024." What makes a sale event-like is that it has associated dates, such as purchase date, shipping date, and delivery date—each date is an event related to the sale. Similarly, a customer table might include dates like created_date and last_modified, which imply events—though the latter can be vague, as it does not specify what aspect (attribute) of the customer record was updated.

More recently, the concept of event sourcing represents an extreme of recording history—every change to individual attributes (e.g., changes to job, address, name) is recorded as a separate log entry.

In this context, every change to a state is treated as an event—which it is. The notion of event sourcing became feasible only after the ability to implement the infrastructure that can process and store such massive data volumes became mainstream (i.e., the cloud).

Prior to that, databases were designed to be as streamlined as possible, and long-term history was a low priority. Today, infrastructures like event streaming and event hubs enable the capture of event streams from countless sources. Similarly, the Data Vault methodology treats all attributes of entities as slowly changing by default, contrasting with dimensional (Kimball or Inmon) data warehouses where SCDs are an optional feature.

IoT (Internet of Things) devices further blur the line between events and states. For instance, an event might be "exceeded speed limit," while a status (a state) might be "traveling over the speed limit," inferred from continuous "heartbeat" signals. In the former case, we can infer that the status has changed (derive a state from an event), while in the latter, we infer that the speed limit was exceeded at some point (derive an event from a state).

Newer data warehousing paradigms like data vault and event sourcing take SCDs to their extremes. These advancements allow for fine-grained historical analysis, enabling precise reconstructions of past states and events. It facilitates "time travel"—where we can rebuild a database to be exactly as it was at some given time in the past. This is critical to fully understand our relentlessly dynamic world. Additionally, over the past decade, regulations like HIPAA and GDPR have reinforced the need for extensive logging toward the goal of exhaustive auditing. These requirements have further emphasized the importance of events, as they fundamentally capture what happened, when, and why.

See Appendix H for more information on Event Sourcing.

Events and Processes

As just discussed, the primary "atoms" of Time Molecules are events—discrete occurrences tied to specific points in time. Events are loosely regular occurrences within the iterations of a process—sequences of events that occur over time—shaped by interacting forces, some natural, some imposed by our human will, such as the workflows of business. Understanding how events and processes relate is essential to appreciating the value of Time Molecules. Each event represents a measurable action or occurrence, such as a customer placing an order, a system logging an error, or a temperature sensor exceeding a threshold.

When events are grouped and analyzed, they manifest cyclical processes—the sequences of actions that define behaviors or systems. They precipitate from out of our databases, shaped by customer behaviors, evolving government regulations, environmental factors, or market trends. Some processes, like workflows or production lines, are explicitly designed and well-documented. Deviation isn't intended nor acceptable in designed systems. Exceptions are detected and dealt with in some manner—whether through a workaround or elimination.

This is process mining. Process mining identifies these evolving or newly emergent processes by analyzing vast collections of event data. It helps us discover the steps that occur, the order they follow, and the typical outcomes. It's the discovery phase—validating how we think the known processes work versus what is really happening, as well as finding the hidden processes that we didn't design and might not even realize exist.

Time Molecules take the next step: they focus on the continued analysis of these processes. Through the transformation of logs of events into compact Markov models, we can quantify the relationships between events, uncovering the probabilities of transitions between events, the timing and variability of those transitions, and the conditions or metrics that influence the process.

Although there is much overlap between process mining and Time Molecules, process mining is evolving. At least for now, process mining leans towards discovery, while Time Molecules lean toward analysis in the time-honored BI tradition.

The Markov Property

The Markov Property describes a process where the next event depends only on the last event—not the full sequence of past events. While this is sometimes referred to as being "memoryless," a more accurate interpretation is that the process has a limited memory, focusing solely on what we last saw.

A familiar example is the popularity of an author's next book. For most authors, the success of their upcoming release significantly depends on how well their most recent book performed. If their last book was a major hit, the next is more likely to ride that momentum. Conversely, if their last book flopped, it could dampen enthusiasm for the new release. Older books, even if they were significant hits or failures, will tend to have diminishing or no influence over time.

This is really the primary principle of MMs. By focusing on the current event rather than the full history, MMs simplify the complexity of modeling processes, making it possible to analyze and predict outcomes efficiently, even at scale.

For those familiar with natural language processing (NLP), a predecessor of LLMs, the notion of the current word (or last few words) predicting the next word was pretty much its big deficiency. It is arguably the insight that attention (context of the conversation), which can span any number of words already spoken in a long conversation, was the breakthrough that raised the ability of a machine to (at least appear to) understand language.[2]

So, as mentioned, the Markov property can fuel the notion that MMs are arcane. In the coming chapters, we'll cover a few features that should ameliorate that perception. But more importantly, there are trade-offs related to simplicity in order to ease compute (training and query) resource appetite and complexity. Such is the case (at the time of writing) with LLMs and their multi-million dollar, weeks to months-long training.

Before continuing, I need to clarify that when I refer to "Markov models" in this book, I am mostly talking about Markov Chains. Markov Chains are a type of Markov model. The Markov Property is the intrinsic characteristic of a Markov Chain. However, I chose to use the broader term, Markov model, since the features I describe could be argued to have moved beyond the strict definition of a Markov Chain.

The Value of Heuristics and "System 1"

Real-life systems are rarely as simple as the Markov Property suggests. As just discussed, most events are influenced by more than just the immediate past. For instance, today's weather may be shaped not only by yesterday's conditions, but also by broader patterns from the day before or even earlier. MMs provide a quick and dirty heuristic—a mental shortcut—that often works surprisingly well.

---

[2] Vaswani, A., Shazeer, N., Parmar, N., Uszkoreit, J., Jones, L., Gomez, A. N., Kaiser, Ł., and Polosukhin, I. (2017). Attention Is All You Need. In Advances in Neural Information Processing Systems (Vol. 30). Curran Associates, Inc.

Heuristics like these are the foundation of System 1 thinking,[3] the fast, intuitive reasoning that helps humans and other animals make effective decisions in complex environments.

For many critters, including us, relying on the most recent events or states for decision-making is not only sufficient but optimal in dynamic situations. Whether it's a predator tracking its prey or a person predicting the success of their next book based on their last one, the ability to make rapid decisions without analyzing the entire history is a critical survival tool. This heuristic approach works because it simplifies complexity into manageable chunks, trading perfect precision for speed and adaptability.

While modern domains such as meteorological science have advanced far beyond basic MMs, incorporating large-scale simulations and intricate dynamics, many systems—especially those that are poorly understood or continuously evolving—can still benefit from the simplicity of MMs. These models offer a quick and adaptable framework to gain insights into a wide variety of systems, making them valuable when resources or information are limited.

One technique for addressing dependencies beyond the current event is high-order MMs. These models extend the heuristic by accounting for the last *n* events—usually a small number like two or three—capturing more nuanced relationships in systems where recent history significantly influences the future. For example, a customer who upgraded their service before contacting support is less likely to leave compared to one who reached out after expressing dissatisfaction.

Heuristics like those embodied in MMs remind us that quick, effective information and reasoning often outperform complex analysis when time is limited and/or the scope is hopelessly large and complex. This type of thinking has served humans and countless other species well, shaping our ability to navigate an unpredictable world with agility and insight.

Transition Matrix

The transition matrix is more like a "crystallized form" of an MM, representing the probabilities of transitioning from one event to another in a neatly organized table. For instance, in the weather

[3] Kahneman, Daniel. Thinking, Fast and Slow. Farrar, Straus and Giroux, 2011.

example for Seattle (Table 4), the matrix captured the likelihood of moving between sunny and rainy conditions.

Why is this representation so powerful? Because it enables us to engage the power of linear algebra to analyze the system. Representing transitions in matrix form unlocks mathematical tools like matrix multiplication, which facilitates a powerful way to examine how the system might evolve over time. This approach is essential for calculating metrics like the stationary distribution, which reveals the system's long-term behavior. For example, consider modeling how customers move through different areas of a retail store: Browsing, Trying On, Purchasing, and Seeking Assistance. Table 6 is the transition matrix for this process:

	Browsing	Trying On	Purchasing	Seeking Assistance
Browsing	0.4	0.3	0.2	0.1
Trying On	0.2	0.4	0.3	0.1
Purchasing	0.1	0.2	0.5	0.2
Seeking Assistance	0.2	0.3	0.2	0.3

Table 6: Transition matrix of a department store sales process.

Table 6 shows, for example, that a customer who is currently Browsing has a 30% chance of moving to Trying On, a 20% chance of Purchasing, and a 10% chance of Seeking Assistance.

With techniques like matrix multiplication and eigenvalue calculations, you can predict system behavior over multiple transitions, identify long-term trends, and uncover insights that are hard to glean from simple visualization. For example, using the transition matrix, you can determine:

- How customer behavior evolves over time.
- What the steady-state distribution looks like (where most customers will end up in the long run).
- How to optimize operations, predict future outcomes, or refine strategies based on these probabilities.

While platforms like Neo4j are excellent for visualizing MMs as a graph, the transition matrix is the analytical format that enables deeper predictions and optimizations. It helps transform today's data into actionable insights for tomorrow, helping businesses streamline processes, enhance customer experiences, and fine-tune strategies for long-term success.

Stationary Distribution

A stationary distribution is a concept that tells us where a system naturally "settles" over time. It answers the question, "If this process ran endlessly, how would things stabilize?" For example, if you roll a fair die countless times, each number will eventually come up very close to the same number of times, resulting in a uniform distribution. This outcome is predictable because we already know the die is fair, and the probabilities for each side are equal. In this case, we don't need to perform the experiment to determine the stationary distribution—it's already defined by the "physics" of the system.

However, for more complex processes in real life, the stationary distribution isn't something we know in advance—it's something we need to discover. Unlike dice, where fairness and independence are baked into the design, real-world processes almost always involve uneven probabilities from poorly understood dependencies and disruptions. Analyzing these processes helps us uncover their long-term behavior, revealing insights we couldn't predict without running the analysis.

Starting with our transition matrix (the table of probabilities shown in Table 6), we can calculate these long-term probabilities. In simple terms, the stationary distribution shows the likelihood of being in each state after many transitions. For example, in our department store scenario, it might reveal at any given instant that a customer would most likely be found in the Purchasing area, followed by Trying On, with fewer customers Browsing or Seeking Assistance. Table 7 shows the stationary distribution calculated from the transition matrix, as shown in Table 6.

State	Browsing	Trying On	Purchasing	Seeking Assistance
Stationary Probability	20.9%	29.7%	32.8%	16.6%

Table 7: Stationary distribution.

The stationary distribution represents the long-term balance of event occurrences. These percentages describe the overall rhythm of the process when it stabilizes. This is very different from the transition matrix:

- **Transition Matrix**: Shows the immediate probability of one event leading to another. Example: A customer Browsing has a 40% chance of continuing to Browse and a 30% chance of moving to Trying On.

- **Stationary Distribution**: Shows the long-term proportion of events in the entire process. Example: Over time, 29.7% of events will involve Trying On, regardless of the initial event. A more intuitive way to state this is, knowing nothing else about the customer or what has gone on, the most likely place to find him is at the purchase counter.

More interestingly, we can use the stationary distribution to calculate the probability of a sequence of events by combining the stationary probabilities with the transition probabilities. For instance, starting from the stationary probability of Browsing (20.9%), the probability of a customer Browsing and then moving to Trying On can be calculated as:

$P(\text{Browsing} \rightarrow \text{Trying On}) = P(\text{Browsing}) \times P(\text{Trying On} \mid \text{Browsing})$

Using the values from Table 6 and Table 7:

$P(\text{Browsing} \rightarrow \text{Trying On}) = 20.9\% \times 30\% = 6.27\%$

This means there is a 6.27% chance that a random customer at some instant will be found Trying On just after Browsing. This approach can be extended to calculate probabilities for longer sequences by multiplying the stationary probability of the initial state with the relevant transition probabilities along the sequence.

Markov Model Manifold

What I call a Markov Model Manifold (MMM) is an interconnected system of MMs. By linking MMs through shared events and generalized terms defined in knowledge graphs (we'll cover in the Enterprise Intelligence chapter), this manifold provides a unified view of the complex interplay between systems—that is, MMs created from the mix of processes of the tapestry of the world. Key components include:

- **Shared Events**: Events such as "Purchase" or "Login" may appear in multiple models. These shared points act as bridges, linking processes that are seemingly separate but inherently interdependent.

- **Ontology-Driven Generalization**: Using a knowledge graph, specific terms (e.g., "checkout" and "cart finalization") can be generalized into broader concepts (e.g., "transaction") to establish connections across diverse Markov models.
- **Dynamic Interaction**: As new events emerge or existing processes evolve, the manifold adapts, continuously refining the links and probabilities.

This manifold concept enables:

- **Global Insights**: By zooming out, we see the big picture of how processes interact, offering insights into systemic trends and emergent patterns.
- **Cross-Domain Analysis**: Linking processes across domains (e.g., sales and customer service) uncovers hidden dependencies and synergies.
- **Enhanced Decision-Making**: A manifold allows decision-makers to evaluate strategies across interconnected models, balancing trade-offs in a complex system.

The MMM links individual Markov models, transforming a set of isolated analyses into part of a broader, interconnected framework—making the invisible threads of systems visible and actionable.

Strategy: The Systems Engineering of Competing Goals

At scale, MMs unlock the ability to analyze systems of processes across vast dimensions of time and subsets of your data's dimensional space. The world is an intricate web of interacting, evolving processes, each shaping and reshaping the others. MMs derived from highly-varied slices of this web reveal the dynamic forces at play, enabling us to engineer systems that work towards coherent strategies in a system of competing goals.

MMs at scale empower the engineering of strategy by transforming the abstract interplay of processes into actionable insights:

1. **Mapping Complex Dimensions**: MMs segmented by time, location, or customer profiles uncover flow patterns across diverse contexts, enabling comparisons that refine understanding and reveal strategic opportunities.

2. **Tracing Evolution**: By studying how MMs change over time (diced by timeframes), we can pinpoint the source of trends, disruptions, and emerging priorities—offering a foundation for proactive adaptation.

3. **Analyzing Variability**: Changes in metrics, like time between events or fluctuations in variability, can signal stabilization, disruption, or volatility, providing cues for intervention or recalibration.

4. **Revealing Systemic Interactions**: MMs expose how one process might influence another, capturing the interplay of goals—like cost vs customer experience or growth vs risk—helping strategists build systems where competing forces work in balance.

At their core, MMs at scale provide more than data and even information—they deliver a systemic lens into the dynamics of emerging and evolving processes—closer to understanding. Strategy is not a linear, one-dimensional plan but the engineering of systems that improve the performance of competing and/or conflicting goals. That is, maximizing value and mitigating risk in a clever way that minimizes the "pain" in the system. For example, how can we increase profit without going into terrible debt, working everyone to their breaking points, and putting good-will customer relationships at risk?

With insights drawn from wide-scale modeling, we can move beyond operational or tactical insights into the domain of true intelligence: designing adaptive systems that thrive amid change, even driving the change. This is the promise of MMs at scale: to see our enterprise as a system of systems, shaping the system, and steering the system toward sustainable success.

Time Series and Sequences

A time series is a sequence of data points of a particular metric, collected or recorded at specific, evenly spaced time intervals. For example, Stock prices recorded at the end of the trading day, daily temperature readings by the minute, or monthly/quarterly/year sales figures. The key feature is the regularity of the intervals between data points, which allows for the analysis of trends and cyclic behaviors over time.

A sequence is a less-specific concept that refers to an ordered list of events or data points, which may or may not occur at regular intervals. For example, a sequence of user actions on a website, events of a crop cycle, or a series of events in a manufacturing process. For example, we can't expect a web user to click on the next page every 15 seconds—they'll click when they're ready. Sequences can include various types of events and can be analyzed to understand patterns, dependencies, and transitions between states.

Since a sequence is a less constrained concept than a time series, a time series is a kind of sequence—just with a couple of restrictions. For this book, I will generally refer to *sequences*, not *time series*. To summarize, the key differences are:

- Interval Regularity: Time series data is collected at regular intervals, while sequences can have irregular intervals.
- Event Types: Time series typically involve a single type of event with some sort of value, whereas sequences can include multiple event types.

The distinction between time series and sequences becomes important when selecting the appropriate ML models for analysis. Time series ML algorithms, such as ARIMA, LSTMs, and Prophet, are specifically designed to handle data with regular time intervals. These models focus on trends, seasonality, and forecasting future values based on past observations. While effective for metrics like stock prices or temperature readings, these algorithms are not well-suited for irregular sequences of processes out in the world.

In contrast, MMs are built to analyze and predict sequences of a set of events based on their transitions. They excel at modeling processes with probabilistic relationships, such as user behavior on a website or steps in a manufacturing process. The flexibility of MMs in handling event-based data makes them particularly useful for studying sequences where the relationships between events matter more than the timing regularity.

Note that IoT data sources often generate continuous time series data (sensor readings at regular intervals), which can be processed through event streaming systems to convert them into discrete events. It's up to a complex event processing system to ingest the time series and analyze it for noteworthy qualities such as significant changes or exceeding thresholds.

Video are "Time Pictures"

In today's world, which is filled with remote conferences, training sessions, sales meetings, and cameras on every phone, street corner, and drone, video has become a massive, if not the most massive, source of unstructured data. These videos capture what happens: people arriving, interacting, debating, and solving problems. Each moment in a video holds potential events, offering a wealth of data at various levels.

If a picture is worth a thousand words, video is at least a thousand times that.

While pictures leave it up to us to infer what might be going on, video goes much further, revealing sequences of actions that unfold over time. It's not just a snapshot—it's the story being told.

Even two years ago, Azure AI enabled us to analyze video frames. Azure AI could detect objects within each frame, identify their proximity, and even summarize the picture. By analyzing consecutive frames, we could then record frame-to-frame changes as events—like someone entering a room or moving within a scene. Trained AI models could detect the sequence of changes in facial expressions, tones of voices, and even classify activities such as walking, running, or waving. Additionally, these models could analyze crowd dynamics by estimating density, tracking movement patterns, and identifying anomalies like sudden gatherings. Further, a transcript extraction could pull key terms spoken by specific people from the audio, enabling us to combine visual and spoken elements into proper context, uncovering patterns or processes.

At the very least, the technology available today through platforms such as Azure AI gives us the parts to start extracting this event-based data from videos. It's all about the automated mining of the possible processes massive videos hold, even if only a few events are detected. In a world filled with unstructured data, this is a powerful tool that brings structure to the chaos, revealing patterns and processes that might otherwise remain hidden.

Markov Models In Machine Learning and AI

MMs haven't been widely recognized or routinely applied in the mainstream BI world—at least at the time of writing. However, they still hold a place in AI due to their ability to model sequential or probabilistic processes efficiently.

Traditionally, MMs have been foundational in areas like Natural Language Processing (NLP) and speech recognition, particularly through n-gram models and Hidden Markov Models (HMMs). Although neural networks and transformers have largely supplanted them in these domains, Markov Decision Processes (MDPs) remain essential in reinforcement learning and decision-making under uncertainty, making them valuable in robotics and control systems. However, the goal of this book is to bring MMs front and center of the BI stage.

MMs are used to model sequential processes where the future state depends only on the current state, relying on transition probabilities. In contrast, Markov Decision Processes (MDPs) build on this framework by adding actions and rewards, enabling decision-making and optimization under uncertainty. While MMs are descriptive and predictive, MDPs are prescriptive, focused on finding optimal policies for complex systems. This book focuses on the practical applications of Markov models, with a little more discussion of MDPs included in Appendix E, as well as future works.

The strength of MMs lies in their interpretability and computational efficiency, which make them useful for sequential data tasks in bioinformatics and anomaly detection. While not currently prominent in BI, MMs have untapped potential in areas like process mining and customer behavior modeling, where understanding time-dependent relationships can provide analytical insights.

At the core, I'm a BI architect and developer. I look at BI as a kind of scientific role in a company that isn't a science-based company. This is similar to how an enterprise such as McDonalds or WalMart has a legal department, although they are not a law firm. The Microsoft campus has cafeterias, although they aren't a food service company.

Most enterprises aren't about hard-core scientific research where scientific investigation is their key role or critical to their success – such as it is for hedge funds and pharmaceuticals. In scientific settings, MMs are very familiar and in modest use. Scientific environments lean on more sophisticated models that might be more accurate but take much time to process. However, a BI environment requires snappy responsiveness.

While MMs are a fundamental concept in probabilistic modeling and AI, their practical application in BI systems is less common compared to more widely familiar ML algorithms such as:

- **Regression Analysis – Forecasting**: At its core, regression analysis is about understanding the relationship between variables to make predictions. In business, this translates to forecasting, where past data (like sales figures or economic indicators) is used to predict future outcomes.
- **Association – Market Basket Analysis**: Association rules find patterns where one item's purchase occurs with another. In retail, this is famously known as market basket analysis, where businesses analyze which products are frequently bought together to optimize product placement, promotions, or recommendations like "customers who bought this also bought..."
- **Clustering – Customer Segmentation**: Clustering in an unsupervised algorithm that groups similar items or customers based on features without predefined categories. In BI, this is commonly applied as customer segmentation, dividing customers into groups/cohorts based on similar behaviors or characteristics for targeted marketing, personalized services, or product development.
- **Time Series – Trend Analysis**: Time series analysis involves studying data points collected over time to identify trends, cycles, or seasonal patterns. In the BI world, this is often known as trend analysis, used for everything from predicting stock levels, understanding seasonal sales variations, and forecasting future market demands or economic conditions.

MMs, while commonly utilized in probabilistic modeling and AI, are less commonly spotlighted in typical BI environments. However, they do have applications that might be familiar to BI professionals:

- **Customer Journey Mapping**: Markov models can be used to predict how customers move through various stages of interaction with a company, from awareness to purchase to loyalty or churn. This can help craft targeted marketing strategies or improve the customer experience.

- **Predictive Maintenance**: In industries where equipment maintenance is critical, Markov models can predict when a machine might fail based on its current state, thus scheduling maintenance before a breakdown occurs, which is crucial for operations planning.

- **Churn Prediction**: By modeling the transitions between customer states (active user to inactive), businesses can identify at-risk customers for retention strategies.

- **Process Optimization**: For workflows or any process that can be broken down into states, Markov models help understand and optimize the flow, reduce bottlenecks, and improve efficiency.

These applications, while not as universally recognized as the previous set of methods in day-to-day BI operations, demonstrate how Markov models can offer insights into sequences or state-dependent behaviors, which are valuable in strategic business decisions. However, their use often requires a bit more technical sophistication or at least a deeper understanding of the system being modeled, which might explain their less frequent direct application in BI toolsets—which is what this book is about.

Given this landscape, the exploration of MMs through Time Molecules is an effort to bring this powerful yet underutilized tool into more practical and scalable use within BI systems. Creating MMs from fact tables and event logs—similar to how aggregations are created in OLAP systems—could open up new possibilities for predictive analytics and real-time decision-making in BI environments. This approach has the potential to offer a competitive edge to businesses that adopt it, providing insights that are currently beyond the reach of standard BI practices.

The TL;DR as a Large Language Model Prompt

Throughout this book, you will frequently interact with large language models (LLMs), particularly in the context of a Retrieval Augmented Generation (RAG) framework. In order for an LLM to assist effectively, it must understand the concept of Time Molecules. Time Molecules is a framework built on Markov models (MMs) that are derived from event data and represent process flows. These models can be generated by all combinations of slices and dices, and cached based on various properties of the events and cases in the database.

In short, Time Molecules provides a scalable solution to analyze and predict how events transition over time, leveraging a scalable Markov model system built from vast datasets. These models are stored in a way similar to OLAP cubes, ensuring efficient retrieval and analysis across a wide range of business processes. By understanding how Time Molecules work, an LLM can better analyze processes, make predictions, and provide deeper insights based on event-driven systems.

Here is a TL;DR that could be used to explain Time Molecules to an LLM:

Time Molecules is a scalable system for generating and caching Markov models (MMs) from a large and diverse database of event data. Events are grouped by cases when possible, and both events and cases possess properties (region, customer type) that describe them. These properties allow for the creation of targeted MMs, which are filtered by specific events or properties at the event and case level.

The system can handle a massive volume of events, making it easy to slice and dice the data based on different event and case properties, even though this might involve processing a vast number of events. Once created, MMs are cached permanently in a database. This caching is somewhat analogous to how pre-aggregated sums and counts are cached in OLAP cubes, although the Markov models are cached only after being generated.

While the default metric calculated for these models is the time between events, other properties can be used as metrics. The models can calculate average, sum, standard deviation, maximum, minimum, and the number of rows across the cases that comprise the model. Custom metrics can also be applied, such as specific input/output measures between event A and event B.

Key points:

- *Events are grouped into cases, with both events and cases having properties that allow flexible slicing for customized models.*
- *The system can generate MMs based on event and case properties, making it highly scalable for large datasets.*
- *Time between events is the default metric, but other properties can be used to generate custom metrics.*
- *Once created, models are cached, enabling efficient reuse.*
- *Metrics like average, sum, standard deviation, and custom inputs or outputs are calculated across the cases.*

CHAPTER 3

TimeSolution

TimeSolution is the implemented realization of the Time Molecules concept, providing an analytical framework designed to unlock the insights hidden within event-based data. Just as traditional BI relies on ETL/ELT processes, data warehouses, and query/visualization tools of the slice and dice nature, Time Molecules revolve around event hubs, event streaming, the TimeSolution database (or warehouse), and associated query patterns.

The term "Solution" itself is a deliberate double entendre:

1. **Solution as a medium:** Just as molecules interact within a chemical solution, Time Molecules represent interrelated processes immersed in the broad environmental context of events, systems, and time.

2. **Solution as a method:** It's also a means of solving analytical challenges, turning raw event data into analytical insights.

At the heart of Time Molecules is the idea that Markov models ("Time Molecules") can be pre-calculated and persisted and/or generated ad-hoc, depending on the analytical need. This flexibility enables a wide array of use cases, from predictive modeling to process optimization. As mentioned, this is in the spirit of pre-aggregated OLAP cubes.

Core features of TimeSolution include:

1. **Precalculated and Persisted Markov Models:** Time Molecules can be created ahead of time and stored for repeated use or calculated dynamically based on real-time data. As with pre-aggregations of OLAP cubes, MMs can be proactively created across ranges of selected properties.

2. **Model Selection:** Users can choose models based on specific parameter criteria, such as event types, time ranges, or custom metrics, ensuring targeted and relevant analysis.

3. **Transition Drillthrough:** Explore what individual events comprise a specific event transition in the MM, allowing for granular analysis of patterns and transitions.

4. **Event Transforms:** Condense multiple events into a single, aggregated event to simplify complex processes or reduce path possibilities, making models more comprehensible.

5. **Selected Events:** Filter the event stream to include only specific events while skipping over others, tailoring the process to focus on the most relevant aspects.

6. **Multiple Metrics:** Beyond the core transition probability and default metric of Time Between Events, other metrics such as consumed fuel, load weight, or custom KPIs can be integrated, enabling multi-dimensional analysis.

7. **Continuous or Long Processes:** Handle long-running processes, such as cases spanning a lengthy or indefinite period.

The Time Molecules Warehouse

Just as a traditional data warehouse is usually an organized dimensional model for optimal BI query performance, the Time Molecules Warehouse provides the infrastructure to store, query, and analyze Time Molecules at scale. This warehouse isn't just a database for event logs—it's a system designed to transform raw event data into interconnected, analytical insights by organizing event streams and storing relationships across time and processes.

Key distinctions of the Time Molecules Warehouse include:

- **Integrated Processes**: Events are not isolated records but part of a larger network of interrelated processes, allowing users to query transitions, drill into specific pathways, and visualize process dynamics.

- **Adaptable Granularity**: Analysts can zoom in to explore detailed transitions between events or zoom out to observe overarching patterns, enabling insights at both micro and macro levels.
- **Efficient Scaling**: Designed to handle billions of events and their relationships, the warehouse supports long-running processes and the complexities of modern business systems.
- **Seamless Integration**: The warehouse integrates seamlessly with event streaming platforms, BI tools, and predictive analytics workflows, bridging the gap between traditional BI practices and modern process analysis.

Bridging Process and Insight

Time Molecules bridges the gap between traditional BI and process mining by elevating processes to first-class objects in BI analytics. While traditional BI emphasizes dimensional attributes and measures (e.g., sales by region or revenue over time), Time Molecules focus on the dynamics of processes—how events interact and evolve over time. This integration empowers organizations to:

- **Visualize Processes in Motion:** Move beyond static metrics to view processes as dynamic, evolving entities.
- **Reveal Hidden Dependencies:** Connect seemingly isolated events and uncover the interplay between processes across domains.
- **Optimize Operational Flows**: Identify inefficiencies, bottlenecks, and opportunities for improvement within key processes.

Prep Work Before Time Molecules

As it is for OLAP cubes, there is much that happens before we get to the point of analyzing Markov models. In the BI world, these are examples of a few major pieces before we have a good OLAP cube to slice and dice through:

1. **Master Data Management (MDM)** – MDM is the practice of creating a unified, consistent, and accurate view of core data entities like customers, products, or locations across an organization. MDM ensures that these data entities are correctly integrated and standardized across multiple systems, providing a reliable foundation for downstream analytics and business processes.

2. **Dimensional Modeling** –Dimensional modeling is the design methodology used to structure data for OLAP cubes, where data is organized into facts (measurable events or transactions) and dimensions (attributes that describe the facts, like time, customers, product, and location). This model facilitates the ubiquitous slicing and dicing query pattern, which aligns with the typical questions posed by managers and analysts.

3. **Extract-Transform-Load (ETL)** – ETL is the process of extracting data from various sources, transforming it into a consistent format, and loading it into a data warehouse or analytical system. ETL ensures that data from disparate sources is clean, consistent, and ready for analysis in systems like OLAP cubes or Time Molecules.

Comparable counterparts to those pre-OLAP steps exist for Time Molecules. My intended vision is that Process Mining is to Time Molecules as MDM and Dimensional Modeling are to OLAP cubes. Just as MDM sorts out the complex mess of entities and relationships across different data sources, process mining works to make sense of the scattered event logs that populate the EventsFact table—grouping event types into what appear to be coherent processes. It is the tool we use to discover the hidden structure within an ocean of events, allowing us to group them into meaningful processes.

Figure 5 illustrates key elements of business intelligence (above the line) and Time Molecules (below the line):

1. **Master Data Management**: Centralized control and governance of critical enterprise data to ensure consistency and accuracy. Process Mining (4) is the Time Molecules counterpart.

2. **Dimensional Modeling**: Structuring data for easy navigation and analysis, typically through star or snowflake schemas.

3. **Extract, Transform, Load (ETL)**: A process to gather, transform, and load data into data warehouses. Event Streaming is the Time Molecules counterpart (5).

4. **Process Mining**: Analyzing event data to discover and improve workflows.

5. **Event Streaming (and Complex Event Processing)**: Real-time data processing from ongoing streams.

6. **OLAP Cube**: A multi-dimensional structure for performing fast, complex analytical queries.

7. **Time Molecules Warehouse**: Markov models that capture event-based sequences, exploring correlations over time for deeper insights. Counterpart to BI's Data Warehouse and OLAP Cube (6).

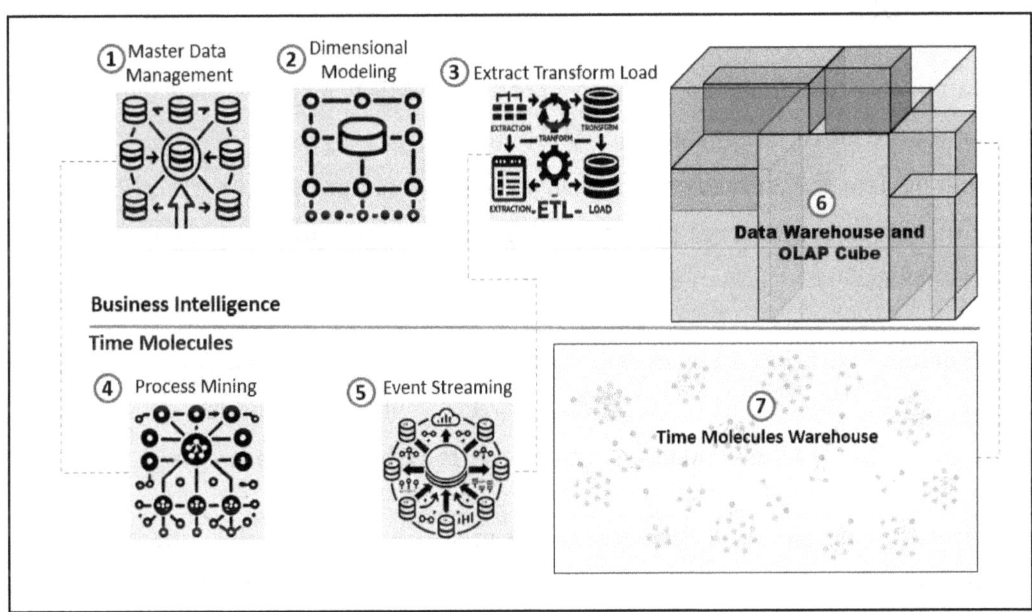

Figure 5: BI vs Time Molecules.

Although those topics are each a book in itself, I will briefly describe process mining (and its cousin, event storming), master data management, and finally, describe the analogy.

Process Mining

Process mining is an essential preparatory part of implementing Time Molecules. In fact, I see process mining as the counterpart to data discovery/profiling/modeling on the BI side. While process mining focuses on analyzing event logs to discover actual workflows, check conformance, and identify inefficiencies, its role within Time Molecules is more specialized—the discovery of what constitutes processes, defining the ontology of cases (what it does, its properties, etc.) which are iterations/cycles of processes, and the inventory of the events of a process.

Just as BI engineers must explore OLTP tables to design clean dimensions and facts, process mining begins with a stage of event discovery, a kind of data discovery tailored to temporal behavior. It's the pre-modeling phase of Time Molecules—just like data discovery precedes cube building in OLAP.

In many real-world scenarios, event data does not arrive neatly organized with case IDs or predefined sets of events. Events may be scattered, irregular, or disconnected, making it challenging to identify cohesive process flows. Process mining addresses this challenge by analyzing sequences, grouping related events, and uncovering implicit workflows that may not be immediately evident.

This utilization of process mining is reminiscent of the way MDM maps disparate data elements into a unified structure for BI analysis. Just as MDM creates a single version of process truth for data, process mining lays the groundwork for advanced process analysis by revealing the hidden connections between events. Once process mining has structured the event data, Time Molecules take over, enabling:

- **Dynamic Transition Analysis**: Process mining identifies the paths; Time Molecules quantify the probabilities of transitions between events. As a reminder, at scale, it means a large number of MMs condensing different parts of the event space.

- **Dimensional Analysis of Processes**: While process mining provides a snapshot of workflows, Time Molecules add the ability to slice and dice these workflows by dimensions like time, event type, or geography.

- **Comparative Process Insights**: Time Molecules leverage the results of process mining to compare how processes evolve over time or differ across regions, customers, or other dimensions.

Without the organization activities of process mining, the chaotic nature of raw event data would make these analyses impossible. By structuring events into cohesive process flows, process mining creates the event map that Time Molecules builds upon to navigate, analyze, and validate the dynamic interplay of processes within systems. This synergy bridges the gap between raw event data and analytical insights, enabling organizations to move from process discovery to process optimization.

Event Storming: Process Mining's 2nd Cousin

Event storming is a technique from the Domain-Driven Design (DDD) world, used to uncover and map out complex business processes by bringing together domain experts (who know the business), technical teams (software developers, architects), and ideally, the front-line workers (who operate in the real world where the theory of experts probably doesn't exactly match reality). It's a collaborative workshop where participants pool their knowledge to identify key events, processes, and constraints.

In a sense, event storming is akin to the "Copenhagen Interpretation" of quantum mechanics—a collective effort where everyone hashes out their current understanding of how things work, revealing connections and insights that may not have been apparent in isolation. Unlike process mining, which relies on event logs and historical data, event storming taps directly into the minds of participants to map out the system as they experience and envision it.

In an event storming session, participants brainstorm significant business events, such as "Order Placed," "Payment Processed," or "Shipment Delivered." These events are typically written on sticky notes and arranged in a timeline or workflow. The goal is to:

1. Discover key events that drive the system or business process.
2. Map the flow of events and actions across different departments or domains.
3. Identify gaps, bottlenecks, or ambiguities in the process by discussing interactions between events.

Key Features of Event Storming:

- **Collaborative**: Involves different stakeholders (product owners, developers, business analysts, field workers) in brainstorming.
- **Visual**: Uses a timeline of events to model processes, making it easy to spot missing pieces or inefficiencies.
- **Exploratory**: Helps teams understand how the business operates by focusing on key events and interactions.

While event storming is primarily associated with designing software systems in DDD, it is also valuable in situations where event logs are unavailable or when processes are poorly documented. Relying on human knowledge uncovers the high-level flow of business operations that may not be evident from data alone.

Event storming, while conceptually similar to process mining in discovering processes, approaches the problem from a different angle. Process mining is more of a data-first approach, analyzing event logs to uncover workflows, while event storming is a people-first approach relying mostly on the collective expertise of participants to manually map processes. This makes event storming more collaborative and human-centric, focusing on brainstorming and discussion rather than data analysis.

Although event storming is not a direct tool of process mining, the two methods can complement each other. Event storming is particularly helpful when event logs are incomplete or unavailable, or when understanding the broader business context is essential. Once a high-level process map is created through event storming, process mining can refine and validate these assumptions using actual event data.

Process mining and event storming share the common goal of discovering processes but differ in their methods. One extracts insights from real data, while the other relies on human expertise to construct a conceptual framework. Both approaches provide clarity on underlying processes, which can then be analyzed further—for example, with Time Molecules.

Master Data Management (MDM)

MDM is the practice of creating and maintaining a consistent, accurate, and unified view of an organization's key data entities, such as customers, products, employees, and locations—called master or golden records. The goal of MDM is to ensure that these core data entities are consistent and correct across various systems, departments, and applications within the organization. MDM processes involve:

1. **Data Integration:** Mapping data from multiple sources (CRM, ERP, financial systems) to create a single, authoritative source of truth.
2. **Data Cleaning and Standardization:** Removing duplicates (dedup), correcting errors, and ensuring that data follows consistent formats.
3. **Data Governance:** Establishing rules and policies to ensure the long-term integrity, quality, and security of the master data.
4. **Data Distribution:** Ensuring that the clean and standardized master data is made available to various business units, applications, and users.

By creating a single source of truth, MDM enables organizations to make informed decisions, improve operational efficiency, and maintain compliance with regulations.

How MDM and Process Mining Are Counterparts

In the BI world, MDM ensures that core data entities like customers, products, and locations are accurately integrated and standardized across systems (e.g., Eugene Asahara in the CRM system matches Eugene A. Asahara in the SCM system). By providing a clean, unified dataset, MDM enables OLAP cubes to reliably slice, dice, and analyze data across domains. Without it, inconsistencies and fragmentation would undermine the trustworthiness of insights.

In the Time Molecules world, process mining plays a similar foundational role but focuses on event-driven processes. Instead of managing entities, process mining discovers, organizes, and integrates processes from unstructured event logs. This step is essential for building coherent Markov models that accurately represent dynamic event sequences, just as MDM ensures trusted data for OLAP.

Here are the key differences and parallels:

- **MDM (for OLAP cubes)**: Integrates and standardizes data entities (customers, products) across systems to create a reliable dataset for BI analysis.
- **Process Mining (for Time Molecules)**: Extracts and structures processes from event logs, forming a foundation for analyzing event sequences and transitions.

In both cases, the goal is the same: to transform complex, messy data into structured, usable information for deeper analysis. While MDM focuses on entities, process mining focuses on processes, enabling tools like OLAP cubes and Time Molecules to generate insights with confidence.

Semantic Web and LLM Integration

The Semantic Web builds on knowledge graphs (KG) to make data more meaningful and interoperable. KGs are an organization of information as entities (e.g., customers, products, locations) connected by relationships (e.g., "purchased," "located in," "created by"). This graph structure allows data to be linked in a way that reflects real-world relationships, enabling advanced querying and pattern recognition.

The Semantic Web extends this concept by providing a framework for global standardization. Tools like Internationalized Resource Identifiers (IRIs) link entities in a KG to public ontologies—structured definitions of concepts and relationships curated by domain experts and organizations. This ensures that everyone uses consistent terms and meanings, fostering interoperability and context.

For example, the term "Country" (the political structure, not the music genre) in an enterprise's data might align with a globally recognized ID in Wikidata or DBpedia, creating seamless connections across datasets.

Figure 6 exemplifies the Semantic Web by showing how an enterprise's KG can link its entities like "U.S.A," "North America," and "HI" to public ontologies using IRIs, ensuring global standardization and interoperability. Whether your enterprise KG says HI, Hawaii, or Hawaya, we're ensuring we know we're talking about Hawaii.

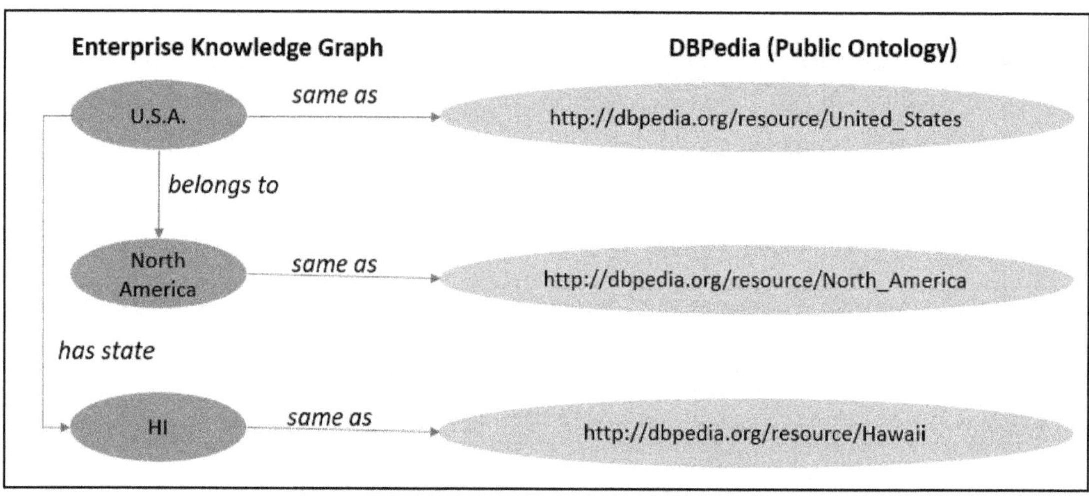

Figure 6: Example of mapping KG nodes to a public ontology.

Think of the Semantic Web as a globally-scoped layer of meaning atop KGs in the same way that MDM standardizes data definitions and instances of entities within an enterprise. This painstaking work of aligning concepts enables organizations to enrich their internal data by embedding it in a broader, universally understood context.

By linking KG elements to Semantic Web standards, enterprises can connect to knowledge transcending their internal systems. Time Molecules leverages this methodology by embedding IRIs (International Resource Identifiers) in its event-driven framework, connecting internal processes to external knowledge. This integration enables more robust analyses, deeper context, and interoperability without requiring every organization to redefine concepts for their specific needs.

In Time Molecules, most dimension/entity tables include columns that facilitate this integration between the Semantic Web and Time Molecules:

1. **Description**: This column holds a detailed explanation of the entity or dimension—it can be free-form text or in a semi-structured format such as JSON. The description can be transformed into a vector embedding, meaning it is transformed into a mathematical representation (a vector) that can be stored in a vector database. These vectors capture the semantic meaning of the descriptions, enabling advanced search capabilities and query understanding by an LLM.

2. **IRI:** This column links the entity to a public ontology, ensuring that the entity is globally identifiable and connected to broader knowledge bases like DBpedia, Wikidata, or other relevant domain ontologies.

3. **DescriptionUserID**: This field identifies the user who composed the description (human, LLM, or some function), adding accountability and traceability for data governance while providing context about who provided specific insights.

LLMs are massive neural networks trained on the vast and varied corpus of humanity's writings. Unlike KGs, which are meticulously curated and deterministic, LLMs assimilate knowledge from immense datasets, mostly text, resulting in an incredibly wide breadth of knowledge—and at least a veil of understanding. This capability allows LLMs to interpret and generate natural language that can mimic real intelligence to an impressive degree. By fine-tuning these "foundational" (they found a base for general knowledge) models with private and/or proprietary enterprise-specific data, LLMs become more adept at answering complex business queries, enhancing decision-making by providing insights directly relevant to the organization.

However, LLMs inherently reflect the perspectives and limitations of their training data, often responding with what is really an aggregated regurgitation of what they've learned, much like a know-it-all friend who might not always think beyond what they've been told. At present, they struggle to "think" outside their training. And "training" (as opposed to curating or even programming) means that there is no *direct* control over what the LLM does.

In contrast, sophisticated AI systems operating in a symbiotic partnership with data-driven and human-curated structures—such as Time Molecules and the Enterprise Knowledge Graph I describe in my book, Enterprise Intelligence—ensure that there is an element of direct control of AI queries and the ability to explore the raw data.

This symbiotic relationship between LLMs and Semantic Web KGs leverages the strengths of both: LLMs provide breadth and natural language understanding, while KGs offer depth, precision, and a structured approach to knowledge, creating a powerful combination for enterprise intelligence.

By integrating the Semantic Web and LLMs, enterprises can extract deeper and more profound understanding from their data, with key benefits including:

- **Improved Query Accuracy**: By vectorizing descriptions and fine-tuning LLMs with enterprise-specific information, the LLM can provide more precise answers to complex queries that go beyond simple keyword matching. This enhances the relevance and accuracy of insights derived from data.

- **Knowledge Context**: Linking entities to public ontologies through the IRI allows for richer contextual understanding, enriching the enterprise's internal data with globally recognized concepts and standards.

- **Data Accountability**: The DescriptionUserID field promotes transparency over who curates data, fosters collaboration, and incentivizes accurate entity descriptions.

I want to emphasize that the primary reason for including human-curated, database-driven structures (such as Knowledge Graphs, Time Molecules, and the EKG from Enterprise Intelligence) is to ensure that people remain the dominant partner in a world where AI has rapidly growing agency—faster than what I feel is the rate that we can wisely adapt. Much like the Senate's slightly greater power compared to the House of Representatives, these carefully managed data frameworks help maintain human control and oversight.

Retrieval-Augmented Generation as an Orchestrator

In the frantically evolving landscape of AI, Retrieval-Augmented Generation (RAG) is a powerful mechanism for iteratively interacting with vast amounts of information from multiple sources. RAG combines retrieval mechanisms with generative AI models (e.g., LLMs), dynamically orchestrating data sources to deliver richer and more context-aware outputs.

RAG is an orchestrator—a specialized function that combines data retrieval and generative AI. It exhibits some characteristics of an AI agent—namely, perceiving (retrieving information) and acting (generating outputs)—but it does not fully embody all aspects of agency, such as autonomous goal-setting or persistence. In practice, many true AI agents rely on orchestrators like RAG to coordinate and integrate insights from multiple data sources. This ensures that the overall system can make context-rich decisions and produce meaningful, timely results.

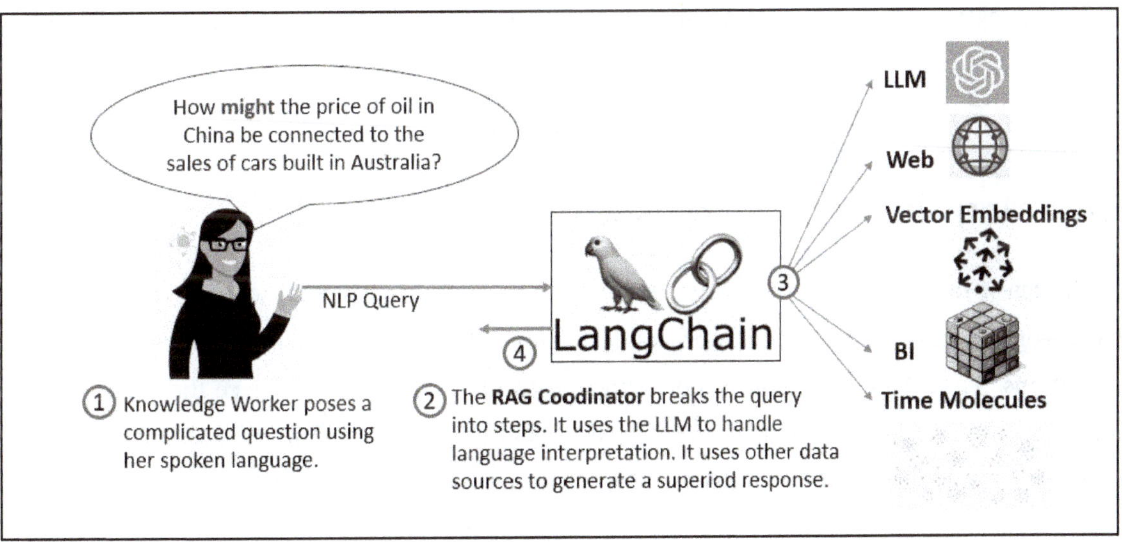

Figure 7: The main idea behind RAG.

Figure 7 illustrates the main idea:

1. **User Question:** A knowledge worker asks a complex question in natural (spoken or written) language.

2. **RAG Coordinator and LLM:** The system (RAG) uses an LLM to interpret and break down the query into logical steps, then plans which data sources are needed.

3. **Data Retrieval:** It pulls information from multiple resources—other LLMs, vector embeddings, BI dashboards, Time Molecules, and the web.

4. **Synthesized Answer:** The RAG Coordinator merges all relevant insights into one coherent response and delivers it back to the user. The merged responses are usually packaged into a big LLM prompt and submitted to an LLM for a final response.

RAG merges the best of both worlds:

- **Retrieval:** The AI agent retrieves facts and data from external, up-to-date sources like databases, specialized documents, or web content—with proper security and privacy measures.

- **Generation:** The AI then uses its LLM capabilities to generate responses that seamlessly integrate the retrieved information with its pre-existing knowledge base.

Exploring Simple Sequences with Time Molecules

In the quest to understand and optimize complex systems, it's essential to start with something basic—one of those simple, everyday processes that form the backbone of much larger, more intricate operations. Time Molecules offer a powerful way to break down and analyze these processes by focusing on their fundamental sequences. By beginning with straightforward examples, we'll establish a solid foundation for understanding more complex interactions later on.

A very simple, "hello world," example is the daily commute to work. The process might start with leaving home, encountering different levels of traffic, and finally arriving at the workplace. While straightforward, this sequence is influenced by various factors—traffic conditions, weather, time of day—that can all be studied to improve efficiency. By analyzing these sequences across a number of days, we can identify patterns that lead to better decisions, such as choosing the optimal departure time or route.

A more complex example, but still simple and familiar, is the routine of dining at a restaurant, as illustrated in Figure 8. You walk in, you're greeted, seated, order drinks, place your food order, get served, receive the bill, pay, and leave.

That sequence, though seemingly mundane, captures a process rich with opportunities for analysis. Each step is a distinct event in the interaction between the customer and the restaurant, from the initial greeting to the final payment. By mapping out these steps, we can start to see patterns—what runs smoothly, where delays occur, or how changes in the sequence might affect the overall experience. And there could be all sorts of unnoticed events somewhere in between leading to curious outcomes.

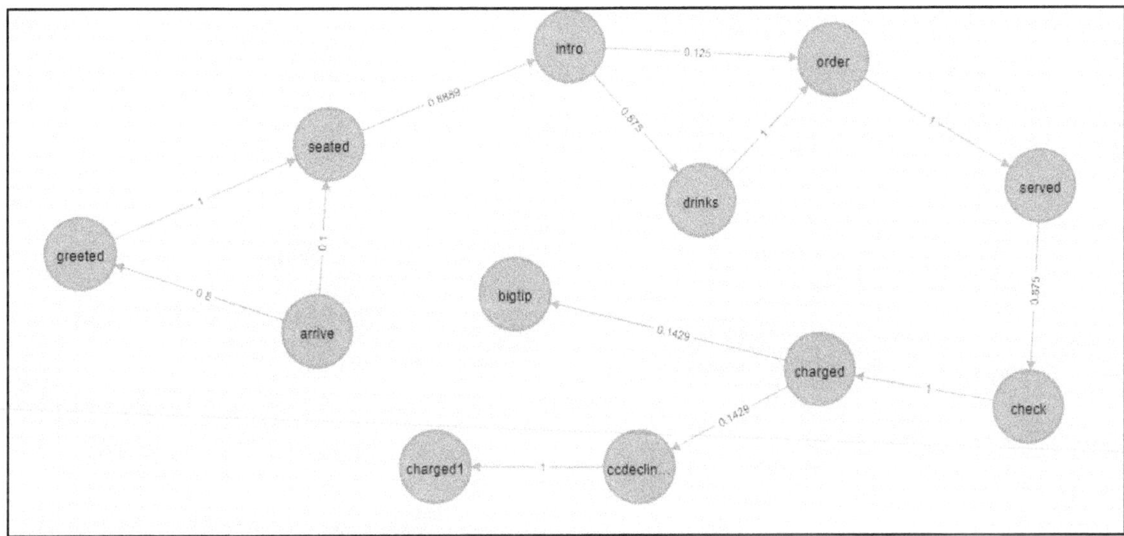

Figure 8: Process of serving customers at a restaurant.

Kicking up the complexity a little more, consider the daily route of a truck making pickups and drop-offs. The restaurant operates in a confined environment where the entities have more control, whereas a truck making its route is subject to more things out of its control—therefore, it's more complex.

The truck follows a regular path through a sequence of locations. Mapping this sequence and studying statistical values along the way provides insight to optimize routes, reduce delays, and promote timely deliveries. Here, Time Molecules help us break down the process into manageable parts—segments from event to event—each with its own set of variables and outcomes, ready for analysis and improvement.

These examples may be basic, but they serve as the building blocks for understanding more complex systems. Starting with these simple sequences, we create a framework that can be expanded to include more complicated or even complex processes later on. Each event in these sequences can be thought of as an atom, and each relationship between events as a bond between atoms of a Time Molecule—computed from statistical computations between events across very many cases (iterations/cycles) that connect to others, forming a succinct, interconnected structure.

Most of the remainder of this book will focus on walkthroughs through the TimeSolution sample found on the GitHub repository. As we work through the TimeSolution examples, these simple sequences will help us establish a clear understanding of how processes unfold over time. They provide a straightforward entry point into the more nuanced and multifaceted systems that we will examine from here. By mastering these fundamental sequences, we set the stage for analyzing and optimizing the more complex processes that drive our world.

CHAPTER 4

TimeSolution Architecture

High-Level Architecture

Time Molecules is a deep dive into leveraging MMs for capturing, analyzing, understanding, and monitoring event-based processes within a business context. The heart of this work lies in the SQL Server TimeSolution, where raw event data is transformed into tangible insights. While standard ETL (Extract, Transform, Load) and/or event streaming processes bring in event data from multiple sources (dozens of databases to millions of IoT devices), the real magic happens when these events are transformed into multi-dimensional arrays of probabilistic Markov models and integrated directly into BI tools and emerging AI frameworks such as RAG.

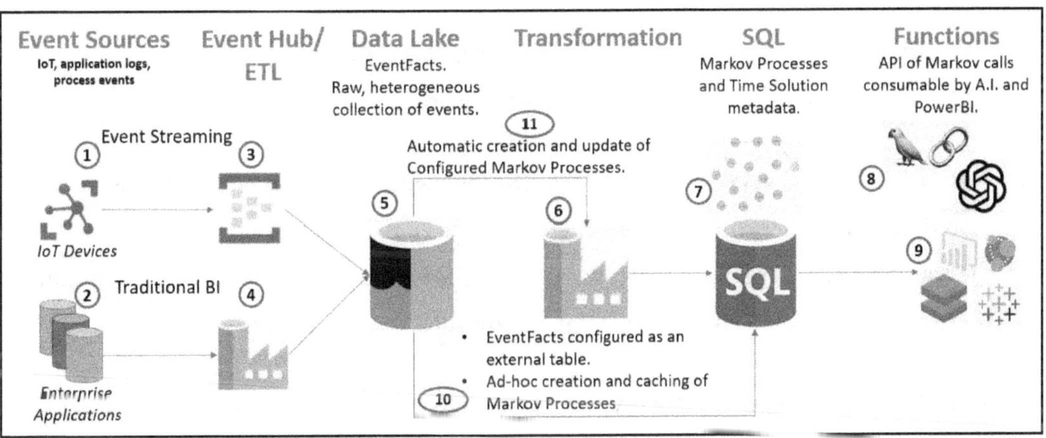

Figure 9: Overall architecture of a Time Molecules Solution.

This book focuses less on the ETL of event streaming data into massive event hubs and more on how these MMs can be used to derive analytical insights that drive decision-making. Figure 9 shows a high-level view of the scale-out Time Molecules environment. The focus on the walkthroughs of the TimeSolution database is represented by item 7.

Here is a description of the items in Figure 9:

1. **IoT Devices (Event Sources):** IoT devices—dozens to millions—serve as key event sources, continuously generating streams of real-time data. This data could include metrics and sensor readings—such as detecting chemicals or RFID (Radio Frequency Identification)—from within whatever it's deployed in.

2. **Enterprise Applications (Event Sources) and Data Warehouses:** Enterprise applications (e.g., SCM, CRM, ERP) and DWs are the incumbent sources of event data. Intuitively, everything with a date is an event—and there are a lot of dates in enterprise applications. Enterprise applications also generate logs, alerts, and events based on various business operations, which are crucial for understanding the internal processes of the organization.

3. **Event Hub:** Receives "real-time" events from what could be thousands (potentially trillions) of IoT devices. It can perform relatively simple transformations on readings over time windows and output aggregated values—for example, instead of saving every single temperature reading from a device, it only outputs the average and/or maximum over the past ten minutes.

4. **ETL (Extract, Transform, Load):** This performs basically the same function as the Event Hub, except its sources are conventional enterprise applications and data warehouses.

5. **Data Lake (EventFacts):** Here, the raw, heterogeneous event data from the Event Hub is stored in its native format. This data lake serves as a repository for EventFacts, which are the foundational elements needed to build Markov processes. The focus is on organizing these events to enable efficient transformation into analytical insights.

6. **Transformation:** This step involves automatically creating and updating Markov models based on the EventFacts. During this phase, selected events are imported into the Time Solution and transformed into configured Markov processes, which are then continuously refined and updated as more data flows in.

7. **SQL (Time Solution):** The core of the Time Molecules framework, the SQL Time Solution handles Markov processes and Time Solution metadata. The SQL layer not only computes Markov models but also manages the metadata that ties these processes together. This structure ensures that Markov processes can be used to predict future states of events and support dynamic decision-making across the organization.

8. **AI/RAG Application:** An AI application that leverages these Markov processes in a RAG setup. This means AI uses these models to retrieve relevant data and incorporate it into generative tasks, allowing for more context-aware responses and predictions.

9. **End-User Consumers (Tableau, Power BI, Neo4j, Databricks):** The final output of the Time Molecules process is consumed by BI tools like Tableau and Power BI, graph databases like Neo4j, and data platforms like Databricks. These tools use the insights generated by the Markov models to create visualizations, graphs, and dashboards that help end-users interpret and act on the data in a meaningful way.

10. **Event data is accessed by the Time Solution as an external table**, and Markov models are created and cached in an ad-hoc manner, providing the backbone for subsequent analysis. This SQL layer is where the events are turned into structured insights that can drive downstream analytics.

11. Processes could be set up to automatically update existing Markov models when new events arrive.

The following are a couple of items that are mostly outside the scope of this book but deserve more commentary.

Internet of Things

Internet of Things (IoT) devices are essential contributors to the TimeSolution. These devices span a massive range of form factors and functionalities—from tiny medical implants (e.g., pacemakers) to sophisticated satellite-linked tags on wild animals to industrial-scale sensor networks (like thousands of sensors deployed in a manufacturing plant).

Modern IoT tags can capture and report multiple metrics (e.g., temperature, location, heartbeat, battery life) at high sampling rates, transmitting data in near real-time for continuous monitoring and analysis. Even today, modern pacemakers generate detailed telemetry on heart rhythms, pacing behavior, and device health, allowing both physicians and patients to detect and address potential issues early. Meanwhile, marine animal tags can measure depth, acceleration, temperature, and location to uncover new insights about life in the open ocean.

Increasingly, IoT devices not only capture and transmit data, but also perform edge computing—processing or filtering information on-device before sending it upstream. This trend will exacerbate as AI "agents"—which could be thought of as much smarter and more powerful IoT devices—become more prevalent, enabling real-time analytics or anomaly detection right at the source, whether that source is inside the human body or in space.

As billions of these devices/agents come online—embedded in homes, cities, factories, and the natural world—IoT will evolve into a highly interconnected ecosystem. Ultimately, these ever-smarter nodes will help form powerful distributed networks that drive automation, optimize resource usage, and enable entirely new classes of products and services.

This vast network of devices generates enormous streams of data that could be fed into the Time Solution pipeline. Each output from IoT devices—whether originating from raw readings or edge-computed analyses—provides a snapshot of a state or noteworthy event, capturing not just what happened, but also when, where, and what was involved. This temporal and spatial context transforms IoT events into building blocks for analyzing workflows, detecting anomalies, and predicting outcomes.

It's important to distinguish between readings and events. IoT devices produce readings at regular intervals, capturing data like temperature, motion, or resource usage. These readings are routine data points, not inherently noteworthy. However, with on-board edge computing, some IoT devices can analyze these readings and emit events when a condition warrants attention—such as a temperature spike or unusual motion. Pacemakers can even detect complicated events such as tachycardias and other arrhythmias beyond just emitting heartbeats and their pacing. An event represents something meaningful, contextualized by time, location, and observation.

Event Logs and Streaming Data

Effective system optimization begins with understanding the events that comprise it. They arrive as part of real-time streams, continuously generated by IoT devices, transactional systems, or user interactions. Events, as the fundamental building blocks, must first be sorted, categorized, and organized into meaningful processes.

In this section, we'll explore how event logs—both historical and real-time—form the foundation for analyzing processes and creating analytical insights.

Events and Subprocesses

Before optimizing a system, we must first sort a variety of distinct event types into a set of hypotheses about the nature of the process. This involves isolating subprocesses—subsets of these distinct events in our database—to create coherent and meaningful MMs. While ingesting events into the TimeSolution should be as unrestricted as possible (allowing data from diverse sources to populate the EventFacts table), the real challenge lies in organizing this soup of events into structured processes.

Sometimes, the task of sorting out event types into processes is straightforward. It might be tacit knowledge obvious to workers or discoverable through the study of enterprise software code. It could even be as simple as asking someone. For example, any member of the wait staff can tell you the events that occur through the process of serving a customer in their restaurant.

However, as we bring many event streams online, we likely will not be familiar with what hidden processes lurk in the massive mix of event data. Understanding how events and things work goes beyond simply recognizing them—indeed, it's the central aim of process mining.

Events are the observable "emissions" from processes—milestones that mark interactions between components as they unfold. These observations are dynamic, capturing interactions between elements at nested levels, from individual tasks to entire workflows. Structuring these events into meaningful taxonomies of subprocesses and processes is critical for understanding system behavior and building accurate models. To achieve this, event logs must be carefully analyzed, categorized, and structured. This process includes:

- **Reading Events**: Measurements, such as a sensor reporting "humidity=60%."
- **Reporting/Logging Events:** Key milestones, like "Mari arrived at the restaurant."
- **Process Events**: Transactions or interactions that include both inputs and outputs, such as a truck arriving and departing.
- **Properties of Events**: Capturing input-output relationships, such as "Player A folded" in poker.

Azure Event Hub: Real-Time Event Streaming

For businesses embracing real-time data, platforms like Azure Event Hub provide a seamless way to stream and process events at scale. Azure Event Hub enables organizations to ingest data from diverse sources such as IoT devices, transactions, and system notifications. Each event, defined by its time-bound nature, becomes part of a continuous flow of information. Events streamed through Event Hub can be processed and stored with highly scalable products such as Azure Stream Analytics and CosmosDB, respectively. A key capability of event processing is the use of windowing functions, which aggregate events over specified timeframes. For example:

- **Total Sales in the Last Hour**: Identify spikes in demand or detect anomalies.
- **Max wind speed in the past 10 minutes**: A terribly high max wind speed could be a signal to visually check an area.

Appendix D provides a detailed comparison of Azure Event Hub and Apache Kafka, helping readers understand their relative strengths and use cases.

Set up SQL Server

Play Along at Home (or not)

Now that we're talking about architecture and will soon be (optionally) setting up software, we're past the background part, into the "2nd Act" of this movie. Unfortunately, that means there will be code. But it will primarily be SQL mostly at a novice level, and I will thoroughly explain what it does.

To be clear:

- You don't need to know the SQL query language to read this book.
- You don't need to play along (load the software and run the code) with the walkthroughs. You can simply read through it. The content is more about the concepts than the code.
- I don't expect many of the end-users of the concepts in this book to be writing in SQL. I expect that data engineers will implement the concepts, as usual, making the utilization transparent to end users through apps of some sort.

However, I believe that if your work is anywhere near data, you should at least have a novice-level skill with SQL. SQL is a language for "declaring" (SQL is a "declarative language") what data you wish to retrieve from databases and the database engine will figure out the best way to accommodate your query. As a declarative language, SQL is constrained in its scope, and therefore, its syntax is simpler than a more generally-scoped language like Java or Python. Therefore, it's probably one of the easiest "coding" languages to learn.

Let's start with a simple example: retrieve the *name*, *occupation*, and *first visit* of customers living in Eagle, ID, who have *college degrees*. SQL is just another way to express that previous sentence that is unambiguously understood by the database. This is how the SQL might look:

```
SELECT Name, Occupation, FirstVisit
FROM Customers
WHERE City = 'Eagle'
  AND State = 'ID'
  AND EducationLevel = 'College'
```

Code 1: SQL of the query mentioned just above.

Here is how SQL maps to the query:

- **SELECT**: Specifies *what* data you want to retrieve.
    - **Mapped to**: Name, Occupation, FirstVisit columns.
    - This is like asking for specific details (like picking items from the menu).

- **FROM**: Specifies *where* the data is coming from—in this case, the table.
    - **Mapped to**: The Customers table.
    - Like specifying which fast food chain you're at because the menus are different.

- **WHERE**: Specifies the *conditions* for filtering the data.

- **Mapped to these columns**:
  - City = 'Eagle' (Filter to only customers in Eagle)
  - State = 'ID' (Limit results to those in Idaho)
  - EducationLevel = 'College' (Only select customers with a college degree)
- This is like narrowing down your order (e.g., only list burgers or drinks), ensuring only the correct conditions are met.

SQL was designed to reflect the way we naturally ask for information. But learning it is more like picking up a second language—you don't need to be ridiculously fluent to get your point across. With a little practice, you can communicate effectively, even if it's not near perfection. For the engineers and SQL experts, the GitHub repository will contain more technically challenging walkthroughs and deeper dives into the code: https://github.com/MapRock/TimeMolecules.

As mentioned earlier, what I've been referring to as "TimeSolution" is a SQL Server database—the traditional, "on-prem" RDBMS (relational database management system) implementation of SQL Server, not the Azure Synapse cloud implementation. I chose SQL Server because it has a free, easily installed "Developer Edition" —at least to SQL Server 2022.

To download it, go to *https://aka.ms/sqldev*, select the Developer Edition, run the installer, and follow the basic setup to install SQL Server and SQL Server Management Studio (SSMS). You'll also want to install SQL Server Management Studio (SSMS) to work with queries and database objects. Download it separately from *https://aka.ms/ssms*. For more detailed and updated setup instructions, see the guide: *https://github.com/MapRock/TimeMolecules/install_timemolecules_dev_env.pdf.*

Later in the book, as we integrate the TimeSolution to the Enterprise Knowledge Graph from my earlier book, *Enterprise Intelligence*, we'll need to install the graph database, Neo4j, which thankfully has an equivalent of a "developer's edition."

Alternatives to SQL Server

If TimeSolution were only limited to ANSI SQL (the standardized, core subset of SQL understood by most relational databases), there would be many alternatives to SQL Server. However, TimeSolution goes beyond basic SQL and involves advanced database objects such as table-valued functions, scalar functions, and stored procedures.

I've spent much effort sticking to standard SQL database features that might be beyond ANSI SQL but are commonly implemented in other advanced SQL database platforms. So, while you won't need to dive deep into code details in this walkthrough, you should be aware that some databases might require slight modifications. Table 8 compares the compatibility of various SQL databases with these features.

Database	Stored Procedures	Temporary Tables	Table-Valued Functions	Views	Scalar Functions	JSON Support
Azure Synapse	Yes	Yes	Yes	Yes	Yes	Yes
Snowflake	Yes	Yes	Yes	Yes	Yes	Yes
Oracle	Yes (PL/SQL)	Yes	Yes	Yes	Yes	Yes
Databricks (SQL)	Yes, in its own way.	Yes, in its own way.	Yes, in its own way.	Yes	Yes	Yes
AWS Redshift	Yes	Yes	Yes (UDFs)	Yes	Yes	Yes

Table 8: Rough idea of compatible relational databases.

Of course, Azure Synapse is the closest in terms of compatibility (since its roots are in SQL Server), but platforms like Oracle and Snowflake should also work well with minimal modifications.

Databricks is the oddball in Table 8. It's not a RDBMS, but in many ways, it's much more powerful for an analytics-based application like Time Molecules. While Databricks does not implement table-valued functions (TVFs) in the RDBMS sense, it offers robust functionality for returning tables through its support for SQL queries, views, and UDFs. Databricks allows users to achieve outcomes similar to that of RDBMS through its Delta Tables, temporary views, or SQL-based data transformations. These features make Databricks a flexible option, especially in environments where scalable, distributed data processing (especially for advanced machine learning) is essential. Though it might require a different implementation approach, Databricks' ability to work with tabular outputs is functionally nearly equivalent to TVFs of relational databases.

At Scale Deployment Considerations

As TimeSolution scales to handle large volumes of event data, deploying on Massively Parallel Processing (MPP) cloud databases becomes a natural fit. Platforms such as Azure Synapse, Snowflake, and AWS Redshift are designed to distribute computational workloads across multiple server nodes. This architecture enables efficient parallel processing of massive datasets while supporting the core features of TimeSolution.

Scalability isn't just about managing enormous datasets and/or expectations of very fast results—it also includes the ability to handle high concurrency (queries from many users at the same time), where many queries are processed asynchronously.

Platforms like Snowflake and Azure Synapse excel at on-demand scaling, which is critical for the real-time or near-real-time processing that TimeSolution demands. By dynamically allocating resources across multiple nodes, MPP environments enable efficient computation of Markov models at varying scales, adapting to changes in data volume, concurrency, or analytical complexity. These platforms support conventional snowflake/star schema architectures, making them a natural fit for traditional data warehousing. Pre-aggregated data and event models can be easily cached and retrieved, ensuring quick access to analytical insights. Furthermore, MPP systems provide advanced workload partitioning and parallelization, which is especially important when managing extremely large or continuous cases.

Certain processes may span long durations, involving millions (to even trillions) of events that exceed the capacity of a single node. These events must be processed in sequence—often using a date sort for continuity—yet still benefit from parallelization across multiple nodes. MPP databases excel here by distributing workloads so that even massive event streams remain coherent and efficiently processed. By leveraging the capabilities of platforms like Snowflake, Synapse, and Redshift, enterprises can integrate Time Molecules into their data ecosystem relatively seamlessly. The distributed architecture and asynchronous processing capabilities of these platforms align perfectly with the requirements of process-centric, large-scale models in TimeSolution. See the GitHub repository for up-to-date scripts and further details on the compatibility of these platforms with *TimeSolution*. In particular, refer to *Partition_Scheme_For_Azure_Synapse.docx* for an example of deployment on cloud-scale MPP databases.

Markov Models on GPUs

In the midst of this AI revolution at the time of writing, I need to at least mention Markov models deployed onto Graphics Processor Units (GPU) as a highly-advanced computation platform.

MMs involve state transitions represented by matrices, and their computations often require matrix-vector multiplications to calculate probabilities of moving between states or achieving equilibrium (stationary distributions). These operations are inherently parallelizable and well-suited for GPUs because GPUs are optimized for massively parallel arithmetic operations like those found in linear algebra. For example:

1. **Transition Matrices**: GPUs can efficiently compute matrix multiplications for dense or sparse transition matrices. Each GPU thread can handle an independent element of the result matrix or vector, enabling rapid parallel updates across the model.

2. **Iterative Computations**: Many MMs rely on iterative approaches, such as the power method to find stationary distributions. GPUs excel at these repetitive, data-parallel workloads by simultaneously performing updates across multiple states.

3. **Monte Carlo Simulations**: For Hidden Markov Models or stochastic simulations, GPUs can execute many independent runs of state sequences in parallel, enabling faster probabilistic inferences or scenario testing.

However, the efficiency of implementing MMs on GPUs depends on the problem size and sparsity of the transition matrices. Sparse matrices, common in real-world Markov models, require specialized techniques (sparse matrix formats and libraries like cuSPARSE) to fully utilize GPU capabilities without excessive memory overhead.

TimeSolution Database

Here we begin the walkthrough of the TimeSolution database, the focus of the walkthroughs to come. While the High-Level Architecture section (referencing Figure 9) provided a broader view of the full pipeline—spanning event streaming, ETL, and data lake integration—these walkthroughs focus specifically on the database layer (item 7 shown back in Figure 9).

To set expectations, this walkthrough does not cover the event streaming or real-time processing components typically associated with Event-Driven Architecture (EDA). Instead, TimeSolution picks up from just after the events are:

1. Sensed by IoT devices or software applications.
2. Picked up by event streaming applications where there might be light processing.
3. Stored in a highly-scalable storage environment such as a data lake or a document database such as MongoDB or Azure CosmosDB.

A comprehensive deep dive into the entire span of the system would significantly expand the scope of this book, potentially doubling its length. For the sake of clarity and practicality, we'll concentrate on the TimeSolution database, which captures the essence of how event data is transformed into informative insights. With that in mind, let's begin by restoring the TimeSolution database so you can follow along and experience its functionality firsthand. This focused approach allows us to dive into the concepts of Time Molecules while acknowledging that the broader pipeline remains an essential but separate topic, which is already well-documented.

Restore TimeSolution Database

To restore the *TimeMolecules.bak* file from GitHub and load it into SQL Server, follow these steps:

1. Download the solution backup file from the repository:
    - Go to https://github.com/MapRock/TimeMolecules/TimeMolecules.bak
    - Download the TimeMolecules.bak file to your local machine.
2. Open SQL Server Management Studio (SSMS) and connect to your server.
3. Right-click on the Databases folder in the Object Explorer and select Restore Database.
4. In the Source section, select Device, and click the ... button.
5. Click Add, then navigate to the TimeMolecules.bak file you just downloaded, and select it.
6. In the Destination section, ensure the Database field is filled in with the desired database name (TimeMolecules).
7. Go to the Options page and choose to Overwrite the existing database if necessary.
8. Click OK to begin the restore process.

Once complete, your TimeMolecules database will be restored and ready for use. Note that all of the examples use SQL Server Management Studio (SSMS). A few need Python, a few need Neo4j. Please see the install guide on the GitHub page if you would like to perform those examples:

https://github.com/MapRock/TimeMolecules/install_timemolecules_dev_env.pdf.

Event and Markov Models Ensembles

The TimeSolution database serves as the foundation for transforming raw event data into analytical insights. It is composed of two primary components:

- **Event Ensemble:** This is an abstract dimensional model designed to organize and integrate event data from diverse sources. At its core is the EventsFact table, which acts as a consolidated repository for all types of events. By consolidating events into a unified structure, the Event Ensemble enables detailed analysis and prepares the data for modeling. It captures the "what," "when," and "where" of events, creating a rich foundation for uncovering process patterns.

- **Markov Models Ensemble:** Building on the structured event data, this component stores Markov models generated from the Event Ensemble. These models reveal the probabilistic transitions between events, offering insights into the dynamics and flow of processes. The Markov Models Ensemble transforms raw event sequences into predictive models that support decision-making and optimization.

Together, these ensembles form the backbone of the TimeSolution database, bridging raw event data and advanced process analytics. They exemplify how structured data and probabilistic modeling can combine to deliver powerful insights into complex, event-driven systems.

I should mention that the Markov Models Ensemble is just one of the ways the Event Ensemble could be used. The Events Ensemble is a data warehouse of integrated events. An example of such a utilization is conventional OLAP cubes founded on slice and dice queries.

The Bronze, Silver, and Gold Medallion Framework for TimeSolution

The Bronze, Silver, and Gold Medallion framework popularized by Databricks provides an analogy for understanding the layers of data and models within TimeSolution, illustrating how raw data transforms into insightful analytical models.

1. **Bronze Medallion**: This layer represents the foundational, pre-processed stage of data. It includes event streaming and complex event processing (CEP), where raw data is captured and processed in real time through platforms like Azure Event Hub or Apache Kafka. At

this stage, patterns such as spikes, outliers, or combinations of events are detected and re-packaged as aggregated events. The data is not yet integrated into the Event Ensemble but often comes from sources like data warehouses or event hubs. It may also involve curated or cleaned datasets that are structured enough for initial processing but not yet tied to specific cases or transitions. The Bronze Medallion serves as the bridge between raw event streams and structured event repositories, providing foundational data preparation and pre-integration analytics.

2. **Silver Medallion (Events Ensemble)**: This layer is the Event Ensemble, with the central EventsFact table. Here, the focus shifts to integrating and structuring event data into a unified system. Events are grouped by cases where possible, and their properties, timestamps, and sources are meticulously cataloged. This layer forms the complete repository of the enterprise's event-driven processes, ready for analytics and modeling. The Silver Medallion is where the streams and curated datasets from the Bronze layer converge, ensuring clean, consistent, and fully traceable event data.

3. **Gold Medallion (MME)**: At this level, we move from structured event data to analytical insights. The MME represents the transformation of the Event Ensemble into probabilistic models. These models reveal patterns, such as state transitions and sequential probabilities, providing rich insights into the dynamics of processes. The Gold Medallion is where value emerges—allowing users to make predictions, optimize workflows, and understand complex event-driven behaviors across the enterprise.

Event Ensemble

The Event Ensemble is a dimensional model data warehouse of abstracted events. There is one fact table, EventsFact. Its two most important dimensions are the date (DateTime) and the Events (DimEvents) dimensions. Figure 10 shows the major tables comprising the Event Ensemble. Here are brief descriptions for each table in the Event Ensemble schema:

- **EventsFact**: Central fact table capturing all events with their timestamps, sources, and related case details.
- **DimEvents**: Dimension table defining event types, their descriptions, and properties.

- **DimDate**: Dimension table for dates, breaking down event dates into components like year, month, and day.
- **DimTime**: Dimension table for time, detailing hours, minutes, and seconds of events.
- **EventSets**: Table managing sets of events, their sequences, and metadata such as descriptions and creation details.
- **Sources**: Table cataloging data sources, their descriptions, and properties.
- **Cases**: Table organizing events into cases, with start and end times, event counts, and case-specific metadata.

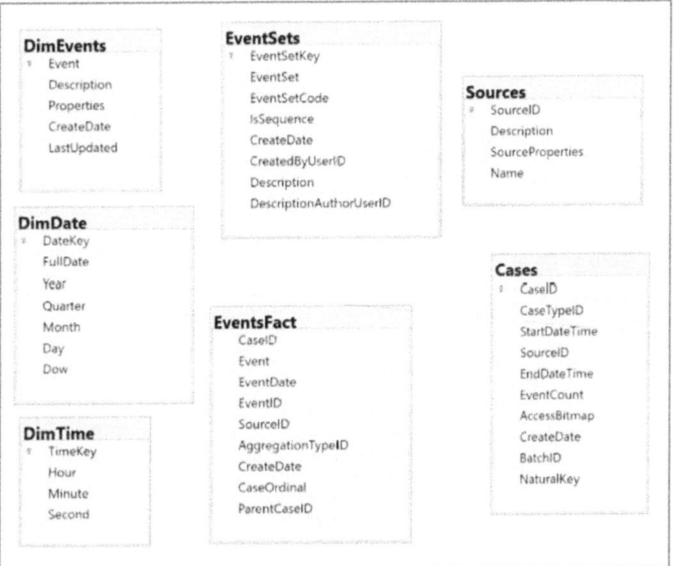

Figure 10: Event ensemble.

Note that the word "event" is used in two distinct but related contexts throughout this schema. In EventsFact, an *event* refers to a specific occurrence in time—a recorded instance with a timestamp (e.g., *"Rainfall recorded on 1/1/25 in Zone A"*). In contrast, DimEvents defines the types of events—the categories or labels used to describe what kind of thing occurred (e.g., *Rain*, *Snow*, *Tornado*). While they share the same term, context makes their meaning clear: one refers to the actual data point, and the other to the classification of that data point.

Markov Model Ensemble

The Markov Model Ensemble (MME) supports the creation and analysis of Markov models created from the Event Ensemble.

The data of the MME could be thought of in the same manner as aggregations of OLAP cubes. Like with OLAP cube sums and counts, Markov models can be created within reasonable timeframes, but caching them preserves compute costs (good for the IT manager) and compute time (good for the user). Figure 11 shows the major tables for the MME.

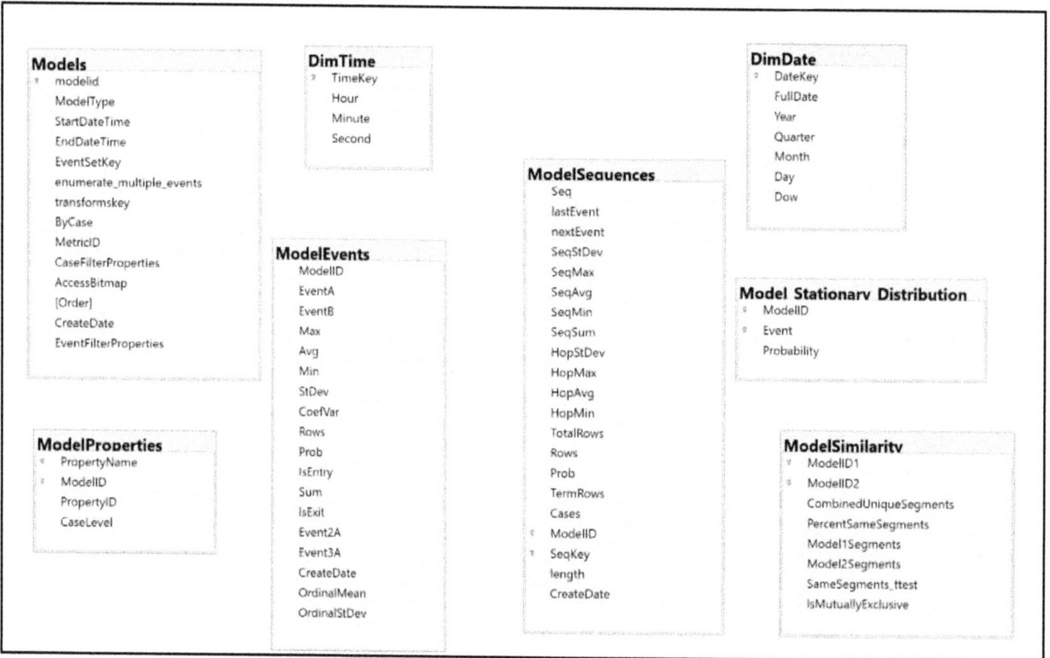

Figure 11: Markov model ensemble.

Here are short descriptions for each table in the MME schema:

- **Models**: Defines the metadata for the MMs, including their type, date range, event sets, and filters.
- **ModelEvents**: Stores the event segments (EventA→EventB) and their statistics (probabilities, averages, and standard deviations) for Markov models.
- **ModelSequences:** Details sequences within a model, including transitions between events and their aggregated metrics.
- **Model Stationary Distribution**: Holds the stationary probabilities for events within a Markov model.
- **ModelSimilarity**: Compares MMs scored by several similarity metrics.
- **ModelProperties:** Defines parameters, properties, and filters for each model.
- **DimDate/DimTime**: Same as Event Ensemble.

CHAPTER 5

The SelectedEvents and MarkovProcess Functions

Although I said I'd only use SQL for code, that is a bit misleading. Most of the SQL we'll see involve stored procedures, Table-Valued Functions (TVF), views, and scalar functions that encapsulate what is fairly complicated SQL. The good news is that all of those functions are written in TSQL (SQL Server's dialect), as opposed to Python or Java.

Think of a TVF as a virtual table defined by code. The underlying SQL code could be as simple as "all rows from the customer table living in 96813 Zip code" to something much more complicated that joins many tables, applies all sorts of filters, and performs all sorts of calculations. In this case, it's more of the latter. The code is fully accessible, exploring the TimeSolution SQL Server database through SQL Server Management Studio.

SelectedEvents and MarkovProcess are the two most prominent functions implemented as TVFs for convenient utilization—they can be used as the source (FROM clause) of a SQL statement. However, there are limitations to TVFs that can result in less performance than if implemented as a stored procedure—stored procedures have fewer restrictions.

The walkthroughs in this book are intended to explain the concepts of Time Molecules. It's not intended to be an exhaustive cookbook on how to use the TimeSolution database. Such detail is the subject of a future book or blog and/or added to the GitHub repository.

Since these two functions are prominent in these walkthroughs, we need to be familiar with their parameters and output.

Some parameters may need clarification—for example, "order" has a specific meaning here. In the Markov context, it refers to how many previous events are considered when predicting the next one, breaking the usual "memoryless" Markov Property that only looks at the last event. Don't worry—walkthroughs later in the book will explore these concepts in more detail. For now, just get familiar with the key functions we'll build on.

SelectedEvents TVF

The SelectedEvents TVF is a core function in the TimeSolution database. It is designed to return a set of events from the Event Ensemble filtered on various criteria such as event sets, time ranges, metrics, and properties. It is flexible enough to handle transformations of event types, multi-occurrence events, and detailed event filtering based on case or event-level properties. This function supports the generation of MMs by retrieving events that occur in specific timeframes and/or filtered by certain attributes. Code 2 is pseudocode for how the SelectedEvents TVF is used in a SQL SELECT.

```
SELECT *
FROM dbo.SelectedEvents(
    @EventSet,                  -- Set of events to analyze
    @enumerate_multiple_events, -- Differentiate multiple event occurrences
    @StartDateTime,             -- Start date for the event selection
    @EndDateTime,               -- End date for the event selection
    @transforms,                -- Event transformations
    @ByCase,       -- Consider each case separately (1) or treat all as one case (0)
    @metric,                    -- Metric for evaluating the events ( Time Between)
    @CaseFilterProperties,      -- Case-level properties to filter the events
    @EventFilterProperties      -- Event-level properties to filter the events
)
```

Code 2: Parameters of the SelectedEvents TVF as used in a SQL SELECT statement.

Following are brief explanations of the parameters of the SelectedEvents TVF. Most are common throughout other major functions and stored procedures, so it's a good idea to introduce them. Note that for the default items, this is the value if NULL is specified as the parameter.

1. **@EventSet** (NVARCHAR(MAX)):
    - **Purpose**: Specifies the set of events you want to select. It can be a comma-separated list of events or a special reference to predefined event sets.
    - **Default**: Select all events.

- **Example**: A CSV listing the event set (e.g., 'leavehome,heavytraffic,moderatetraffic,arrivework') or the code for a defined eventset (e.g., restaurantguest).

2. **@enumerate_multiple_events** (INT):
   - **Purpose**: Controls how the function deals with events that occur multiple times within the same case. If set to a value greater than 0, it enumerates each occurrence of the event within a case.
   - **Default**: Multiple occurrences are not explicitly enumerated unless specified. Automatically sets to 1.
   - **Example**: If set to 2, two occurrences of an event, say an event called "charged", will be labeled as charged1 for the first occurrence and charged2 for the second occurrence.

3. **@StartDateTime** (DATETIME):
   - **Purpose**: The start date and time for selecting events. Only events that occur on or after this date will be included.
   - **Default**: '01/01/1900' (a very early date, effectively including events from the earliest possible time).
   - **Example**: '01/01/2020' to select events from the start of 2020 onward.

4. **@EndDateTime** (DATETIME):
   - **Purpose**: The end date and time for selecting events. Only events that occur on or before this date will be included.
   - **Default**: '12/31/2050' (a far future date, effectively including all events up to the farthest reasonable future).
   - **Example**: '12/31/2024' to select events occurring before the end of 2024.

5. **@transforms** (NVARCHAR(MAX)):
   - **Purpose**: Specifies any transformations you want to apply to the event set. This is useful for aggregating similar event types or renaming event types to a common format.
   - **Default**: No transformations.

   - **Example**: This JSON snippet, '{"fromKey": "heavytraffic", "toKey": "traffic"}', will rename heavytraffic to traffic.

6. **@ByCase** (BIT):
   - **Purpose**: Determines whether events should be grouped by case. If set to 1, the events will be returned in the context of the case they belong to. If set to 0, all events are treated as if they belong to a single case.
   - **Default**: 1 (group events by case by default).
   - **Example**: Set to 0 if you want to treat all events across different cases as a single sequence.

7. **@metric** (NVARCHAR(20)):
   - **Purpose**: Specifies the metric you want to track for each event. The metric could be any event-level property, such as "Fuel," or it could be time between events (default).
   - **Default**: 'Time Between' (measures the time between events by default).
   - **Example**: 'Fuel' to track fuel consumption for each event.

8. **@CaseFilterProperties** (NVARCHAR(MAX)):
   - **Purpose**: Allows filtering events based on case-level properties. These are passed as JSON key-value pairs that describe specific attributes of the case, such as an employee ID or a customer ID.
   - **Default**: No filtering based on case properties.
   - **Example**: '{"EmployeeID":2, "CustomerID":2}' to filter events only from cases where EmployeeID is 2 and CustomerID is 2.

9. **@EventFilterProperties** (NVARCHAR(MAX)):
   - **Purpose**: Allows filtering events based on event-level properties. Similar to @CaseFilterProperties, but applies to individual event characteristics.
   - **Default**: No filtering based on event properties.
   - **Example**: '{"Player":"JohnDoe", "GameType":"Poker"}' to filter only poker events related to the player JohnDoe.

MarkovProcess TVF

The MarkovProcess TVF is the central function in the TimeSolution database that generates Markov models for a given set of events over a specified timeframe. It incorporates the SelectedEvents function to pull the relevant events, then computes the probability of transitions between events, along with other statistical metrics such as average time between events, standard deviation, and more. This function can generate first-order, second-order, and third-order MMs, allowing for deeper analysis of event sequences.

Code 3 is pseudocode showing the parameters for the MarkovProcess TVF.

```
SELECT *
FROM dbo.MarkovProcess(
    @Order,                       -- Order of the Markov model (1, 2, or 3)
    @EventSet,                    -- Set of events to analyze
    @enumerate_multiple_events,  -- Differentiate multiple event occurrences
    @StartDateTime,               -- Start date for the event selection
    @EndDateTime,                 -- End date for the event selection
    @transforms,                  -- Event transformations
    @ByCase,      -- Consider each case separately (1) or treat all as one case (0)
    @metric,                      -- Metric for evaluating the events ( Time Between)
    @CaseFilterProperties,        -- Case-level properties to filter the events
    @EventFilterProperties,       -- Event-level properties to filter the events
    @ForceRefresh                 -- Force recalculation or use cached results
)
```

Code 3: Parameters of the MarkovProcess TVF as used in a SQL SELECT.

Most of the parameter explanations are the same as it is for SelectedEvents, so I'll just describe those as "Same as SelectedEvents":

1. **@Order** (INT):
    - **Purpose**: Specifies the order of the Markov process.
        1. First-order Markov Model, considers only the previous event.
        2. Second-order Markov Model, considers the last two events.
        3. Third-order Markov Model, considers the last three events.
    - **Default**: 1 (first-order).
    - **Example**: 2 to consider the last two events in each transition.
2. **@EventSet** (NVARCHAR(MAX)): Same as SelectedEvents.
3. **@enumerate_multiple_events** (INT): Same as SelectedEvents.

4. **@StartDateTime** (DATETIME): Same as SelectedEvents.
5. **@EndDateTime** (DATETIME): Same as SelectedEvents.
6. **@transforms** (NVARCHAR(MAX)): Same as SelectedEvents.
7. **@ByCase** (BIT): Same as SelectedEvents.
8. **@metric** (NVARCHAR(20)): Same as SelectedEvents
9. **@CaseFilterProperties** (NVARCHAR(MAX)): Same as SelectedEvents
10. **@EventFilterProperties** (NVARCHAR(MAX)): Same as SelectedEvents
11. **@ForceRefresh** (BIT):
    - **Purpose**: If set to 1, forces the function to regenerate the Markov model even if a cached version exists.
    - **Default**: 0 (use the cached model if available).
    - **Example**: Set to 1 to force recalculation of the Markov model.

CHAPTER 6

Dimensional TimeSolution Data

With the TimeSolution SQL Server database set up and a bit of background of the two most important functions, we can begin playing with the solution. We'll start out focusing more on concepts and then begin a lab walkthrough in *Explore Time Solutions*. We'll start with the dimension tables, which are the entities (the things) of the system.

DimDate and DimTime

Without date and time, MMs wouldn't make any sense—it's about the probability of what comes *next*, so with no time, there's no next.

The separation of date and time is a typical BI practice. The reason is to mitigate the size of a combined DateTime dimension that would otherwise have one row for every time period. For example, a DateTime dimension with ten years down to the level of seconds (86,400 seconds per day) would result in over 300 million rows. That's huge for what is usually thought of as a very small table, since the BI time granularity has usually been at the day or higher level. But over the past decade, BI use cases have required date/time granularity down to even the millisecond level.

By splitting up into the DimDate and DimTime table, for ten years, there will be 3,650 days and 86,400 seconds, respectively. This optimization is even more evident if your use cases take you to the millisecond level (86 million milliseconds per day times 3,650 days—yikes!).

In this time of AI and IoT, there will be many processes at least at the millisecond level. If we have processes related to life sciences (e.g., protein folding), that could go down to the picosecond level!

In the EventsFact table, the EventDate column is a DateTime column. Specifically, it's the high-precision "datetime2(7)" column:

- Precision: The (7) indicates that the datetime2 column can store date and time data time down to the 100 nanosecond level. This should be adequate for most non-scientific applications, not for protein folding or nuclear accelerators, which, as mentioned, could go down to the picosecond, 1/1000 of a nanosecond.
- Range: datetime2 supports a broader range of dates compared to the datetime data type. It can store dates from 0001-01-01 through 9999-12-31 and times from 00:00:00.0000000 to 23:59:59.9999999.
- Storage Size: Depending on the precision you choose, the storage size can range from 6 to 8 bytes:

DimEvents Table

The DimEvents table defines the distinct types of events that occur within the system, not the events themselves—that's the role of the EventsFact table. This dimension table acts as a catalog of possible event types, providing a structured way to categorize and analyze the actions or occurrences that take place within each case. For example, in the restaurant context we've discussed, events like *seating a customer*, *taking an order*, *serving food*, and *processing payment* would be defined here, while the specific occurrences of these events are recorded in the EventsFact table.

The DimEvents table includes columns such as event identifiers, descriptions, and possibly hierarchical information to group events into a taxonomy.

Window Functions in Event Streaming

Most events landing in Time Molecules will have passed through event streaming systems, which will usually be the source or raw data for TimeSolution. However, the raw events are usually combined to form aggregated events. This class arises from the application of "window functions," which process streams of events by first grouping them into defined time windows or other criteria, and then applying an aggregation function to that group of events.

These window functions allow events to "flow through" dynamically, applying aggregation or analytical logic to continuous data in real time. By segmenting streams into meaningful windows, event streaming systems can summarize, analyze, or act on data within these intervals, enabling the creation of derived insights or actions. These aggregation functions are generally deterministic, predefined logic to data streams, transforming raw events into a compact, insightful value.

As an example, say you're having a serious conversation with your boss and you finally say, "You've said 'that would be great' eight times during our five-minute conversation." The fact that your boss said "that would be great" in the conversation is the salient event, not the individual utterances.

Let's look at common functions—first, the window functions, the range of events upon which we will apply an aggregation function:

1. **Tumbling Window**: Fixed-size, non-overlapping windows that group events within a set interval (e.g., 1-minute windows).
2. **Sliding Window**: Overlapping windows that slide by a specified amount, allowing events to appear in multiple windows (e.g., sliding by 30 seconds).
3. **Session Window**: Based on periods of activity separated by gaps of inactivity (e.g., grouping all events until a 5-minute inactivity period is detected).
4. **Count-based Window**: Groups events after a fixed number of occurrences rather than time (e.g., every 100 events).

Now let's look at the common aggregation functions that are applied to events grouped by the window functions:

1. **COUNT**: Counts the number of events within a tumbling window, such as "10 orders placed in a 1-minute window."
2. **SUM**: Totals a metric within the window, such as "total revenue from all orders placed in a 1-minute window."
3. **AVERAGE**: Calculates the mean value of a metric, such as "average transaction size for all orders in a 1-minute window."
4. **MIN/MAX**: Finds the minimum or maximum value within the window, such as "highest transaction amount in a 1-minute window."

These window functions, combined with aggregation functions, are foundational in event streaming systems. They allow for the summarization of real-time data streams, identification of trends, and triggering of actions based on observed patterns—whether it's detecting anomalies, generating alerts, or analyzing user activity.

IsState Flag

As discussed earlier, under Markov models, events result in some change of state. The DimEvents.IsState column indicates whether the DimEvent row is an event or really a state.

For example, think of our restaurant set of events (arrive, greeted, seated, intro, …). After a customer arrives at the restaurant (an event, cause, action), the state of the customer is "waiting to be greeted". Eventually, the host greets the customer (the next expected event). They have a short conversation and so the customer's next state is "waiting to be seated".

Although the TimeMolecules MMs are based on events, we could create "pseudo events" that are really states—the result of an event. For example, in poker, after a player takes an action (an event), the state of the game changes—the pot size is different, another player has a turn, and maybe the last player folds. The next player (a good player) should react to the new state of the game, not the action of the previous player.

Why aren't all event sets like this—alternating events and the resulting state (a.k.a. cause and effect)? Because event streaming generally only processes events. Event streaming generally doesn't assess the state of its surroundings after each event.

For example, an IoT device deployed on a beach could submit events such as "detected rain." But it doesn't immediately assess how the beach has changed after detecting rain—e.g., Is the beach now void of people? It might send a photo that could be analyzed by an AI asynchronously. It would be very nice if the IoT device could say, "Detected rain, no one still at the beach, …" That's what a human would say with a similar task, and as AI continues to proliferate, that should become more common.

Synthetic Events from Machine Learning

What I'm calling "synthetic events" are created by analyzing real-time data and clustering it into significant patterns or conditions. These are events we make up from other events. For example, in a poker tournament, we can collect data after each player's turn, such as the number of players still in the game, the pot size, and the current bets. By analyzing the current metrics of the game, we can generate synthetic events that signal key scenarios like "high-risk play," "bluffing opportunity," or "critical pot size." Here's how that might be done:

1. **Collect Data from Each Player's Turn**: In the example (the gamestate_properties table in the TimeSolutions database), the data consists of game metrics after each player's turn. This includes properties like:
   - **Players_In**: The number of players remaining in the hand.
   - **Pot Size**: The total amount of money in the pot.
   - **Current Bet**: The current bet amount during the player's turn.

2. **Cluster Similar Game States**: By clustering game states based on these properties, we can identify patterns that frequently occur together. For example:
   - A small number of players with a large pot size might indicate a "high-stakes showdown."
   - A situation where many players are still in, but the pot size is low, might indicate "early cautious play."

3. **Define Synthetic Events**: Once clusters of similar states are identified, we can assign understandable labels to them. These labels are abstractions, making it easier to recognize important game conditions that otherwise might go unnoticed in real time.
   - **Example Synthetic Event**: A game state where Players_In < 3 and Pot > 10000 could be labeled as **"Endgame High Stakes"**.
   - Another scenario where Players_In > 5 and Pot < 2000 could be labeled as **"Cautious Early Play."**

4. **Leverage These Events**: Once these synthetic events are defined, they can be used to trigger specific actions, inform decision-making, or refine strategies. For example, a poker player could use these synthetic events to guide betting strategies in future hands.

Table 9 shows the five discovered game states and their property values. These values were created by analyzing logs of poker games through a k-means cluster algorithm.

	GameState-0	GameState-1	GameState-2	GameState-3	GameState-4
Players_In	6.31374	4.0961	2.92737	2.7282	2.29818
Pot	1452.957	8101.354	35046.61	1773.978	2686.583
current_leader_chips	20066.8	130527.1	59122.6	15730.16	12088.66
game_turn	1.00811	1.13213	1.58659	1.17625	2.80774
game_bet	212.4045	988.1622	13668.53	66.75294	1233.452
current_bet	602.0491	3220.48	14665.98	685.2137	636.012
chips_remaining	10976.91	46528.15	5956.603	8818.535	5981.484
cards_on_table_value	1.1362	1.42843	1.14507	1.16201	1.23559
pct_pot	0.10911	0.08636	0.44779	0.04893	0.45
pct_current_leader_chips	0.58337	0.36346	0.07239	0.61427	0.5554

Table 9: Game State clusters found with KNN.

LLMs could assist in analyzing the possible meaning of the cluster. Here are possible interpretations of the game states created by ChatGPT when submitting Table 9 along with a simple prompt—*"Please write a summary for each Game State based on an analysis of very many Texas Holdem hands."*:

- ***GameState-0:*** *An early game state with moderate player engagement. The pot size is relatively small, and players still have a decent amount of chips. Decisions are likely cautious, with lower bets and minimal risk.*
- ***GameState-1:*** *An increasingly active state, with fewer players remaining and a significant rise in the pot size. Players are starting to make more impactful bets, but the leader's chip count has surged significantly.*
- ***GameState-2:*** *A high-stakes state where the pot size has grown dramatically, but few players remain. Players are likely making bold moves, and the bets are at their highest, reflecting a pivotal moment in the game.*
- ***GameState-3:*** *A state of moderate activity, with a decrease in the pot size after a peak. The game has stabilized somewhat, with players making smaller bets, and the current leader has fewer chips than in previous states.*
- ***GameState-4:*** *A late-stage game state where only a few players remain. The pot size is still significant, but player chips and bets have decreased, signaling the final stages of the game. Decisions here are crucial for the outcome.*

These summaries represent the progression of a typical tournament from start to finish, with each game state indicating a deeper stage of player engagement and risk.

Synthetic events enable us to derive new insights from existing data by clustering and analyzing patterns that wouldn't be readily evident from studying raw events alone. By applying techniques like clustering to game states in a poker tournament, we can label scenarios such as "Endgame High Stakes" or "Cautious Early Play." These synthetic events provide a higher level of abstraction, enabling more informed decisions and actions. This approach can be applied to various domains, turning unstructured data into meaningful events that can guide strategy and process optimization.

Sources Table – Data Sources Dimension

The Sources table organizes the event data sources that feed into the TimeSolution. Data sources encompass any system, database, or stream where events are stored, such as Azure CosmosDB, SQL Server, Kafka streams, or log files.

These sources can range from the sources of real-time event streams, like those processed by Azure EventHub, to batch-loaded datasets from enterprise applications (e.g., log files). Each source represents a distinct pipeline of event data that contributes to the broader, integrated analysis within the TimeSolution, ensuring that every event—and case-level and event-level properties—are traceable back to its origin. By cataloging these sources, Sources facilitates traceability, scalability, and transparency in event ingestion and processing.

DimObservers Table - Observers

As the old koan goes: If a tree in the forest fell and no one heard it, did it really happen? I mention that as a reminder that most of what happens in the world isn't recorded in some database. For something to get into a database, an observer must first observe the event to record it into a data source. Observers can be:

- **Software systems, such as CRM or ERP:** These aren't really the "edge" observers, but events are loaded into them from people (the "edge devices"), other systems, or the systems generate events on their own. These OLTP systems I've mentioned probably play a dual role of observer and data repository (what we'll call "sources" from TimeSolutions point of view).
- **IoT device:** Sensors out in the field. They can be passive, just recording things, such as the temperature and chemical levels. What they pick up is emitted from hardware embedded in them. Or they could be more intelligent, performing edge-computing, programmed to spot incoming ICBMs, discerning them from flocks of birds.
- **Video cameras:** We can't forget these. It seems like everything is passively recorded, including images and sounds. If needed, we can run this video through multimodal AI to transcribe the sounds and pluck out recognized objects, and generative AI can automatically compose a summary of what's happening.

Processes can involve multiple observers from different teams, departments, or enterprises. For example, a sales process involves salespeople, customers, payment approvers, inventory personnel, shipping, and many others.

Observers and sources could overlap in functionality but operate at different levels:

- **Observers**: Capture and record individual events (IoT devices, cameras, and users entering data into a CRM).
- **Sources**: Process and organize event data from observers into structured pipelines or repositories (databases, event streams).
  While a source can contain data from multiple observers, the observer is the first point of contact for an event entering the system.

EventSets Table

Event sets are curated lists of event types (from the DimEvents table) used to create Markov models for process analysis—they define which event types are included in a Markov model. A unique given code identifies each event set and serves to include or exclude events, depending on the level of detail required for the analysis.

The purpose of event sets is to filter and focus on certain aspects of a process, skipping over events that are not relevant to the current objective or not relevant to the process itself.

For example, in a restaurant setting, you might create an event set that includes just the key stages—{seated, ordered, served, paid}—to analyze how efficiently customers are served and leave. Alternatively, you might create an event set that only tracks arrival and departure times for a high-level view of customer flow. In this way, event sets are really the definition of relevant granularities of processes—whether you're zooming in on granular process steps or zooming out for a broader overview.

When working with raw, unfamiliar, stews of event logs, a good part of the process mining effort involves fleshing out the event set—identifying the event types that form the "language" of a process. This discovery is essential, as it defines the structure and meaning necessary to analyze the data. Conversely, when the events are from already well-understood processes—such as a sales log grouped by case and event—the event set can often be directly defined by Subject Matter Experts (SME). Whether discovered or predefined, event sets are the primary grouping that allows us to build MMs and analyze and interpret processes.

The object called an Event Set is really just a convenience, so we don't need to specify the list of events when a new MM is created. We reference an Event Set using a unique code. For example, the events involved with serving a customer are: *arrive, greeted, seated, intro, drinks, ccdeclined, charged, order, check, seated, served, bigtip, depart.* For the walkthroughs, this event set is named *restaurantguest*—much less verbose than the list of each event. We'll meet this event set soon. Code 4 is an example of explicitly listing the events.

```
--[START Code 4 - Filtering events by a list of events.]
DECLARE @eventset NVARCHAR(1000)=
      'arrive, greeted, seated, intro, drinks, ccdeclined, charged, order, check,
seated, served, bigtip, depart'
SELECT
      *
FROM
      dbo.SelectedEvents(@eventset,0,NULL,NULL,NULL,1,NULL,NULL,NULL)
ORDER BY
      CaseID,[Rank]
```

Code 4: Filtering events by a list of events.

Alternatively, so that we don't need to always explicitly spell out that set, as mentioned, we could define the event set with a code name (*restaurantguest* –we'll see how to do that later) and reference that code name, as shown in Code 5. Both will return the same results, which is a list of all specified events.

```
--[START Code 5 - Filtering events by event set.]
SELECT
       *
FROM
       dbo.SelectedEvents('restaurantguest',0,NULL,NULL,NULL,1,NULL,NULL,NULL)
ORDER BY
       CaseID,[Rank]
```

Code 5: Filtering events by an event set.

The ability to reference either a list of events or an event set gives us flexibility to specify ad-hoc lists of events, which is especially beneficial when exploring specific scenarios or asking targeted questions. For example, suppose we were only interested in how long it takes for a customer to leave. We could define an ad-hoc set, specifying "seated, depart" to retrieve only the events when they were seated and when they left. This mode of exploration allows us to zoom in on particular aspects of a process—in this case, how long a table is occupied—without being muddied by unrelated events.

Transforms and Abstraction

One of the most powerful (if not most powerful) feature of our brain is our ability to abstract—to generalize and categorize—before we formulate predictions. Abstraction enables us to focus on the essence of something, stripping away the noise of unique traits to understand what is common and fundamental across a population of things. In our world, most things are spawned from a template, a pattern, even though particular instances have their own unique traits and attachments.

The word "generalization" can sometimes carry a negative connotation, such as when it's used to oversimplify or stereotype people. However, abstraction is not about rigidly defining something forever—it's about creating a flexible framework that helps us make sense of the world. The key is to remain adaptable, treating abstractions as tools for quick, foundational understanding, not as immutable truths.

In fact, most things we observe are subject to not just one, but many very different abstractions—different points of view and countless ways to categorize something. The problem is the limitations of our current information systems that prevent it. For example, we're given forms with limited categories to check off. If none apply, we go into the "Other" category, which strips the beautiful complexity of the world. There is always some way each human falls into the "Other" category.

In the context of this book, transforms are about the abstraction of events—such as merging earthquake, tremor, and seismic events into "earthquake". I mention this because "transformer" is a very overloaded term in the AI and data world. For example, it's a keyword in the realm of LLMs (i.e., Transformer architecture), and *transform* is the "T in ETL or ELT" of the BI world.

These transforms imply similarity between two different events of a couple of types:

- They describe what could be the same thing (*sameAs* in knowledge graphs).
- One is a sub-category of the other (*aKindOf* in knowledge graphs).

Across a large ecosystem of processes, there are likely to be synonymous events with different names. They can be euphemisms, such as all the ways we say we're going to the restroom without saying, "I'm going to the restroom." In business, domains often have their own word for the same thing based on their domain lingo. For example:

- **HR Domain:** Fired – let go, terminated, offboarded, down-sized, separated—sacked, made redundant (for the UK readers).

- **Cross Domain terms that mean "Customer Order":**

    - **Sales:** *Order,* the act of closing a sale or winning a deal.
    - **Warehouse/Logistics:** *Fulfillment Request,* the need to ship the product based on the order information.
    - **Finance:** *Invoice,* the need to bill the customer for the product or service.

These complications make categorization and standardization critical but also challenging when done manually. In this context, transforms—abstractions of events—become a powerful tool for specifying the grouping and aligning of similar events.

To automate such abstraction, the DimEvents table in the TimeSolution database includes columns like *description* and *IRI.* The description column provides a succinct summary of each event type, while the IRI column maps those events to external ontologies/vocabularies (e.g., SKOS, DBPedia, FOAF), anchoring them within the Semantic Web framework. Together, these columns allow for a systematic approach to abstraction and grouping, leveraging modern tools like vector embeddings to automate much of the work.

Vectorized Transforms for Aggregation

As we just discussed, most dimension and reference tables in the TimeSolution database include a description and an IRI column. This includes the DimEvents table, which makes sense since transforms are fundamentally about abstracting and grouping events.

The description column provides a succinct summary of the entity—preferably under 100 words. It should have enough to provide searchable context. This description is then vectorized—converted into a numerical representation, 1536 dimensions using one of the OpenAI LLM models—and stored in a vector database. This enables the system to quickly identify entities that are semantically similar, even if they originate from diverse sources. The IRI column links the entity to objects of the Semantic Web, enabling the mapping of synonyms and variations to standardized entities.

With these tools, the system can:

1. **Link Data Across Sources:** By grouping events based on semantic similarity, the system can link events from different sources, even if they are named and/or described differently.

2. **Event Standardization:** Events that are conceptually identical but labeled differently can be aggregated into a single, standardized form. For instance:
    - *twister, funnel cloud, cyclone → tornado:* All variations are grouped together to represent the same underlying entity.

3. **Interoperability:** The IRI column facilitates linking events to external ontologies, ensuring compatibility with other Semantic Web frameworks and systems—like a molecular docking site in self-assembling structures, allowing components to recognize and bind with each other in precise, meaningful ways.

Using embeddings generated from the description column in the DimEvents table, the system can automatically detect and group similar events across disparate data sources. This facilitates the abstraction of entities, reduces noise, and enhances the coherence of MMs, allowing for wider and deeper-scoped analysis and insights.

Figure 12 illustrates the process for embedding descriptions:

1. **Search Query:** An analyst types in a query in English.

2. **Generate Embeddings:** A pre-trained language model (e.g., OpenAI's embedding model) generates an embedding of the search query of item 1.

3. The embedding is a 1536 dimensional vector using OpenAI's API.

4. **Store in Vector Database:** These embeddings are stored in a vector database (Pinecone, Weaviate) to enable efficient similarity searches and grouping of related entities.

5. The embedding is used to quickly find similar embeddings. There isn't a need for painstakingly precise query syntax, and the response doesn't need to be a frustratingly exact match. The "fuzzy" response is more like what you'd expect from a human—reasoning with approximate, imprecise, or partial input.

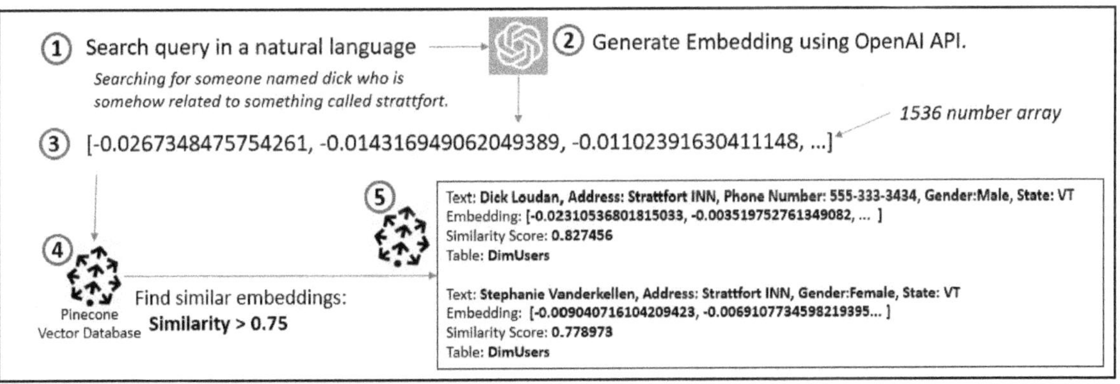

Figure 12: Storing entity descriptions as embeddings.

CHAPTER 7

Events

Events are individual occurrences within a process or workflow tied to specific cases, such as a customer order or a manufacturing lot. Events are also nested. For example, even major ones, such as hurricanes, earthquakes, and stock market crashes, are events within a larger process cycle. We just might not notice the process because the process is kind of on a different facet of existence than the daily lives of most of us.

A case serves as a container for each cycle/iteration of a process, providing context to the sequence in which they occur. The *Cases* table holds essential information about each cycle of a process, such as case identifiers, timestamps, and metadata related to the process duration or its categorization.

For example, in the context of a restaurant, a case could represent the entire dining experience of a customer. Each individual action within that experience, such as being seated or served, is an event that belongs to that case. These events are tracked and imported into the *EventsFact* table, which captures the essential details of the event (such as date, time, type, and the specifics of the case, such as the server, customer, and ticket number).

In this way, events are analyzed as part of the larger narrative of a case, allowing you to track the full sequence of actions, understand dependencies, and identify patterns within the process. This allows for greater insights into the behaviors and transitions that we can generalize across many iterations of a process—whether it's customer service, order processing, or any other domain where sequences of events unfold over time.

For BI or DW practitioners, the EventsFact table isn't much different from the fact table of a star or snowflake dimensional model. After all, facts in fact tables are generally events—a sale, a website visit, or a series of clicks. The key difference is that a traditional fact table typically consolidates data from a single source or a few closely related sources (e.g., sales, web clicks), whereas the EventsFact table in Time Molecules is designed to hold events from a very large variety of sources. In its most stripped-down form, the table is abstracted to the essential properties of an event: date, event type, and case ID.

Events are indications of change. While they may involve objects, they are not primarily about the interaction between objects—they are about salient changes to the "system" (the interacting objects of a process) that occur. To support this flexibility and richness, TimeSolution provides a mechanism for adding variable sets of properties at both the case and event levels. This means that while the foundational structure of EventsFact remains lean, it can dynamically adapt to the diverse and evolving needs of event-driven analysis by appending properties specific to a given process or dataset.

This approach ensures that the EventsFact table can handle the complexity of integrating events from disparate systems without being overwhelmed by rigid schema requirements. It also allows for deep customization, making it a versatile tool for process mining and advanced analytics.

Cases

In the context of Time Molecules, a case represents a cycle, an iteration of a process—usually a process relevant to some enterprise. Examples include a sales cycle, a new employee onboarding, or a project sprint. A case consists of the events that occur within the case and the properties associated with the case.

This distinction between cases and events can sometimes be confusing. For instance, is a hurricane or doctor visit an event or a case? On the surface, both might seem like single events—a hurricane occurs at a point in time, and a doctor's visit happens during a specific appointment. But both are clearly themselves composed of multiple events.

Hurricane Katrina, for example, sounds like an event, but what about all the events that unfolded while it was going on and all the events in its aftermath? A hurricane is not just one event but a series of sub-events over time: formation, intensification, landfall, and dissipation. Each phase of the hurricane's life cycle involves distinct characteristics—such as wind speed, pressure, and location—that define the hurricane at different stages.

Similarly, we say, "I saw the cardiologist last Wednesday." That sounds like an event. But the visit is made up of events—driving there, checking in, waiting in the lobby, walking to the exam room, waiting …

Together, these events form a cohesive process cycle—a case—that captures the full sequence of interactions or changes over time.

The term *case* should be familiar to data scientists, as most ML models are created from datasets where each row is often referred to as a case. However, a key difference in the EventsFact table is that it integrates many types of cases within a single table, where each case represents a distinct process cycle and may involve vastly different sets of attributes and event types. In contrast, typical ML datasets represent a single type of case, with a fixed schema of attributes (columns) across the entire dataset—for example, each row represents a patient in a cohort and the patients' features. This flexibility in EventsFact allows for the representation of diverse cases—such as sales cycles, hurricane processes, or doctor visits—each with unique properties and event sequences within a unified structure.

This perspective shifts how we model and analyze these cases of events. It reveals that cases are not isolated but are cyclical and composite—meaning cases are linked to other cases and even nested within a larger, hierarchical system. By understanding cases as collections of related events, we can uncover patterns, dependencies, and insights that would otherwise remain hidden. Whether it's the phases of a hurricane or the stages of a doctor visit, analysis at the case and event level enables us to see the interconnectedness of events and how they evolve within a larger context.

Categorizing Characteristics of Events

In both the hurricane and doctor visit scenarios, events are not entirely random but emerge from recognizable patterns within a process. These patterns can be analyzed based on how their characteristics are related to the event or process. We can broadly categorize these characteristics as follows (using a doctor visit as the example).

- **Prime Characteristics:** These are the essential features that define the case type. Without these characteristics, the event cannot be classified as such. Consulting with a healthcare provider is the defining characteristic. Without this, it isn't a doctor visit, regardless of other events like scheduling or tests.

- **Associated Characteristics:** These are features that frequently occur during the event and are integral to its execution, though they may not define it entirely. They form the backbone of the process. Scheduling the appointment, checking in, and the actual consultation are associated characteristics—they are core steps that typically occur together to complete the visit.
- **Context-Dependent Characteristics:** These are optional or situational features that may or may not occur during the event or process. They depend on the specific circumstances of the case. Diagnostic tests, follow-up scheduling, or discussions about lifestyle changes are context-dependent—they may happen during some visits but are not required for a visit to be considered complete.

This framework helps distinguish what is core to the case, what is typically associated with it, and what is more variable or context-dependent. It also aids in modeling events more effectively, allowing for clearer analysis and improved insights. This framework helps use set-up transforms that create MMs at different levels—for example, a higher-level MM of only prime and associated characteristics or a very detailed one that includes all permutations of doctor visits.

Time Crystals

When I came up with the term *Time Molecules* about three years ago, I wondered if anyone had ever thought of it. It seemed like a unique idea. Even the domain *timemolecules.com* was available, which surprised me. During my search, I came across something interesting—*Time Crystals*, a relatively new concept in physics that started as a thought experiment by Nobel laureate Frank Wilczek.[4] Time crystals are hypothetical structures that repeat in time without any additional energy, just as photons continue to move without needing input. They simply "do what they do."

Business processes are somewhat like time crystals in that they're designed to follow a set sequence of actions. But unlike time crystals, they require constant energy input—resources, effort, and human intervention—and to put it mildly, they don't always execute perfectly or consistently. This is where *Time Molecules* (Markov models) come in: they help us analyze and understand these business

---

[4] Time Crystals (frankawilczek.com): https://www.frankawilczek.com/single-post/2017/12/06/new-time-crystals.

processes, potentially guiding them toward their "ideal" state—closer to the perfection of a time crystal (mechanistic business process), where variability and inefficiencies are minimized.

I also find myself wondering if *Time Crystals* in physics interact with each other, much like photons can interact. Similarly, we understand business processes as interacting systems that form larger systems. My assertion is that by studying how *Time Molecules* interact, we can find new ways to optimize processes, leading them toward greater efficiency and seamless operation, just as we might imagine ideal interactions between time crystals.

For a sneak peek, see Appendix F on the GitHub repository. It is about non-deterministic finite automata as the "time crystal complement" of time molecules.

Perfect Cycles

At least for now, our business processes are not the same as the cycles of machines. Business processes are exposed to and must cope with the cold, cruel world—where they voluntarily or involuntarily interact with other processes, each with objectives of their own. So business processes rarely work exactly as intended—like a car on a very bumpy dirt road. The analysis we perform mainly optimizes existing business processes in an evolutionary manner and develops new business process strategies in a revolutionary manner (or, more likely, something in between). Let's compare a typical cycle of a business process with that of a machine.

Figure 13 shows the sequence of events for a perfectly operating machine, a four-stroke engine. The probability for every transition is 1.0. Of course, in reality, it's not really 1.0 because machines do wear down and break, and they have dependencies (e.g., oxygen in the atmosphere).

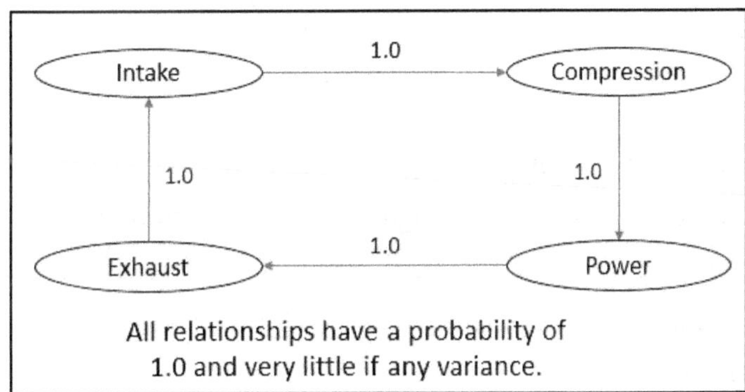

Figure 13: Example of a machine cycle. Four-stroke engine.

Figure 14 is an example of the sales cycles of a business in the form of an MM. The thicker arrows show the sales cycle if everything goes well. That is the "intended cycle". But in reality, the processes don't always work as intended.

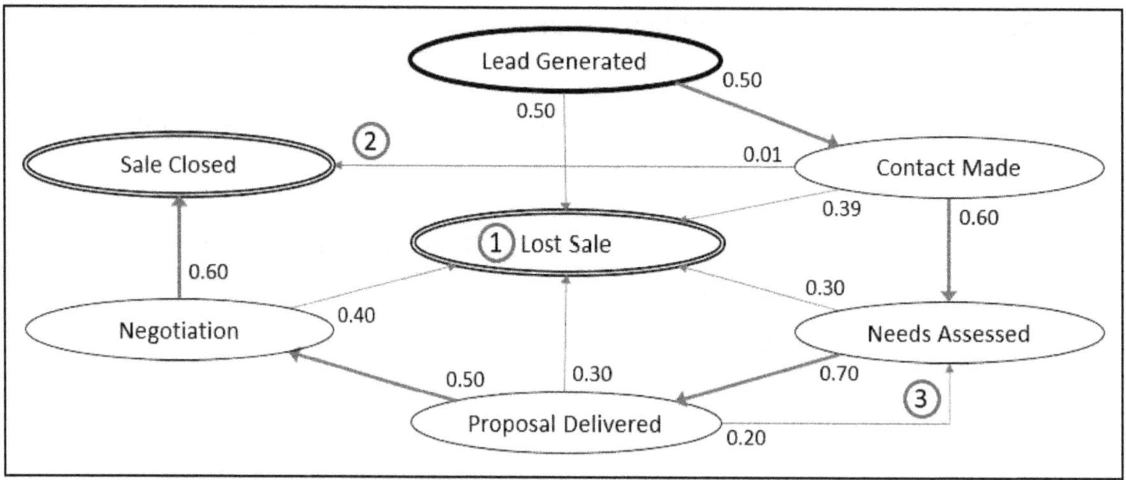

Figure 14: Imperfect but flexible cycle. Sales is exposed to countless factors.

The world is a messy place, so our intended sales cycles could deviate in countless ways. Here are a few of those ways, represented by the numbers in Figure 14:

1. All along the way, there is a risk the sales cycle will come to a halt. This is a characteristic of imperfection. Things go wrong along the way and the process prematurely terminates.
2. On rare occasions, contact is made and the customer buys our product, no questions asked. This (and item 3) is an example of flexibility in the process.
3. We regularly need to re-assess customer needs after delivering a proposal.

But a process having multiple paths doesn't make it chaotic. Most machines have some sort of built-in ability to self-adjust—self-heal. What we would be interested in is which segments might not run so smoothly and why/how.

Machines without mechanisms to self-heal (e.g., no single points of failure) are brittle—unyielding systems that wear down over time or fail outright when faced with unplanned conditions. Life and business processes, on the other hand, are resilient but imperfect. This resilience is what allows business processes to adapt to uncertainty (up to now, almost exclusively through our intervention with our human intelligence).

We can measure resilience by analyzing the standard deviation of metrics. However, if the standard deviation (or its relative measure, the coefficient of variation) is small, it *suggests* that the segment operates smoothly and predictably. When the coefficient of variation is moderate, but the process continues without errors, it indicates that the system is under uncertain conditions but is able to adapt and remain functional. This adaptability is the hallmark of resilient systems, distinguishing them from the rigid cycles of machines. However, if the coefficient of variation is large, the system is exposed to wild conditions, and so the system is at risk for failure.

Cases Table

The Cases table serves as the foundation for grouping events into distinct scenarios or processes. Each row in the Cases table represents a unique instance or "case," such as servicing a customer, processing an order, or completing a manufacturing cycle. These cases are central to the analysis, as they provide the context in which sequences of events occur.

CaseTypes Table

This table defines the type of process each case represents—for example, the process of servicing a restaurant customer. In essence, each case is an instance of a broader process. It could be argued that "Process" might have been a more appropriate name for this table, as it captures the idea that cases are executions or iterations of a defined process or system.

Table 10 shows the case types used in the walkthroughs.

CaseTypeID	Description	Name/Code
1	The process of serving a customer in a typical sit-down restaurant.	Meal
2	A route of some delivery or pickup vehicle, such as a package delivery or a garbage truck pickup.	Truck Trip
3	Commute to Work by a typical U.S. commute in a big city.	Commute to Work
4	Texas Hold'em game.	PokerGame

Table 10: The case types used in the walkthroughs.

Note that the description column is succinct, but descriptive enough for the fuzzy search through the vector database as just discussed.

Case Properties Table

The CaseProperties table holds additional details that describe the specific attributes of a case. The CaseProperties table allows us to store contextual information about each case in a flexible, semi-structured JSON format. This data can be used to analyze and differentiate cases beyond just the event timeline.

Examples of Case Properties:

1. **Employee Performance Review (HR Case)**
    - {"EmployeeID": 123, "ReviewDate": "2023-12-01", "Reviewer": "ManagerA", "Rating": "Exceeds Expectations", "Department": "Sales"}
    - Describes the performance review of an employee, including identifiers, dates, and evaluation details.

2. **Customer Support Ticket (Support Case)**
    - {"TicketID": 56789, "CustomerID": 789, "Priority": "High", "Status": "Open", "AssignedAgent": "AgentB", "Product": "Software Suite X"}
    - Captures key information for a customer support case, including ticket details, customer information, and current status.

3. **Sales Transaction (Sales Case)**
    - {"TransactionID": 9823, "SalesPersonID": 45, "StoreID": 3, "TotalValue": 1500.75, "ItemsSold": 4, "CustomerType": "VIP"}
    - Describes a sales transaction, with properties detailing the salesperson, store, and transaction specifics like the value and type of customer.

These properties add richness and context to the analysis of events, allowing insights at both the event and case level, such as correlating employee review performance with sales results or identifying patterns in customer support tickets.

EventsFact Table

This is a generalized table for any kind of event. That is, any event that happens in the universe has at its core the date and time of when it happened, a classification of the event (DimEvents), and ideally, some sort of process template (Cases table). That is the minimum definition of an event.

The EventsFact table is the central fact table in TimeSolution, designed to integrate events imported from a wide variety of sources. It captures the fundamental details needed to construct MMs and other analyses by organizing events within cases. The key columns of the table include CaseID, Event, and EventDate.

In addition to these key columns, the table tracks the ordinal position of each event within a case, the source from which the event was captured, and the aggregation type related to streaming processes such as windowing functions. Table 11 lists the columns of the EventsFact table.

Column Name	Data Type	Description
CaseID	int	Identifies the unique case or process to which the event belongs.
Event	nvarchar	Describes the specific event that occurred within the case.
EventDate	datetime	The date and time when the event occurred.
SourceID	int	Links to the **Sources** table, indicating the origin or system where the event was captured.
AggregationTypeID	int	Links to the **AggregationType** table, representing the type of aggregation applied (e.g., windowing, rolling averages). This column supports streaming and event processing functions.
CaseOrdinal	int	Represents the ordinal position of the event within its case, ordered by **EventDate**.
ParentCaseID	int	Identifies the parent case if the event is part of a **nested** or **hierarchical case structure**.
BatchID	int	The **ETL batch number** indicating when this event was loaded into the system.

Table 11: The Events Fact table.

The EventsFact table is the core of the creation of MMs and other process-related analyses. Events from this table are grouped by CaseID and then analyzed based on the event sequence, event date, and other metrics across a large number of cases. The ability to integrate source, aggregation, and parent case information makes this table highly versatile for handling complex, multi-source event streams in real-time or batch-processing contexts.

Event Metrics

Event Metrics are quantitative measures that capture the characteristics and dynamics of events within a process, providing a flexible framework for analyzing event-driven systems. These metrics include native measures, such as counts and time between events and transition probabilities. However, they also extend further, enabling the analysis of changes in custom metrics across event sequences, such as fuel consumption, inventory levels, or sales revenue. This allows Time Molecules to track not only how events unfold, but also how key metrics change from one event to the next, enriching both diagnostic and predictive insight.

In MMs, counts are the traditional and ubiquitous metric, forming the foundation for calculating the probability of the next event. This probability is calculated by comparing the distribution of transition counts from one event to the subsequent events that are recorded.

For example, consider predicting what might happen to a customer after arriving at a restaurant: address the host, walk in directly to meet a friend already seated, or just leave. Table 12 summarizes the history of customer service events over the past month based on their next actions.

Customer Arrives	Next Event	Count	Probability
	Addresses the Host	80	0.90
100	Walk in to Meet Friend Already Seated	15	0.15
	Immediately Leaves	5	0.05

Table 12: Historic count of customer orders for July 2024.

Table 12Table 13 shows that of 100 customer arrivals, 80 addressed the host, 15 joined a friend already seated, and five immediately left. These counts are the basis for predicting the probability of a new customer taking a similar action. Such probabilities provide valuable insights into behavioral patterns and guide decision-making processes and optimizations.

Count is core to the concept of MMs. While event metrics such as time between events, fuel consumption, or other measures provide additional valuable information, they are not required to define a basic MM. Therefore, count is always part of every MM.

Time Between Events – The Default Metric

Although predicting what will happen next is valuable, in a dynamic world, "when" something might happen is often just as important. Understanding the time between events offers deeper insights into processes and can drive more nuanced decisions.

Table 13 is sort of similar to Table 12 above. Instead of describing the probability of the next event, it shows the time between arriving and what happens next.

Arrived Count	Next Step	Total Minutes Between Events	Mean Time Between Events (minutes)
80	Greeted by Host	40	0.50
15	Seats Themselves	3	0.20
5	Departed	50	10.00

Table 13: Mean time between customer arrival and next event.

The mean time between events highlights important insights, such as why some customers leave. For example, the long 10-minute average wait for customers simply departing suggests an issue with service efficiency that needs to be addressed to reduce churn.

Metrics Table

The time between events is the default metric. However, other metrics can provide context and enrich the analysis. Examples include fuel consumption, weight changes, or even financial metrics like stock prices.

Table 14 lists the metrics already entered into the TimeSolution database.

MetricID	Metric	Method	UoM	Description
1	Time Between	$n_1 - n_0$	sec	Time between the previous and current event. This is the default metric based on the EventDate.
2	Fuel	$n_1 - n_0$	liter	Fuel consumed
4	Weight	$n_1 - n_0$	tons	Weight change between events
5	Close	$(n_1 - n_0) / n_0$	NA	Day over Day Closing Stock price

Table 14: Metrics table.

The Method column defines how values are calculated for specific metrics. For example:

- **(n_1-n_0) –Time between events (1):** The difference in timestamps for consecutive events. For Fuel (2), this is the difference between starting and ending fuel levels during a journey. For Weight (4), this is the net gain or loss of cargo between stops.
- **(n_1-n_0)/ n_0 –Close (5):** This is the difference between the value of an event (n_1) compared to the value of the prior event (n_0). For example, the stock closing price of today (n_1) versus the stock closing price of yesterday (n_0).

Metric Statistics

In TimeSolution, event-to-event metrics are summarized using a range of statistical values, enabling detailed analysis. This includes:

- **Sum:** Total metric value across all cases (total time or fuel).
- **Max:** Maximum metric value (longest time or greatest consumption).
- **Min:** Minimum metric value.
- **Avg:** Mean (average) metric value.
- **StDev:** Standard deviation, reflecting variability in the metric.
- **CV or CoefVar:** Coefficient of Variation, normalizing the standard deviation as a percentage of the mean.

The Coefficient of Variation (CV) is particularly useful for comparing variability across different event-to-event transitions. It is calculated as the ratio of the standard deviation to the mean, expressed as a percentage:

$$CV = \left(\frac{\text{Standard Deviation}}{\text{Mean}}\right) \times 100$$

For example, if the average time between events, say being greeted to being seated, is 5.0 minutes with a standard deviation of 1 minute, the Coefficient of Variation is:

$$CV = \left(\frac{1}{5}\right) \times 100 = 20\%$$

A Coefficient of Variation of 20% indicates that the time between events varies by 20% of the average (with a standard deviation of 5.0, this ranges from 4 to 6 minutes), reflecting moderate variability from the time you are greeted by the host and the time you are seated.

Open Schema Properties

Although anything with a date is an event, a date alone isn't really that useful without more context. The TimeSolution database is "abstract" at its core in that it consolidates events across a wide range of event types into a "lowest common denominator" form (date, event type, case ID). In other words, events of many types across many sources co-exist in a single database. That's the minimum we need to generate MMs.

But this abstraction comes with a trade-off—it limits how we can analyze across various dimensions of events. For example, we could create sales MMs from events sliced by different salespersons, different stores, or even by a salesperson at a certain store. However, across all imaginable events, there are countless properties or attributes associated with these events. Some properties, like "location" or "time of day," are common and broadly applicable across many types of events. Other properties are highly specific to event types, like the discount code used for a sale or the weather conditions during a delivery. The diversity of potential properties reflects the complexity of the real world and the unique contexts in which events occur.

We don't attempt to "model" all these attributes with their own columns in TimeSolution—that would quickly grow into a data modeler's nightmare with tables of thousands of columns. Instead, we rely on the flexibility of the key-value, open-schema data modeling technique.

That is, we create one table with two main columns: a key column along with a value. The key represents a property identifier, enabling us to store properties without needing to create a column for each. Unfortunately, for relational databases, this technique comes with a terrible performance penalty—very many self-joins.

That has been a big problem in the data modeling world. However, JSON and document databases (e.g., MongoDB) represent an "open-schema" platform that has drastically mitigated the problem.

Fortunately, we don't need to adopt yet another type of database for open-schema support. Most major large-scale data warehouse vendors have implemented an "unstructured column type" optimized for handling semi-structured data such as JSON. As I write this, Azure Synapse just announced such a column type. This was one of Snowflake's primary differentiators a few years back. It's not just a matter of having such a column type but also implementing the ability to query this data effectively.

The Open Schema mechanism in TimeSolution balances flexibility, query efficiency, and schema adaptability by incorporating both JSON-based storage and key-value tables (KVTs) for structured querying.

Two tables store raw JSON data as received, preserving all attributes for future use while allowing selective extraction into structured formats when needed:

- **CaseProperties** – Stores case-level properties as a single JSON object, allowing the system to retain all attributes without prematurely filtering out potentially useful data.
- **EventProperties** – Stores event-level properties in semi-structured JSON format, ensuring that metadata remains flexible and adaptable to future changes.

In contrast, there are two Key-Value Tables (KVTs)—counterparts to the tables listed just above—that store *selected* attributes parsed from the two tables. This removes a layer of processing since the case and event properties are now in a "native" relational table format, and we can avoid unnecessary processing of properties that may not be of value for MMs:

- **CasePropertiesParsed** – Extracts key-value pairs from CaseProperties, enabling efficient querying of specific case-level properties without requiring full JSON parsing.
- **EventPropertiesParsed** – Extracts key-value pairs from EventProperties, optimizing event-level analysis by making structured attributes directly available.

Another properties table is ModelProperties. It stores model-level properties as a direct key-value table rather than JSON since these properties are set at the time of Markov model creation and do not require schema flexibility. This design achieves a balance between schema flexibility and query efficiency. The JSON tables allow dynamic and evolving attributes to be stored without rigid constraints, while KVTs provide structured, high*er*-performance (we'll talk about outrigger tables for high performance soon) access to frequently queried properties.

Event Properties

Four different sets of event properties land in the EventProperties table (as separate JSON). They are stored in these four columns of the EventProperties table:

- **ActualProperties:** Represent what truly happened during the event, capturing the state of the world at that moment the event triggered. For instance, in a logistics scenario, the actual fuel level or cargo weight of a truck at a specific stop might be recorded. These properties provide a factual baseline against which other values can be compared.
- **IntendedProperties:** This is what we want to happen. In contrast to actual properties, encapsulate the goals or targets established before the event. These values reflect human or organizational intent, such as reaching the next destination or maintaining a specific service level. They define the objectives that guide actions, offering a critical link between planning and execution.
- **ExpectedProperties:** These are predictions or estimates, often generated by machine learning models or other analytical tools. These values aren't necessarily what we hope for, but what we expect will happen. These values are dynamic and may be recalculated in real time as circumstances change. For example, an AI might predict that a vehicle has enough fuel to travel only 30 miles when the intended destination is 50 miles away. This discrepancy would flag a decision point, requiring intervention to align actions with goals.
- **AggregationProperties:** This is the function that is used to summarize patterns or trends over a group of events, mostly using techniques like windowing functions in event streaming. These aggregated insights might calculate metrics such as average response times or cumulative totals, providing a broader context for understanding individual events. For example, a property of the event might be FuelConsumed. This would be a value, which is the sum from the start of the route to the time of the event.

The concept of the four property sets reflects a semantic and dynamic approach to capturing event-time information that bridges the gap between real-world occurrences, goals, and predictions. These properties are recorded and updated at the time an event takes place, making them a vital resource for real-time decision making and performance analysis.

One special type of ActualProperty could be the rule or logic that triggered the event. This might include the ID of a business rule, a Prolog clause[prlc], or the name of a decision function in a business rules engine. Capturing this identifier allows for traceability—linking outcomes back to the logic that produced them—and supports auditing, debugging, and the refinement of automated decisions over time.

Open Schema Properties to an Outrigger Dimension Table

To further enhance performance—beyond parsing the case and event properties from semi-structured JSON into KVTs—and streamline analysis, attributes from open schema properties can be selectively flattened into an outrigger dimension table. An outrigger dimension table is a construct of dimensional modeling that consolidates multiple selected attributes formatted in a single table, where each row contains the selected attributes. This reduces the need for query-time parsing (JSON) and joins (KVT-one join for each property), optimizing data retrieval and making it particularly effective when speed and simplicity take precedence over normalization.

In dimensional modeling, an outrigger dimension refers to a secondary dimension table linked to a primary dimension table to provide additional, related attributes. For example, consider the case of our restaurant visit. A visit involves numerous attributes, such as menu items ordered, customer demographics, server details, and time of visit. Rather than repeatedly querying semi-structured data, the most relevant attributes—like customer type, meal category, server, and visit duration—can be extracted and flattened into one table.

The main idea behind this approach is to minimize query complexity while improving performance, particularly in scenarios where data is frequently accessed in a structured format. Instead of repeatedly parsing JSON or joining multiple tables at query time, pre-flattened attributes allow for direct querying of the most relevant fields. This method is especially useful when working with large-scale event data, where reducing the number of joins and function calls can significantly impact processing speed and resource consumption.

This approach loses the flexibility of the open schema but gains the performant advantages of structure. Consolidating key attributes into a single table enables faster queries and easier-to-write SQL while preserving the raw JSON schema for exploring less frequently accessed attributes.

Although this modeling strategy is well-established in the BI world, it is outside the primary focus of this book.

Models Table

The Models table serves as the root structure for organizing and analyzing processes, decisions, and their interrelationships within a system. Each row in the table represents a distinct model that can be of one of four types: MarkovModel, BayesianProbability, Workflow, and NFA (Non-Deterministic Finite Automata).

These models enable complementary analytical capabilities, including understanding observed behaviors, intended processes, probabilistic predictions, and pattern recognition. By storing essential metadata and configuration details, the Models table supports a holistic exploration of both real-world dynamics and aspirational designs.

For this book, we focus on two primary types of models—MarkovModel and BayesianProbability. We've already talked about MMs, but BayesianProbability is new. BayesianProbability models are the probability of some event happening given that another particular event has occurred. In the context of this book, by BayesianProbability, I'm actually referring to conditional probabilities, incorporating prior knowledge to refine forecasts. It supports decision-making under uncertainty by quantifying the likelihood of various outcomes. For example, predicting flight delays based on weather conditions and historical data.

While the WorkFlow and NFA model types are important tools for structuring and analyzing processes, they are not the primary focus of this book. Instead, we concentrate on the foundational concepts behind Time Molecules and how they relate to uncovering and analyzing patterns in event-driven data. NFAs will be briefly touched upon later in the book, but their deeper exploration, along with workflows, will be reserved for future works.

Workflows differ from MMs in that Workflows are purposefully designed processes, reflecting the designed sequence of events rather than patterns observed in the field. However, MMs can play a crucial role in guiding the creation of new workflows or validation of existing workflows. By analyzing event data through MMs, we can uncover the actual dynamics of a process as it happens in the real world. These insights can then inform the design of workflows, enabling them to better align with real-world behaviors or address inefficiencies.

In this way, workflows could possibly be seen as an end product of process mining, starting with MMs to understand what a process truly looks like in practice and then transforming into workflows as a formalized, optimized representation of that process. Table 15 lists the important columns of the Models table.

Column Name	Type	Description
ModelID	BIGINT	Unique identifier for the model.
ModelType	VARCHAR	Specifies the type of model: MarkovModel, BayesianProbability, WorkFlow, or NFA
StartDateTime	DATETIME	Start date and time of the model's scope.
EndDateTime	DATETIME	End date and time of the model's scope.
EventSetKey	VARBINARY	Identifier for the associated event set, used primarily in MarkovModel models.
Order	INT	Specifies the order or complexity of the model—first-order, second-order Markov model.
MetricID	INT	Identifier for the metric that the model evaluates or tracks.
CaseFilterProperties	NVARCHAR	Conditions for selecting specific cases the model applies to.
EventFilterProperties	NVARCHAR	Conditions for selecting events relevant to the model.
Description	NVARCHAR	Human-readable summary of the model, including its purpose and scope. Used to create LLM embeddings.
TransformsKey	VARBINARY	Identifier for any transformations applied to events in the model. See *Transforms and Abstraction.*
ByCase	BIT	Indicates whether the model evaluates cases individually or whether a case is actually a continuous process—for example, time.
DistinctCases	BIGINT	Number of unique cases involved in the model.
EventFactRows	BIGINT	Number of rows in the event fact table used to build the model.

Table 15: Important columns of the Models table.

ModelEvents Table

The ModelEvents table stores a row for each segment (EventA→EventB) of created models, mostly applicable to MMs. It provides detailed information on event transitions and their associated metrics, enabling a thorough snapshot of how processes unfold over time. In dimensional modeling terms, if Models is a dimension table, ModelEvents is the primary fact table.

For MMs, in addition to the transitions between pairs of events (EventA to EventB), each row contains statistical metrics like probabilities and time-based statistics. These metrics are essential for analyzing the probability and variability of transitions. The table also supports higher-order MMs by including columns for events that occurred two or three steps prior to the current event, enabling more fine-grained analysis of dependencies in sequences. The columns in the table are logically grouped into three main categories as described in the following sub-topics.

Segment Columns

Table 16 lists the group of columns that capture the structural details of each transition within an MM. It defines the events involved in the transition of EventA→EventB and includes additional fields to support higher-order MMs (columns Event2A and Event3A). These columns are crucial for understanding the flow of processes and identifying entry and exit points in the sequence. Table 17 describes how the EventA, Event2A, Event3A, and EventB columns are affected by the value of the Order parameter.

Column Name	Data Type	Description
ModelID	BIGINT	The ID of the associated Markov model.
EventA	nvarchar	The starting event in the transition.
EventB	nvarchar	The ending event in the transition.
Event2A	nvarchar	Used if Order=2. The event preceding EventA (used for higher-order models). If Order=1, this will be "------".
Event3A	nvarchar	Used if Order=3. The event two steps before EventA (used for higher-order models). If Order=1 or 2, this will be "------".
IsEntry	int	A flag indicating whether this transition is ever an entry point for a case (1 = Yes).
IsExit	int	A flag indicating whether this transition is ever an exit point for a case (1 = Yes).
Rows	BIGINT	The number of rows that include this event transition.

Table 16: Segment columns.

Order	EventA	Event2A	Event3A	EventB (*n*)
1	Transition From (*n*-1)	------	------	Transition to
2	One Event Prior (*n*-2)	Transition From (*n*-1)	------	Transition to
3	Two Events Prior(*n*-3)	One Event Prior (*n*-2)	Transition From (*n*-1)	Transition to

Table 17: How the higher-order columns work.

Transition Analysis Metrics Columns

This set of columns of the ModelEvents table holds statistical metrics for analyzing the characteristics of event transitions across qualifying cases. Each row in the table represents a unique transition between events of a model and aggregates data from all observed instances of that transition across the qualifying cases. The metrics—such as probability, maximum, average, and standard deviation—offer a comprehensive view of transition patterns, including their frequency, variability, and distribution. These insights are crucial for uncovering patterns, detecting anomalies, and understanding process dynamics at scale.

Table 18 lists these statistical metrics. Remember that each metric is calculated for the transition across all cases in the dataset, providing a holistic understanding of process behavior and variability.

Column Name	Data Type	Description
Prob	float	The probability of transitioning from EventA→EventB.
Max	float	The maximum value for the metric between EventA→EventB.
Avg	float	The average value for the metric between EventA→EventB.
Min	float	The minimum value for the metric between EventA→EventB.
StDev	float	The standard deviation of the metric between EventA→EventB.
CoefVar	float	The coefficient of variation for the metric, representing relative variability.
Sum	float	The sum of the metric values for this transition.
Skew	float	The skewness of the metric distribution, showing how asymmetrical the data is.

Table 18: Columns for transition analysis.

Sequence and Ordinal Statistics Columns

This group of columns of the ModelEvents table holds statistics on the sequence of transitions within a case, focusing on their ordinal position (when they usually occur in the process) and the variability of these positions across cases. These statistics provide valuable insights into the typical flow of events and their timing within a process, helping to identify deviations or patterns that may impact performance or outcomes.

Table 19 lists the columns associated with the ordinal statistics.

Column Name	Data Type	Description
OrdinalMean	float	The average ordinal position of this transition in a sequence of events within a case.
OrdinalStDev	float	The standard deviation of the ordinal position, indicating variability in event sequence.

Table 19: Sequence and ordinal statistics.

For example, in a restaurant scenario, serving guests generally follows a predictable path: guests are seated, place their order, receive their food, and pay. However, variations can occur:

- A customer may order additional items later in their visit, or friends may arrive later, resulting in multiple rounds of ordering.
- A payment process might need to be repeated if a credit card is declined.

The value of this is we can quickly determine the "gist" of the order of a process by simply looking at sorting events in an MM for OrdinalMean. Figure 15 illustrates this order for ModelID 1.

```
SELECT
    [EventA],
    [Rows],
    [OrdinalMean]
FROM
    ModelEventsByOrdinalMean(1)
ORDER BY
    [OrdinalMean]
```

	EventA	Rows	OrdinalMean
1	arrive	10	1
2	greeted	8	2
3	seated	9	2.5
4	intro	8	4
5	drinks	7	5
6	order	8	5.88
7	served	8	6.5
8	check	7	8
9	charged	7	9
10	bigtip	1	10
11	ccdeclined	1	10
12	charged1	1	11

Figure 15: The "gist" of the order of restaurantguest MMs.

By analyzing the OrdinalMean, you could identify that the payment process typically occurs as the 5th step in a sequence but occasionally happens again later in cases where payment issues arise. The OrdinalStDev can show how consistent or variable these positions are across cases, highlighting if certain events, like reordering or repeated payments, are common exceptions or outliers.

ModelSequences Table

The ModelSequences table captures the exact sequences of events as they occurred in the EventsFact table, providing a highly granular view of process flows. Each row represents a unique progression of events (e.g., *arrive → greeted → seated → drinks → order → served → check*), preserving their true order within individual cases.

This level of detail makes the ModelSequences table significantly larger than the ModelEvents table because it moves beyond analyzing aggregations of events and transitions. Instead, it records every unique sequence and all its variations. For instance:

- A single event like *order* might appear in dozens of distinct sequences depending on what happened before or after, such as whether drinks were ordered first, if additional items were added later, or if payment issues occurred.
- Similarly, loops and repetitions, like a customer ordering additional items or retrying payment, create even more unique sequences.

In contrast, MMs condense these sequences into aggregated probabilities between states, abstracting away the detailed paths while retaining transition likelihoods. This abstraction makes MMs compact, as they focus only on the probability of moving from one event to another rather than capturing the exact order or context of all sequences.

This table is invaluable for understanding the complete process flow, including rare or unexpected paths, making it a critical resource for workflow analysis and process optimization. However, its detailed nature also results in significantly larger data volumes compared to the more abstracted ModelEvents or MMs.

Figure 16 shows an example of an event set (restaurant guest) and most of the sequences that happen in our data (15 of the 20).

Seq	lastEvent	nextEvent	Rows	Prob	TermRows	Cases
arrive	arrive	seated	1	0.1	NULL	1
arrive	arrive	greeted	8	0.8	NULL	8
arrive	arrive	depart	1	0.1	1	1
arrive,greeted	greeted	seated	8	1	NULL	8
arrive,greeted,seated	seated	order	1	0.125	NULL	1
arrive,greeted,seated	seated	drinks	7	0.875	NULL	7
arrive,greeted,seated,drinks	drinks	order	7	1	NULL	7
arrive,greeted,seated,drinks,order	order	served	7	1	NULL	7
arrive,greeted,seated,drinks,order,served	served	check	7	1	NULL	7
arrive,greeted,seated,drinks,order,served,check	check	depart	6	0.8571	6	6
arrive,greeted,seated,drinks,order,served,check	check	bigtip	1	0.1429	NULL	1
arrive,greeted,seated,drinks,order,served,check,bigtip	bigtip	depart	1	1	1	1
arrive,greeted,seated,order	order	served	1	1	NULL	1
arrive,greeted,seated,order,served	served	depart	1	1	1	1
arrive,seated	seated	depart	1	1	1	1

Figure 16: Event sequences for restaurantguest event set.

Table 20 provides a brief description of the columns shown in Figure 16.

Column Name	Description
Seq	Represents the full sequence of events, maintaining their exact order.
lastEvent	Denotes the final event in the sequence before the transition.
nextEvent	Represents the event that occurs immediately after the lastEvent.
Rows	Indicates how many times this specific sequence (Seq) occurred in the dataset.
Prob	The probability of the transition, calculated as the fraction of the transition's count over all transitions from the lastEvent to nextEvent.
TermRows	Captures terminal events (events without a subsequent nextEvent), useful for identifying end states in workflows or sub-processes.
Cases	The number of distinct cases in which this specific sequence of events occurred.

Table 20: Event sequences for restaurantguest event set.

Note that the ModelSequences mechanism is designed to be loosely coupled to the core MM mechanisms. This is so that Model Sequences can be optional due to their high demands on storage and computation (much more than the Markov models). While it provides valuable detailed insights into exact event chains, it is not required for generating and analyzing MMs, as these rely on aggregated probabilities between events rather than the full sequences. For many use cases, the abstraction provided by MMs is sufficient without the additional complexity of managing full sequence data. Although this book will only touch on this aspect, the GitHub repository will contain deeper dives. At the least, model sequences can be created ad-hoc, on demand, and optionally stored—as opposed to automatically stored along with the MM.

CHAPTER 8

Explore the Time Solution

Now that we've had an overview of the TimeSolution pieces, this chapter begins the actual lab walkthrough designed to guide you through the main steps involved in using the TimeSolution database. While this is structured as a hands-on lab, it's written so you can either "read along" or "play along," depending on your preference.

The walkthrough will cover the following major steps:

1. **Procuring Data:** Setting up the ETL process for populating the Time Solution database.
2. **Creating Sample Markov Objects:** Generating Markov models from the data.
3. **Markov Model Utilization:** Basic querying patterns for analyzing the models.
4. **Advanced Analytics:** Extending insights with additional analytical techniques.

Although this book doesn't cover the selection or building of a fully interactive UI application, such as an administrative tool like SQL Server Management Studio (SSMS) or an end-user-friendly analytical platform like Power BI and Tableau, many of the database functions described here can be implemented within ETL systems like Azure Data Factory or as an API through serverless compute services such as Azure Functions. These approaches remain current and applicable for modern data pipelines.

Each exercise in this walkthrough should be viewed as representing a particular aspect of functionality. As mentioned, the gory details of the operations performed within the TimeSolution database are typically encapsulated as table valued functions, stored procedures, or scalar functions. These serve as modular units of functionality, making it easier to integrate the database processes into broader systems or pipelines.

Function Example

Let's start with a simple example of a function call to TimeSolution. Code 6 shows how to add an event set using the InsertEventSets function (stored procedure). If you're not a programmer, this might seem complex. This code simply inserts a defined event set into the system:

1. Two variables are defined:
   - @EventSetKey is a placeholder for the unique identifier of the event set.
   - @EventSet contains a comma-separated list of events and a name for the set (in this case, 'pickuproute').
2. The InsertEventSets stored procedure is called with these parameters:
   - @EventSet as the input for the list of events. In this case, it's a set of events for truck route stops.
   - @EventSetKey OUTPUT to capture the unique key generated for the event set.
   - 0 to specify that the set is not a sequence of events.

```
--[[START Insert Event Sets]
DECLARE @EventSetKey VARBINARY(16)
DECLARE @EventSet NVARCHAR(200)=
      'leavesite,walmart1,lv-walmart1,walmart2,lv-walmart2,csv1,lv-csv1,csv4,
      lv-csv4,csv5,lv-csv5,walmart3,lv-walmart3,homedepot1,lv-homedepot1,csv2,
      lv-csv2,returnsite'

EXEC [dbo].[InsertEventSets]
      @EventSet=@EventSet,
      @EventSetCode =NULL,
      -- Key of the inserted event set returned in @EventSetKey.
      @EventSetKey=@EventSetKey OUTPUT,
      @IsSequence=0 -- IsSequence is a set, not a sequence.
PRINT @EventSetKey
```

Code 6: Example of inserting a new event set defined by the variable, @EventSet.

For those who have worked with SQL databases (not just SQL Server, but others such as Oracle, MySQL, and Postgres), Code 6 should be easy to interpret. For those who are not familiar with SQL databases, the caption pretty much captures what it does. InsertEventSets encapsulates a substantial amount of code to perform that task which can be succinctly stated as "inserts an event set specified by the variable, @EventSet."

LLMs and Code Generation

Even though what is shown in Code 6 is much simpler compared to all the code it encapsulates, it's still kind of cryptic and tedious to write by hand. To illustrate how these functions can be written with much less tedium, we'll use Code 6 as an example of a code snippet that could be submitted to a LLM for assistance in code generation. You can quickly generate boilerplate code or refine complex SQL logic by providing an LLM prompt with a sample of the required functionality.

This approach not only accelerates development but also demonstrates the potential of AI-driven tools to augment traditional development processes. Each code snippet and exercise in this walkthrough is designed to showcase both functionality and the possibilities of automating parts of the development workflow.

Code 7 is a prompt I submitted to ChatGPT asking it to create a new event set based on the provided example.

Based on this example code, please write code to insert an event set of 'wakeup, coffee, emails, breakfast, coding, lunch, writing, dinner, sleep' named myworkday. Example code:

```
--[[START Insert Event Sets]
DECLARE @EventSetKey VARBINARY(16)
DECLARE @EventSet NVARCHAR(200)=
       'leavesite,walmart1,lv-walmart1,walmart2,lv-walmart2,csv1,lv-csv1,csv4,
       lv-csv4,csv5,lv-csv5,walmart3,lv-walmart3,homedepot1,lv-homedepot1,csv2,
       lv-csv2,returnsite',
       'pickuproute',

EXEC [dbo].[InsertEventSets]
       @EventSet,
       @EventSetKey OUTPUT, -- Key of the inserted event set returned in this
variable.
       0 -- IsSequence is a set, not a sequence.
```

Code 7: Prompt to ask ChatGPT to create code based on an example using Code EE1 as an example.

Code 8 is the code composed by ChatGPT.

```
-- Insert 'myworkday' event set
DECLARE @EventSetKey VARBINARY(16);
EXEC [dbo].[InsertEventSets]
    'wakeup,coffee,emails,breakfast,coding,lunch,writing,dinner,sleep', -- EventSet
    'myworkday',                              -- EventSetCode
    @EventSetKey OUTPUT,                      -- Output EventSetKey
    0;                                        -- IsSequence: 0 for set, 1 for sequence
```

Code 8: Code composed by ChatGPT.

I will not get into an excruciating code walkthrough in this book. My intent for including any code here is to provide what is essentially an alternative way to express the intent of the TimeSolution concepts—SQL versus English.

The GitHub repository will provide detailed information on these stored procedures and functions via in-line comments.

Procuring Events

This is really the ETL of the Time Solution. As shown back in Figure 9, events could be sourced from IoT devices, conventional enterprise applications, and data warehouses. In the interest of mitigating the size of this book, I've provided "toy" data of events from a variety of sources:

- **Restaurant:** An enterprise application that is primarily an IoT edge device at a restaurant.
- **Truck Route:** This is an IoT example of events from trucks on a route.
- **Poker hands:** This could be an IoT (real-time) or read from logs of online poker.
- **Stocks:** A data warehouse of stock quotes of the past few decades.

Additionally, I've included a few examples that use Microsoft's ubiquitous AdventureWorksDW database. As a comprehensive but simple sample of a retail database, it is a good place to start to explain the process of procuring events.

I use the restaurant source frequently as examples throughout this book. That's because restaurants, more than most businesses, operate in a world where fundamentals matter deeply. Margins are tight, competition is fierce, and success depends on getting the basics right: timing, quality, and customer experience. As Ram Charan expressed in *What the CEO Wants You to Know*, the principles of running a street vendor's stand or a Fortune 500 company are (or should be) surprisingly similar. In that spirit, I view every business—whether a high-tech enterprise or a neighborhood diner—as governed by the same core forces. Restaurants simply offer a vivid, relatable backdrop to illustrate those forces in motion.

AdventureWorksDW Example

Code 9 is a simple SQL that will return a row for each sale in the FactInternetSales table. It is the "E" of ETL—extracting data from a source database. Although we normally think of a sale itself as a transaction, each sale really is a set of events. Customers don't just buy something—there is a process that starts before the customer gets to the store (marketing) and ends when the items are delivered to the customer—although there might be returns and other support issues as well.

Remember, an event has a date/time. In this case, every sale in the FactInternetSales table has an order date and ship date. There could also be other dates, such as delivery dates.

```
USE AdventureWorksDW2017
GO
SELECT
  [OrderDate], [ShipDate],
  [SalesOrderNumber]+'-'+CAST([SalesOrderLineNumber] AS VARCHAR(20)) AS NaturalKey,
  ROW_NUMBER() OVER (ORDER BY [SalesOrderNumber], [SalesOrderLineNumber]) AS CaseID
,
  '{"SalesAmount":'+CAST(SalesAmount AS VARCHAR(20))+
    ',"OrderQuantity":'+CAST(OrderQuantity AS VARCHAR(20))+
    ',"CustomerKey":'+CAST(CustomerKey AS VARCHAR(20))+
    ',"ProductKey":'+CAST(ProductKey AS VARCHAR(20))+
  '}' AS Properties
INTO #ETLADW -- Write to temp table for follow-ups to the data.
FROM [dbo].[FactInternetSales]
-- Note that some values are packaged in a JSON, as discussed regarding event
properties.

-- Display the result.
SELECT * FROM #ETLADW
-- Drop #ETLADW temp table later.
```

Code 9: Code for importing sales events from AdventureWorksDW into temporary table.

Figure 17 displays the first few rows of the results from Code 9, which extracts sales data from the FactInternetSales table in the AdventureWorksDW2017 database. Each row:

1. Represents a sale row from the FactInternetSales table.

2. Is treated as a case (note the CaseID column).

3. Will yield two events—OrderDate and ShipDate.

	OrderDate	ShipDate	NaturalKey	CaseID	Properties
1	2010-12-29 00:00:00.000	2011-01-05 00:00:00.000	SO43697-1	1	{"SalesAmount":3578.27,"OrderQuantity":1,"CustomerKey":21768,"ProductKey":310}
2	2010-12-30 00:00:00.000	2011-01-06 00:00:00.000	SO43705-1	9	{"SalesAmount":3399.99,"OrderQuantity":1,"CustomerKey":11011,"ProductKey":344}
3	2011-01-02 00:00:00.000	2011-01-09 00:00:00.000	SO43713-1	17	{"SalesAmount":3578.27,"OrderQuantity":1,"CustomerKey":27601,"ProductKey":310}
4	2011-01-03 00:00:00.000	2011-01-10 00:00:00.000	SO43721-1	25	{"SalesAmount":3578.27,"OrderQuantity":1,"CustomerKey":13590,"ProductKey":310}
5	2011-01-06 00:00:00.000	2011-01-13 00:00:00.000	SO43729-1	33	{"SalesAmount":3399.99,"OrderQuantity":1,"CustomerKey":11238,"ProductKey":346}
6	2011-01-08 00:00:00.000	2011-01-15 00:00:00.000	SO43737-1	41	{"SalesAmount":3578.27,"OrderQuantity":1,"CustomerKey":13261,"ProductKey":311}
7	2011-01-10 00:00:00.000	2011-01-17 00:00:00.000	SO43745-1	49	{"SalesAmount":3578.27,"OrderQuantity":1,"CustomerKey":16514,"ProductKey":311}
8	2011-01-11 00:00:00.000	2011-01-18 00:00:00.000	SO43753-1	57	{"SalesAmount":3578.27,"OrderQuantity":1,"CustomerKey":16482,"ProductKey":310}
9	2011-01-13 00:00:00.000	2011-01-20 00:00:00.000	SO43761-1	65	{"SalesAmount":3578.27,"OrderQuantity":1,"CustomerKey":16493,"ProductKey":310}
10	2011-01-16 00:00:00.000	2011-01-23 00:00:00.000	SO43769-1	73	{"SalesAmount":3578.27,"OrderQuantity":1,"CustomerKey":21659,"ProductKey":312}
11	2011-01-17 00:00:00.000	2011-01-24 00:00:00.000	SO43777-1	81	{"SalesAmount":3578.27,"OrderQuantity":1,"CustomerKey":16515,"ProductKey":311}
12	2011-01-19 00:00:00.000	2011-01-26 00:00:00.000	SO43785-1	89	{"SalesAmount":3578.27,"OrderQuantity":1,"CustomerKey":11601,"ProductKey":311}
13	2011-01-19 00:00:00.000	2011-01-26 00:00:00.000	SO43793-1	97	{"SalesAmount":3399.99,"OrderQuantity":1,"CustomerKey":11000,"ProductKey":344}
14	2011-01-21 00:00:00.000	2011-01-28 00:00:00.000	SO43801-1	105	{"SalesAmount":3578.27,"OrderQuantity":1,"CustomerKey":13583,"ProductKey":311}
15	2011-01-23 00:00:00.000	2011-01-30 00:00:00.000	SO43809-1	113	{"SalesAmount":3578.27,"OrderQuantity":1,"CustomerKey":16350,"ProductKey":310}

Figure 17: Extract and transform Internet sales to events.

Table 21 is a breakdown of the columns shown in Figure 17.

Column Name	Description
OrderDate	The date when the customer placed the order. This represents the starting point of the sales event.
ShipDate	The date when the order was shipped to the customer. This provides an additional event tied to the sales transaction.
NaturalKey	A unique identifier for each sales line item, created by combining the SalesOrderNumber and SalesOrderLineNumber.
CaseID	A sequential number assigned to each sales event, generated using the ROW_NUMBER() function for easier referencing.
Properties	A JSON string capturing additional attributes of the sales event, including: - SalesAmount: The monetary value of the sales transaction. - OrderQuantity: The quantity of items purchased in the transaction. - CustomerKey: The key identifying the customer associated with the sale. - ProductKey: The key identifying the product being purchased.

Table 21: Column descriptions of Figure 17.

Code 10 adjusts the CaseID values in the temporary table (#ETLADW) by adding an offset equal to the current maximum CaseID in the CaseProperties table. This ensures CaseID values remain unique across all cases in the database. This is a very minor transform ("T" of ETL).

```
DECLARE @CaseID_OffSet INT=(SELECT MAX(CaseID) FROM
[TimeSolution].dbo.CaseProperties)
UPDATE #ETLADW SET
       CaseID=CaseID+@CaseID_OffSet
```

Code 10: Update CaseID with an offset so we don't write over existing CaseIDs.

Code 11 inserts the cases into the TimeSolution case tables. This (and Code 12) comprise the load for this example, the "L" of ETL—loading the events into the TimeSolution DW.

```
--Retrieve metadata (SourceID and CaseTypeID) for the data source
DECLARE @DatabaseName NVARCHAR(128)='AdventureWorksDW2017'
DECLARE @SourceID INT =
  (SELECT SourceID FROM [TimeSolution].[dbo].[Sources] WHERE [Name]=@DatabaseName)
DECLARE @CaseTypeName NVARCHAR(128)='Internet Sale'
DECLARE @CaseTypeID INT =
  (SELECT CaseTypeID FROM [TimeSolution].[dbo].CaseTypes WHERE [Name]=@CaseTypeName)

--Insert data from #ETLADW into CaseProperties and Cases tables.
INSERT INTO [TimeSolution].dbo.CaseProperties (CaseID, [Properties])
       SELECT CaseID, [Properties] FROM #ETLADW
INSERT INTO [TimeSolution].dbo.Cases
  (CaseID, NaturalKey,SourceID,CaseTypeID,AccessBitmap)
  SELECT CaseID, NaturalKey,@SourceID AS SourceID,@CaseTypeID, 7 FROM #ETLADW
```

Code 11: Insert sales from AdventureWorksDW into the Cases tables of Time Solution.

Code 12 inserts sales events (SaleOrder and SaleShip are each an event) into the EventsFact table.

- Each event is associated with a CaseID and assigned a sequential CaseOrdinal (1 for OrderDate and 2 for ShipDate).
- Combines order and ship events using a UNION ALL to create a consolidated timeline for each case.

```
INSERT INTO [TimeSolution].[dbo].[EventsFact]
       (CaseID, [Event],EventDate,CaseOrdinal)
       SELECT CaseID, 'SaleOrder' AS Event, OrderDate AS EventDate, 1 AS CaseOrdinal
              FROM #ETLADW
              WHERE OrderDate IS NOT NULL
       UNION ALL
       SELECT CaseID, 'SaleShip' AS Event, ShipDate AS EventDate, 2 AS CaseOrdinal
              FROM #ETLADW
              WHERE ShipDate IS NOT NULL
       ORDER BY CaseID,CaseOrdinal
```

Code 12: Insert (Load) into the Events fact table.

Code 13 generates and displays a Markov model created from the EventsFact table using the MarkovProcess TVF that calculates transition probabilities and other statistical metrics between events (SaleOrder → SaleShip). It also will display a few metrics—maximum, average, minimum, standard deviation, and probability for transitions between event pairs.

```
SELECT ModelID,Event1A,EventB,[Max],[Avg],[Min],[StDev],CoefVar,[Sum],[Rows],Prob
FROM dbo.[MarkovProcess](1,'SaleOrder,SaleShip',0,NULL,NULL,NULL,1,NULL,NULL,NULL,0)
```

Code 13: Display Markov model created from AdventureWorksDW2017 Internet sales.

Figure 18 shows the result of Code 13. It's a very simple MM since there are only two event types—SalesOrder and SalesShip. The most important information is the Prob of 1—meaning every sales order was shipped. Of course, that only happens in the synthetic world of AdventureWorksDW.

ModelID	Event1A	EventB	Max	Avg	Min	StDev	CoefVar	Sum	Rows	Prob
NULL	SaleOrder	SaleShip	10080	10080	10080	0	0	608811840	60398	1

Figure 18: Markov model created from Internet sales process.

Code 14 will clean up this exercise from your database in case you'd like to try this again, perhaps with more event types.

```
--Clean up this exercise.
DECLARE @SourceID INT=5 -AdventureWorksDW database in TimeSolution.
DELETE FROM [TimeSolution].[dbo].[EventsFact]
WHERE CaseID IN
  (SELECT CaseID FROM [TimeSolution].[dbo].[Cases] WHERE SourceID = @SourceID)

DELETE FROM [TimeSolution].[dbo].[CaseProperties]
WHERE CaseID IN
  (SELECT CaseID FROM [TimeSolution].[dbo].[Cases] WHERE SourceID = @SourceID)

DELETE FROM [TimeSolution].[dbo].[Cases] WHERE SourceID = @SourceID
```

Code 14: Delete the Internet Sales events from the Time Solution database.

Event Granularity

Events are a nested phenomenon. They could be singular moments in time (e.g., Hurricane Katrina) or the sequence of events in a process that unfolds over its duration (e.g., all the events of a sales cycle). In some cases, they serve as simple markers—like signs on a highway that indicate we've passed a specific point during a road trip. Directional signs or mile markers are noted briefly but don't represent a broader context or interaction; they might merely be thought of as timestamps of our higher-level road trip event.

In everyday life, what we think of as events are often more complex and involve multiple steps across a period of activity. For instance, a birthday party, a doctor's appointment, or a meal isn't just a singular moment—it's a sequence of interconnected actions and interactions that make up the event. In the TimeSolution framework, these types of extended activities are captured as *cases*, where each case represents a cohesive cycle of a process.

For example, consider a truck route. At a lower granularity, you might only track the truck's arrivals at key locations—WalMart-A, CVS-B, and WalMart-D, as shown in Case 1 of Figure 19. Here, events are simple markers of time indicating arrival points. However, when you drill down to a lower granularity, as in Case 2, you can include more details—in this case, we added when the truck departed from each location. We could add even finer detail, adding events such as unloading, loading, delays, refueling, and other activities.

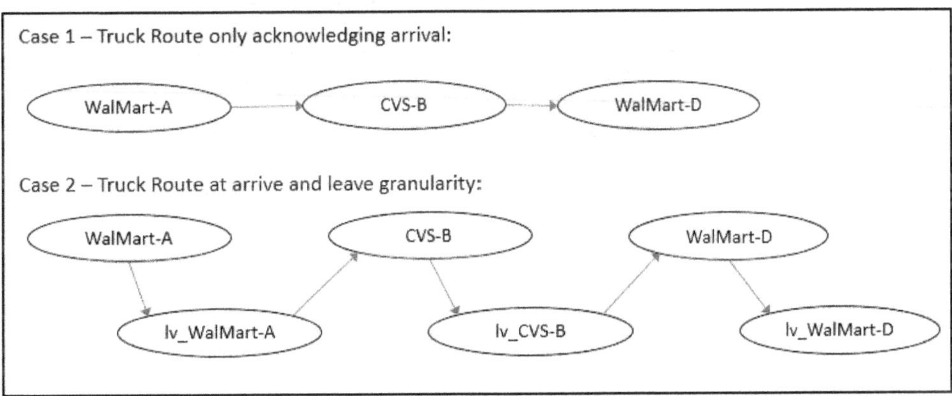

Figure 19: High granularity versus lower granularity.

Event as an Effect

An "effect" is a change of state we hopefully can attribute to some event (what caused the effect). For example, we're aware that we had a routine dental checkup last Tuesday and another visit scheduled for next week on Thursday. Why? A cavity was discovered and now it should be filled—it's an effect of your routine dental checkup. Discovery of the cavity is a change to the state of the awareness of your health. Before last week Tuesday, the state of your awareness of your health didn't include a cavity that must be filled.

By introducing the concept of effects into event modeling, we can move beyond timestamps and capture richer details. For instance, injected effects—like a customer's satisfaction with a taxi ride—can provide meaningful context to an event, turning it into something more dynamic. This approach allows us to see events not just as points in time, but as interconnected processes with causes and outcomes, uncovering more analytical insights and better decision-making. Figure 20 shows a model with injected effects (dashed ovals)—events we created to supplement our event stream with more detail. In this case, it's the reaction of the customer to our delivery/pickup.

1. I pick up Cust-A.
2. I drop off Cust-A.
3. The injected event is that Cust-A is happy and gave us 5-stars on the app.
4. I'm rewarded by being routed to a more profitable pickup, Cust-B.
5. We hit unexpectedly terrible traffic, which unfairly upsets Cust-B.
6. Cust-B gives me three of five stars on the app.
7. As punishment, I'm routed to a short and unprofitable pickup.

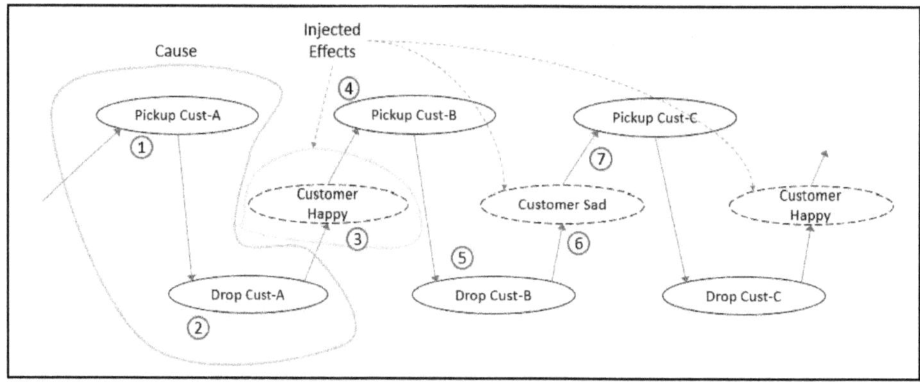

Figure 20: Injected effect calculated from properties of the visit to WalMart-A.

The injected effects tell a much richer story. Without the injected effects, we wouldn't know what really happened. Figure 21 is another example of injected events (the dashed ovals—Game_state). The difference is that the injected event isn't just an effect but becomes a cause as well. It shows the last round (River) of a Texas Hold'em Poker game.

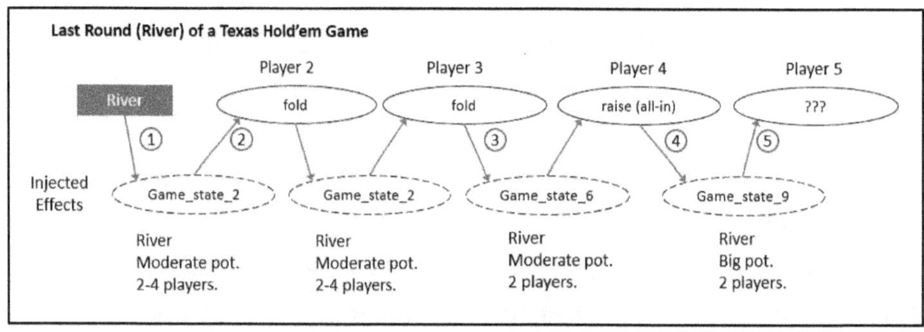

Figure 21: Injected effect is also a "cause" for the next player.

In the raw data, only:

1. The last card of the game is thrown down by the dealer. That act is the "cause" with the effect of the game in a state we call "Game_state_2"—At the river, a moderate pot on the table, and 2-4 players still in.
2. Game_state_2 is then the "cause" affecting Player 2. Player 2 is enticed to fold.
3. Player 3 folds as well. The effect is that the game state is now what we call "Game_state_6"—River, moderate pot, but just the last two players still in.
4. With only two players left, Player 4 goes all-in. The pot is now big.
5. The resultant game_state_9 affects Player 5's action—forced into a do-or-die situation.

With the injected events and the ML-computed state of the game, the information is much richer. When a player folds, checks, raises, or calls, it's meaningless if we don't know what they are reacting to.

Date Best Practices for Events

Managing dates effectively is crucial for ensuring accurate analysis of events, particularly in ETL workflows and streaming systems. Key principles include (which apply to BI/DW and event streaming):

- **Store Dates in UTC, Display in Local Time:** Always store timestamps in UTC to avoid ambiguity across time zones, daylight saving changes, or shifts in local time. Local time zones should be applied only at the presentation layer (dashboards, reports) based on user preferences or business rules. This ensures consistency in analytics, especially when aggregating global data.
- **Track Multiple Timestamps**: Have separate dates for when events happened (logical event date), when they were loaded (system load date), and when they were last updated (update date).
- **Handle Late-Arriving Events**: Set up processes to manage events arriving after their expected date and refresh any affected Markov models to maintain accuracy.
- **Use Cutoff Windows and Watermarks**: Define time limits (cutoff windows) for processing events and markers (watermarks) to track what has been processed, ensuring timely analysis while allowing late data to be included later if needed.

These best practices help maintain the integrity of event-based systems like Time Molecules. For a deeper exploration of ETL considerations and handling late-arriving events, see Appendix G on the GitHub Repository.

Create Sample Markov Objects

After procuring events ("ETL-ing") into the EventsFact table, we need to review the setup of the supporting information before demoing use case capabilities. The exercises discussed in this chapter are in the SQL Script file on the GitHub repository named *create_demo_markov_chains.sql*. You can find the code samples shown in this book by searching that SQL script for the "*--[[START*" tags at the beginning of each listed code. For example, in Code 15 that's coming up, the first line is: --*[[START Set up DimEvents]*

Create DimEvents

The DimEvents table is a dimension table that contains the definitive list of valid event types in the dataset. It ensures that the Event column in the EventsFact table references a clean, standardized set of unique event names. The purpose of the DimEvents table (this goes for all dimension tables) is to provide an authoritative list of valid events for the entire system. It ensures validation and consistency by serving as the definitive reference for what constitutes a valid event, ensuring all related data aligns with this standard. Code 15 inserts events from EventsFact that are not yet in the DimEvents table.

```
--Automatically generate the DimEvents table from the EventsFact table.

DECLARE @UnknownSourceID INT=(SELECT SourceID FROM dbo.Sources WHERE
[Name]='Unknown')
INSERT INTO [DimEvents] ([Event],SourceID)
   SELECT DISTINCT
       ef.[Event],
       COALESCE(ef.SourceID,@UnknownSourceID) AS SourceID
   FROM [dbo].[EventsFact] ef
   WHERE
       NOT EXISTS
       (SELECT de.[Event] FROM dbo.[DimEvents] de WHERE de.[Event]=ef.[Event])
```

Code 15: Populate the DimEvents table from the loaded EventsFact table.

Note that Code 15 doesn't use TSQL's MERGE key word. This is an example of using standard SQL to mitigate cross-platform issues. However, most major SQL systems have implemented MERGE, and it is generally more optimized for the intent of Code 15.

Figure 22 shows a partial list of the events added to DimEvents using Code 15.

Event	Description	CreateDate	LastUpdated	IRI	SourceID	IsState
arrive	User arrives at location	2024-12-29 08:27:15.117	2024-12-29 08:27:15.117	NULL	2	0
bigtip	User gives a big tip	2024-12-29 08:27:15.117	2024-12-29 08:27:15.117	NULL	2	0
ccdeclined	Credit card was declined	2024-12-29 08:27:15.117	2024-12-29 08:27:15.117	NULL	2	0
charged	User charged for a purchase	2024-12-29 08:27:15.117	2024-12-29 08:27:15.117	NULL	2	0
check	Player checks	2024-12-29 08:27:15.117	2024-12-29 08:27:15.117	NULL	2	0
depart	User departs from location	2024-12-29 08:27:15.117	2024-12-29 08:27:15.117	NULL	2	0
drinks	User orders drinks	2024-12-29 08:27:15.117	2024-12-29 08:27:15.117	NULL	2	0
greeted	User was greeted	2024-12-29 08:27:15.117	2024-12-29 08:27:15.117	NULL	2	0
intro	Introduction event	2024-12-29 08:27:15.117	2024-12-29 08:27:15.117	NULL	2	0
order	User places an order	2024-12-29 08:27:15.117	2024-12-29 08:27:15.117	NULL	2	0
seated	User takes a seat	2024-12-29 08:27:15.117	2024-12-29 08:27:15.117	NULL	2	0
served	User is served	2024-12-29 08:27:15.117	2024-12-29 08:27:15.117	NULL	2	0

Figure 22: DimEvents table showing just the events for the restaurantguest event set.

Parse Case and Event Properties

Cases and Events can have unique properties. These properties are used to filter cases and events when creating MMs. For example, a sales cycle can include case-level properties such as the customer, the salesperson, the primary product, etc. At the event level, properties for meeting events can include the location and type of meeting.

As previously discussed, these unique properties are loaded into TimeSolution in the form of a JSON. For example:

- **Case:** {"EmployeeID":2,"CustomerID":2} – The case is a route driven by EmployeeID:2 for CustomerID:2.

- **Event:** {"Fuel":50,"Weight":23000} - This is the amount of fuel and weight of the truck when arriving at a site. When the truck arrives at the customer site, this is how much fuel is remaining and what the truck weighs.

Parsing JSON into relational tables allows for efficient querying of semi-structured data. Code 16 illustrates how to use the InsertCaseProperties stored procedure to parse these properties into a table, making each property its own searchable row.

```
EXEC [dbo].[InsertCaseProperties] @CompleteRefresh=1 --1 means to truncate
CasePropertiesParsed
EXEC [dbo].[InsertEventProperties] @CompleteRefresh=1
```

Code 16: Parse JSON properties for the cases and events.

Code 17 will display the parsed properties for one case—Case 1.

```
SELECT * FROM [dbo].[CaseProperties] WHERE CaseID=1
SELECT * FROM [dbo].[CasePropertiesParsed] WHERE CaseID=1
```

Code 17: Compare unparsed and parsed.

Figure 23 shows the results of Code 17—CaseProperties on top and CasePropertiesParsed below.

CaseID	Properties	TargetProperties	NaturalKey	CreateDate
1	{"EmployeeID":1,"CustomerID":2}	NULL	NULL	NULL

CaseID	PropertyName	PropertyValueNumeric	PropertyValueAlpha	SourceColumnID
1	CustomerID	2	NULL	25
1	EmployeeID	1	NULL	30

Figure 23: Example of the properties of one case.

At the time of writing, I'm using SQL Server 2022, which includes support for querying JSON using functions like OPENJSON and JSON_VALUE. While SQL Server has come a long way in supporting semi-structured data since 2016, it still lacks a native JSON data type — JSON is stored as NVARCHAR, and parsing is done at query time. This works fine for light to moderate workloads, but performance can degrade with heavy or complex JSON queries since SQL Server doesn't index inside the JSON structure and can't optimize those paths as it does for traditional columns.

In contrast, modern data warehouse platforms like Snowflake treat semi-structured data as a first-class citizen. Snowflake stores JSON and other formats (like XML, Avro, and Parquet) in a flexible VARIANT type, enabling native querying with dot notation (data.key.subkey) and built-in functions like OBJECT_KEYS() and ARRAY_SIZE() — all without requiring a full relational transformation. The engine can optimize execution plans and storage even with mixed structured and semi-structured data, making it far more efficient and seamless for workloads that rely heavily on nested or hierarchical data structures.

That said, I could have bypassed the JSON parsing stage entirely by importing case and event properties directly into key-value tables. The reason I opted not to do this was the possibility of having many properties that might not be valuable for building Markov models but could still be worth storing for other purposes.

Create Event Sets – InsertEventSets Stored Procedure

Code 18 is an example of how to add a named event set—in this case, an event set named "pickuproute" defining the events for a truck route making its rounds to various stores.

```
--InsertEventSets Parameters: @EventSet NVARCHAR(MAX), @EventSetCode NVARCHAR(20),
@EventSetKey VARBINARY(16) OUTPUT, @IsSequence BIT
DECLARE @EventSetKey VARBINARY(16)
EXEC [dbo].[InsertEventSets]
       'leavesite,walmart1,lv-walmart1,walmart2,lv-walmart2,csv1,lv-csv1,csv4,
          lv-csv4,csv5,lv-csv5,walmart3,lv-walmart3,homedepot1,
          lv-homedepot1, csv2,lv-csv2,returnsite',
       'pickuproute',
       @EventSetKey OUTPUT,
       0 -- IsSequence is a set, not a sequence.
```

Code 18: Insert an event set named pickuproute.

Figure 24 is a list of most of the event sets I've already created for the walkthrough.

EventSetKey	EventSet	EventSetCode	IsSequence
0x0888B97F18FEB280485557D2B0A778A6	leavehome,heavytraffic,moderatetraffic,lighttraffic,arrivewo...	NULL	0
0x0C9294682D92CC4CF747B36DE8AB499B	websitepages	NULL	0
0x281CE40AD3A51DE5CAC588793498CBCA	raises,folds,calls,bets,checks	pokeractions	0
0x384060D658FDAE2CB57186A008234AF6	arrive,bigtip,drinks,greeted,order,check,seated,served,dep...	NULL	0
0x510AB328E43FF6BA4BC5E6D10CD74AB2	arnold1,arnold2,receipt,abandonedcart	NULL	0
0x527C1854FE4C32C22484FAA8B87A7A10	restaurantguest	NULL	0
0x5516AAD0BCE7F243D1ABA7374810FBB8	NEW_GAME,collected,GameState-0,GameState-1,GameS...	poker	0
0x5D0816B650DD51E53E19B74C7771783F	pokeractions	NULL	0
0x6578313A71A8B642E194BEBA703F6AB9	GameState-0,GameState-1,GameState-2,GameState-3,G...	pokergamestates	0
0x6CD99510BCA54729CBC41BBF6C6320C8	leavehome,heavytraffic,lighttraffic,arrivework	NULL	0
0x7447CED91DCCF7B553493E939027E522	heavytraffic,moderatetraffic,lighttraffic	NULL	0
0x802DFFE5A341446AF7FD1E338FAFE937	leavehome,heavytraffic,moderatetraffic,lighttraffic,arrivework	commute	0
0x825604E51A843EE181BA50DC7DEDD5F8	arrive,depart	NULL	0
0x8DCE23308B0F60FD22313BB8E0324D07	leavesite,walmart1,lv-walmart1,walmart2,lv-walmart2,csv1...	pickuproute	0
0x9CEFF06A049CFA042C10BE4D19C3B82D	pickuproute	NULL	0
0x9DE13992AFDFAF8295228CFCA1AF216B	leavesite,returnsite	NULL	0
0xBD23A78FC79F9CB0E798F435CF6DD4C9	bigtip,drinks	NULL	0
[illegible]	poker	NULL	0
0xC87DC9835A4FC6421B983C7E9CC22654	pokergamestates	NULL	0
0xF55D96AAC5C1BB4F0DF26587CD8CC1C2	arrive,greeted,seated,intro,drinks,ccdeclined,charged,orde...	restaurantguest	0
0xF97EDF2773B674FCED4E9B4BF58C00CC	homepage,chocprotein,arnold1,keto1,chocproteinbars,cart...	websitepages	0

Figure 24: Event sets.

Here is a brief description of the columns shown in Figure 24:

- **EventSetKey:** Hash of the sorted EventSet. We sort the EventSet before creating the hash so they are the same. This way, you don't need to worry about the order.
- **EventSet:** The event set as the comma-separated list we submitted (not sorted or otherwise prepped).
- **EventSetCode:** Easy code to reference this event set. Many event sets don't have a code because they are created automatically during processing when new event sets are encountered.
- **IsSequence:** Is this a sequence or set? If it's a sequence, the order matters.

The EventSet and EventSetCode columns are pretty self-explanatory. However, IsSequence and EventSetKey need a little more clarification.

IsSequence

The IsSequence flag indicates whether an EventSet represents an unordered set or an ordered sequence.

If IsSequence=0 (False), an Event Set is a collection of events where the order does not matter. It defines the set of events that can occur in a process, focusing on the inclusion of events rather than their temporal order. For example, the Event Set named restaurantguest includes the following events:

arrive, depart, greeted, intro, drinks, ccdeclined, charged, order, check, seated, served, bigtip

In this case, all events listed are included in the analysis, but the specific order in which they occur is not considered.

If IsSequence=1 (True), the Event Sequence is an *ordered* list of events that specifies the exact flow of a process. Sequences are used when the order of events carries meaning, such as in workflows or any process where a defined temporal progression is critical for analysis. For instance, the Event Sequence buying a drink from a vending machine is always in this order:

Insert money, select item, confirm payment, dispense item, return change (if applicable), retrieve item, walk away

The purpose of an event set where the order matters—a sequence—is if I wish to search for cases that reflect this exact sequence using a succinct EventSetCode (code name for the sequence) without having to type in the whole sequence.

EventSetKey

Because not all event sets will have an EventSetCode, the actual primary key for each event set is the combination of the hash key generated from the EventSet value and the IsSequence flag, which determines whether the event set is treated as a sequence or an unordered set.

While the actual event set (the comma-separated list) is unique, it can be verbose and impractical for use as a key. For example, SQL Server indexes have a key length limit of 900 bytes, which some complicated event sets could exceed.

To ensure consistent hashing, the function, EventSetKey, always alphabetically sorts the items in the event set before generating the hash key, regardless of whether a set or sequence. This guarantees that the hash is consistent for equivalent sets, even if they are provided in a different order.

Code 19 shows the code for the logic that accounts for three key scenarios for generating the hash key:

1. **Event Set (Unordered, No Sequence)**:
    - When @IsSequence is NULL or 0, the event set is treated as an unordered collection. The function alphabetically sorts the items to ensure that the order does not affect the hash value.
    - For example, the sets 'arrive,greeted,seated,order,served,check,depart' and 'arrive,check,depart,greeted,order,seated,served' both generate the same hash key: 0x0CD81FF42053BE46A03E9CACA3D4D451.

2. **Event Set (Pre-Sorted)**:
    - Even if the event set is pre-sorted alphabetically ('arrive,check,depart,greeted,order,seated,served'), the function still sorts the items again to ensure consistency. As a result, the hash key for this pre-sorted set is the same as for any equivalent unordered set: 0x0CD81FF42053BE46A03E9CACA3D4D451.

3. **Sequence (Ordered)**:
   - When @IsSequence is 1, the function treats the event set as a sequence, where the order of the items is critical. In this case, the function generates the hash key directly from the input order without re-sorting.
   - For example, the sequence 'arrive,greeted,seated,order,served,check,depart' generates a different key than that of item 1: 0x68202A5558621FC045E6EBB091C4AD1F, as the specific order of events is preserved.

```
DECLARE @SetByOccurence NVARCHAR(50)='arrive,greeted,seated, order,
served,check,depart'
DECLARE @SetPreSorted NVARCHAR(50)=' arrive,check, depart,greeted,order,
seated,served'
DECLARE @NotSequence BIT=0
DECLARE @IsSequence BIT=1
--These two sets return 0x0CD81FF42053BE46A03E9CACA3D4D451
SELECT  [dbo].[EventSetKey](@SetByOccurence, @NotSequence) AS [Set_BCD]
SELECT  [dbo].[EventSetKey](@SetPreSorted, @NotSequence) AS [Set_BCD]

--This sequence returns 0x68202A5558621FC045E6EBB091C4AD1F
SELECT  [dbo].[EventSetKey](@SetByOccurence, @IsSequence) AS [Seq_CBD]
```

Code 19: Three ways the event set key is created.

Transforms

Transforms are mappings between one event and another, enabling connections between events that are differently named but related within a process. For example, a transform might map the viewing of different web pages about hurricanes, monsoons, and cyclones—topics that are essentially the same but labeled differently. These mappings are critical for grouping or linking related events, and simplifying or consolidating actions within the broader process analysis.

Transforms act as a tool for categorization, generalization, and abstraction—key capabilities of human cognition. By applying transforms, we can combine events that are functionally equivalent but might otherwise be treated as separate. For instance, while hurricanes, cyclones, and monsoons may each individually occur too infrequently to indicate a trend, combining them under a single mapping allows their collective significance to emerge. This enhances the ability to create more cohesive and accurate MMs, capturing relationships that would otherwise be fragmented or overlooked.

Code 20 shows how to create a transform named "merge-heavy-mod," intended to combine heavytraffic and moderatetraffic events encountered by a commuter into a single event named "traffic".

```
--[[START Insert Transform]
DECLARE @transformskey VARBINARY(16)
EXEC [dbo].[InsertTransforms] -- Transform both heavytraffic and moderatetraffic to
"traffic"
      '{"heavytraffic":"traffic", "moderatetraffic":"traffic"}', -- @Transforms
      'merge-heavy-mod', -- @Code - The code of this transform.
      @transformskey OUTPUT
```

Code 20: Insert a transformation.

Figure 25 shows the few transforms in Time Solution. The highlighted row is the transform we just added with Code 20.

transformskey	transforms	Code
0x903FBEFEFB94CFAD7968...	{"arnold1":"arnold","arnold2":"arnold","keto1":"dietpage","weig...	arnold
0xC770BBCA21A3457DA37A...	{"heavytraffic":"traffic","moderatetraffic":"traffic","returnhome":"...	NULL
0xCABA46EC39DAF9D421E4...	{"arnold1":"arnold","arnold2":"arnold"}	NULL
0xCD3D15AFB1CCD3EAF4E...	{"heavytraffic":"traffic", "moderatetraffic":"traffic"}	merge-heavy-mod

Figure 25: Transform that we just created is highlighted.

Similar to event sets, transforms can be identified by both a hash primary key (transformskey) and an optional code (Code). Before generating the transform key, the transform (stored as JSON in the transforms column) is sorted by its JSON keys. This ensures that transforms with identical content but different key orders do not produce duplicate transformskey values. Code 21 and Code 22 will return an MM without using the transform and another using the transform, respectively.

```
SELECT Event1A, EventB, Prob,[Rows] FROM dbo.[MarkovProcess](0,
      'leavehome,heavytraffic,moderatetraffic,lighttraffic,arrivework,returnhome',
-- Event Set.
      0,NULL,NULL ,NULL, 1, NULL, NULL, NULL, 1)
```

Code 21: Markov model without using the transform.

```
SELECT Event1A, EventB, Prob,[Rows] FROM dbo.[MarkovProcess](0,
      'leavehome,heavytraffic,moderatetraffic,lighttraffic,arrivework,returnhome',
-- Event Set.
      0,NULL,NULL ,
      'merge-heavy-mod',
      1, NULL, NULL, NULL, 1)
```

Code 22: Markov model using the transform.

Figure 26 shows a comparison of the two SQL from Code 21 and Code 22.

Without Transforms

Event1A	EventB	Prob	Rows
heavytraffic	arrivework	0.875	7
heavytraffic	returnhome	0.125	1
leavehome	heavytraffic	0.4706	8
leavehome	lighttraffic	0.2353	4
leavehome	moderatetraffic	0.2941	5
lighttraffic	arrivework	1	4
moderatetraffic	arrivework	1	5

With Transforms

Event1A	EventB	Prob	Rows
home	lighttraffic	0.2353	4
home	traffic	0.7647	13
lighttraffic	arrivework	1	4
traffic	arrivework	0.9231	12
traffic	home	0.0769	1

Figure 26: Results without transforms and with transforms.

Note how the right results (With Transforms) have fewer rows. That's because *heavytraffic* and *moderatetraffic* were merged into a single event, *traffic*. In the upcoming section, *Compare Two Markov Models*, we'll look at a more complicated scenario—web page clicks.

Create Markov Process

The function to create and update Markov models (CreateUpdateMarkovProcess) is the heart of the TimeSolution. Code 23 shows the code for creating an MM—in this case, a MM for restaurantguest, across all time.

```
DECLARE @Include NVARCHAR(100)='restaurantguest' -- Name of an Event Set for Total
in-and-out time.
DECLARE @ModelID INT
EXEC CreateUpdateMarkovProcess
        @ModelID OUTPUT, @Include,1, NULL,NULL, NULL, 1,NULL, NULL, NULL, NULL
```

Code 23: Create a Markov model.

Figure 27 shows the event-to-event segments of the created MM in table form.

	ModelID	EventA	EventB	Rows	Prob	IsEntry	IsExit	Max	Avg	Min	StDev	CoefVar
1	2	arrive	depart	1	0.1	1	1	5	5	5	NULL	NULL
2	2	arrive	greeted	8	0.8	1	0	16	7.38	3	5.07	0.69
3	2	arrive	seated	1	0.1	1	0	1	1	1	NULL	NULL
4	2	bigtip	depart	1	1	0	1	4.98	4.98	4.98	NULL	NULL
5	2	ccdeclined	charged1	1	1	0	0	2	2	2	NULL	NULL
6	2	charged	bigtip	1	0.1429	0	0	0.02	0.02	0.02	NULL	NULL
7	2	charged	ccdeclined	1	0.1429	0	0	1	1	1	NULL	NULL
8	2	charged	depart	5	0.7143	0	1	33	13.2	3	13.01	0.98
9	2	charged1	depart	1	1	0	1	7	7	7	NULL	NULL
10	2	check	charged	7	1	0	0	5	4.43	2	1.13	0.26
11	2	drinks	order	7	1	0	0	5	4	1	1.73	0.43
12	2	greeted	seated	8	1	0	0	5.5	1.72	0.5	2.19	1.27
13	2	intro	drinks	7	0.875	0	0	3.25	2.75	1	0.78	0.28
14	2	intro	order	1	0.125	0	0	0.17	0.17	0.17	NULL	NULL
15	2	order	served	8	1	0	0	35	19.18	9	8.04	0.42
16	2	seated	depart	1	0.1111	0	1	4	4	4	NULL	NULL
17	2	seated	intro	8	0.8889	0	0	3.5	1.43	0.25	0.98	0.69
18	2	served	check	7	0.875	0	0	40	22.71	15	8.06	0.35
19	2	served	depart	1	0.125	0	1	20	20	20	NULL	NULL

Figure 27: Markov model for restaurantguest event set.

Figure 28 is a graph view representing the model, with the transition probabilities on the lines.

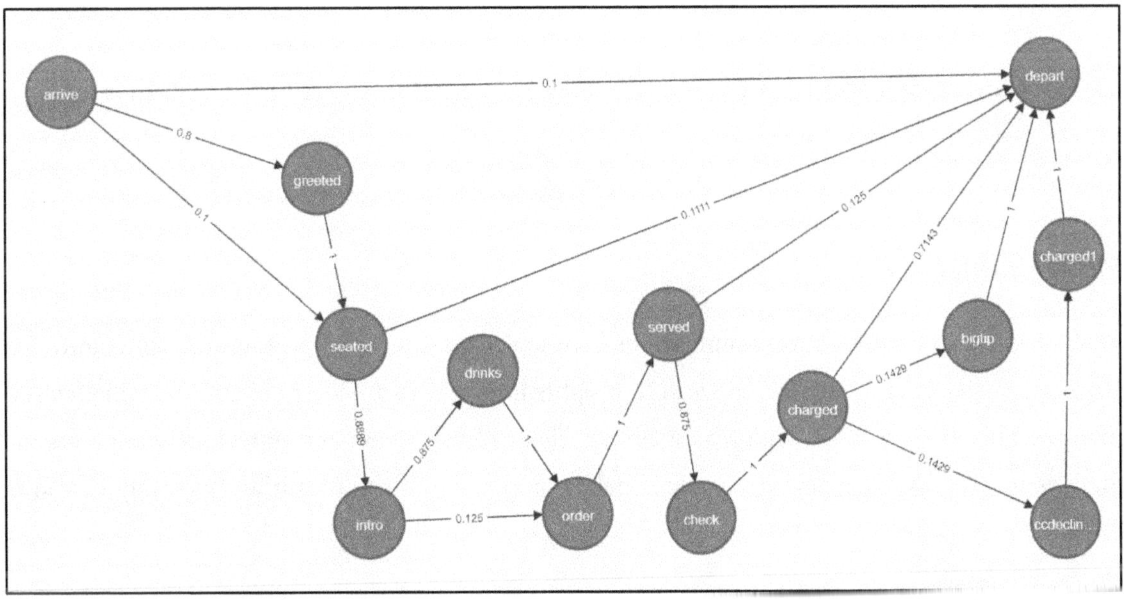

Figure 28: Look at the Markov model in a graph view.

Most of the parameters of CreateUpdateMarkovProcess are shared among many of the other major functions and stored procedures, which warrants a brief explanation of each:

1. **@ModelID INT=NULL OUTPUT** - Identifies the Markov model; if NULL, a new model is created.
2. **@EventSet NVARCHAR(MAX)** - Specifies the set of events for building the Markov model—comma-separated list or event set code.
3. **@enumerate_multiple_events INT=0** - Indicates whether to consider multiple occurrences of the same event.
4. **@StartDateTime DATETIME=NULL** - The start date and time for filtering events.
5. **@EndDateTime DATETIME=NULL** - The end date and time for filtering events.
6. **@transforms NVARCHAR(MAX)=NULL** - JSON object specifying transformations of event data.
7. **@ByCase BIT=1** - Determines whether the Markov process is calculated per case (1) or globally (0).
8. **@metric NVARCHAR(20)=NULL** - Specifies the metric for analysis. Will default to "Time Between", the number of seconds between the event transitions.
9. **@CaseFilterProperties NVARCHAR(MAX)=NULL** - JSON object for filtering cases based on properties.
10. **@EventFilterProperties NVARCHAR(MAX)=NULL** - JSON object for filtering events based on properties.
11. **@InsertSequences BIT=1** - Indicates whether to insert model sequences, which can be time and compute intensive.

Model Similarity

Analyzing the similarities and dissimilarities between MMs generates profound insights into how processes evolve over time. That can lead to insights into how to avoid or enhance certain effects of changes. This analysis is particularly valuable in fields like business and fintech, where even small changes in process efficiency or customer behavior can signal significant and possibly cascading shifts.

Everything changes. That's because every process interacts with other processes. Or at least if a process doesn't change, it's because we've successfully deflected any forces affecting it. The tires of our cars wear down from interaction with the ground, but we proactively change the tires to maintain continuity of service. Similarly, business processes are in constant flux, whether we actively manage the change or passively observe it.

In the context of MMs, comparing models from different time periods or other dimensional slices allows us to spot shifts in probabilities between events. Perhaps steps in a process are becoming less likely, or new steps are emerging while others fade away. This kind of comparison analysis allows us to discern underlying trends and shifts in behavior, both for customers, operational workflows, and supply chain management.

Here are a couple of examples.

Fraud Detection in Fintech

Think of a fintech company tracking its fraud detection workflow. An MM from 2023 might show the common process of a transaction being flagged, reviewed, and either approved or denied. However, upon comparing the 2024 MM, the company may discover that the probability of denying transactions has decreased, and the time between review and final decision has widened, perhaps suggesting the implementation of a more extensive fraud review process step.

Furthermore, the company might notice that some steps are entirely missing from the 2024 model, such as manual escalation, indicating that the process has become more streamlined, but possibly less thorough. This kind of insight—before and after comparisons—is critical for helping the company assess whether these changes are beneficial or indicate a problem in the fraud review system.

This is important because any improvements to fraud detection will result in highly motivated fraudsters evolving their tactics. In the adversarial world, all changes open new doors.

Car Dealership Sales Process

Consider a car dealership analyzing the process of selling vehicles. A 2023 MM might show that customers visiting the dealership typically follow a common path: browsing vehicles, negotiating terms, applying for financing, and completing the purchase. The model might reveal a high probability of customers dropping out at the negotiation step due to dissatisfaction with pricing or terms.

In contrast, the 2024 MM may show significant changes. For example, it might indicate that more customers are proceeding directly to financing after browsing vehicles, skipping the traditional negotiation step. This could suggest the dealership introduced a no-haggle pricing policy, simplifying the process but potentially alienating customers who value negotiation.

Additionally, the model might highlight a new step in the 2024 process: customers taking a longer test drive or using an online tool to finalize their financing options before visiting the dealership. These changes could explain an increase in the average time between the initial visit and the purchase, potentially signaling improvements in customer satisfaction and decision-making time, or it might point to inefficiencies introduced by the new step.

By comparing the 2023 and 2024 MMs, the dealership can identify areas to refine—such as optimizing the test drive process or enhancing the online financing tool—to ensure a smoother customer experience while maintaining sales performance.

Key Metrics for Comparison

When comparing MMs from different periods, these are a few metrics to focus on:

- **Probabilities Shifting:** Are customers or systems moving from one event to the next at the same distribution as before?
- **New or Missing Steps:** Are there now steps that didn't exist before, or are old steps now irrelevant?
- **Changes in Time Consistency:** Have the coefficient of variations between key events widened or narrowed? This can show if a process has become more or less reliable.
- **Shifts in Process Flow:** Are more people stopping or dropping out at certain steps than they used to? If fewer cases are making it past a specific point, it may signal a new roadblock or change in behavior that's affecting flow.

By studying metrics like those listed above, businesses can answer vital questions such as whether processes are becoming more efficient, whether the chaos is encroaching in the form of a wider variance in customer response times, or if new regulatory steps are introducing friction. These insights are especially valuable in fintech, where changes in regulatory compliance, fraud detection, or loan approval processes can have significant financial implications.

Setting Up Similarities

The ModelSimilarity table captures metrics that quantify the similarity between two MMs. These metrics provide insights into how closely the event transitions, probabilities, and sequences in one model resemble those in another. This comparison is crucial for identifying patterns, understanding relationships, and validating models in similar contexts.

This functionality is essential for understanding the relationships between different MMs and how they represent variations in event sequences across cases or scenarios. This helps answer the consultant's critical question (usually after "What's the problem?"), "What has changed?"

The InsertModelSimilarities stored procedure calculates these metrics by:

1. Extracting transitions and probabilities from the ModelEvents table for each model.
2. Comparing these values to compute structural and probabilistic similarities.
3. Inserting or updating the results in the ModelSimilarity table.

Code 24 creates three pairs of similarity analysis.

```
--[[START set model similarity]
EXEC InsertModelSimilarities @ModelID1=1, @ModelID2=7
EXEC InsertModelSimilarities @ModelID1=5, @ModelID2=6
EXEC InsertModelSimilarities @ModelID1=13, @ModelID2=14
```

Code 24: Analyze and add similarity score between pairs of models.

Figure 29 shows the three comparisons that were created with Code 24.

ModelID1	ModelID2	CombinedUniqueSegments	SameSegments_ttest	CosineSimilarity
1	7	10	NULL	0.96056685680073
5	6	10	NULL	0.987762965329069
13	14	5	-19.3850815029327	1

Figure 29: Scores for the three comparisons.

The similarity scores shown in Figure 29 include:

1. **CombinedUniqueSegments**: This represents the total number of unique event transitions (EventA → EventB) across both models being compared. It combines the segments from both models, including those that are common and unique to each.

2. **PercentSameSegments**: This is a measure of the overlap between the two models. It is calculated as the proportion of shared event transitions between the two models out of the total combined unique segments. A higher percentage indicates greater similarity in transitions.

3. **SameSegments_ttest**: The t-test value provides a statistical measure of whether the average probabilities for shared segments (EventA → EventB) differ significantly between the two models. A low value suggests that the probabilities are similar for the shared transitions, indicating a stronger similarity.

4. **CosineSimilarity**: This metric calculates the cosine similarity between the probability vectors of the two models. Cosine similarity ranges from 0 to 1:

    - **1** indicates the models are perfectly aligned in terms of probabilities.
    - **0** indicates no similarity in their probability vectors.

    This measure focuses on the direction of the vectors rather than their magnitude.

Figure 30 shows the segment analysis for the 2nd model created in Code 24.

m1_EventA	m2_EventA	m1_EventB	m2_EventB	m1_Avg	m2_Avg	m1_Rows	m2_Rows	m1_Prob	m2_Prob
arrive	arrive	greeted	greeted	7.38	5	8	1	0.8	1
bigtip	bigtip	depart	depart	4.98	4.98	1	1	1	1
charged	charged	bigtip	bigtip	0.02	0.02	1	1	0.1429	1
check	check	charged	charged	4.43	5	7	1	1	1
drinks	drinks	order	order	4	5	7	1	1	1
greeted	greeted	seated	seated	1.72	0.5	8	1	1	1
intro	intro	drinks	drinks	2.75	3	7	1	0.875	1
order	order	served	served	19.18	20	8	1	1	1
seated	seated	intro	intro	1.43	1.5	8	1	0.8889	1
served	served	check	check	22.71	20	7	1	0.875	1

Figure 30: Comparison of common segments in ModelID 1 (m1) and 7 (m2).

MM similarities in the TimeSolution are calculated on demand to avoid overwhelming computational and storage costs. Automatically comparing all pairs of models would require a massive cross-join of MMs, creating an unmanageable number of comparisons as the number of models grows. Moreover, not all models are logically comparable; similarities only make sense for models with shared contexts, such as overlapping event sets or related processes. Blindly calculating similarities would produce noise without more analytical insights.

Model Stationary Distribution

The stationary distribution of an MM describes the long-term probabilities of being in each event, irrespective of the initial event. Over time, the transitions stabilize, and the probabilities converge to a steady state. This makes the stationary distribution a key analytical tool for understanding equilibrium behavior in processes like customer journeys, operational workflows, or system state transitions.

The stationary distribution is calculated in the TimeSolution framework using the script *TimeSolution.py*, which is available on the GitHub repository. This script connects to the SQL Server database, extracts the transition matrix for a given model, and computes the stationary distribution through iterative matrix multiplications. The transition matrix represents the probabilities of moving from one event to another. By repeatedly multiplying the matrix by itself, the probabilities converge to the stationary distribution.

For example, consider a simplified customer support system with three states: "New," "In Progress," and "Resolved." The transition matrix might look like Table 22.

	New	In Progress	Resolved
New	0.5	0.4	0.1
In Progress	0.3	0.6	0.1
Resolved	0.0	0.2	0.8

Table 22: Transition matrix for a simple customer support system.

After iterative computations, the stationary distribution converges to what we see in Table 23.

State	New	In Progress	Resolved
Probability	0.25	0.50	0.25

Table 23: Stationary distribution for the customer support system shown in Table 22.

This means that in the long run, at any given time, 25% of tickets remain "New," 50% are "In Progress," and 25% are "Resolved" (then archived away after a few days). These probabilities guide resource allocation, such as optimizing staffing levels to match where effort is most needed.

The stationary distribution bridges the gap between raw event data and analytical insights, providing a summary of long-term behavior in systems modeled as MMs. Its computation requires high-quality data with no missing events or zero probabilities.

The *TimeSolution.py* script on the GitHub repository automates this computation and stores the results in the database for further analysis. For larger datasets or complex MMs, because these are matrix computations, GPU-based computation could significantly enhance performance, as discussed earlier in this book.

Markov Model Utilization

This section showcases how to leverage the concepts we just discussed for practical insights and applications through a series of demonstrations. Each demo highlights key capabilities of the framework, including constructing and analyzing MMs, exploring transition probabilities, calculating stationary distributions, and comparing model similarities. These examples illustrate how TimeSolution can be used to extract analytical insights from event-driven data.

All demonstrations are consolidated into the script file *time_molecules_code_from_book.sql*, available on the accompanying GitHub repository.

Basic Markov Model

For this "hello world" demo, we'll request an MM for the process of servicing restaurant guests.

Code 25 will retrieve the raw events as per the parameters of the SelectedEvents TVF, which basically requests all events in the event set named *restaurantguest*.

```
--The individual Events for @EventSet=restaurantguest.
SELECT *
FROM dbo.SelectedEvents('restaurantguest',0, NULL,NULL,NULL,1,NULL,NULL,NULL)
ORDER BY CaseID,[Rank]
```

Code 25: Basic request for a Markov model.

Figure 31 is a partial result, but we at least see all the events for CaseID 1, from arrive through depart. The full result set includes ten cases (ten customers serviced), 85 rows.

CaseID	Event	EventDate	Rank	EventOccurance	EventID	MetricInputValue	MetricOutputValue
1	arrive	2023-01-01 17:00:00.0000000	1	1	1	NULL	NULL
1	greeted	2023-01-01 17:05:00.0000000	2	1	2	NULL	NULL
1	seated	2023-01-01 17:05:30.0000000	3	1	3	NULL	NULL
1	intro	2023-01-01 17:07:00.0000000	4	1	4	NULL	NULL
1	drinks	2023-01-01 17:10:00.0000000	5	1	5	NULL	NULL
1	order	2023-01-01 17:15:00.0000000	6	1	6	NULL	NULL
1	served	2023-01-01 17:35:00.0000000	7	1	7	NULL	NULL
1	check	2023-01-01 17:55:00.0000000	8	1	8	NULL	NULL
1	charged	2023-01-01 18:00:00.0000000	9	1	9	NULL	NULL
1	bigtip	2023-01-01 18:00:01.0000000	10	1	85	NULL	NULL
1	depart	2023-01-01 18:05:00.0000000	11	1	10	NULL	NULL
2	arrive	2023-01-01 17:00:00.0000000	1	1	11	NULL	NULL
2	greeted	2023-01-01 17:06:00.0000000	2	1	12	NULL	NULL
2	seated	2023-01-01 17:06:45.0000000	3	1	13	NULL	NULL
2	intro	2023-01-01 17:08:00.0000000	4	1	14	NULL	NULL
2	drinks	2023-01-01 17:15:00.0000000	5	1	15	NULL	NULL
2	order	2023-01-01 17:16:00.0000000	6	1	16	NULL	NULL
2	served	2023-01-01 17:25:00.0000000	7	1	17	NULL	NULL

Figure 31: Results of Basic Markov Model.

The full results of Figure 31 are in the GitHub repository: *data_output/Basic_Markov_Chain.csv*

Code 26 goes a step further, creating an MM from the same raw events we see in Figure 31 and returns the statistics-based columns. Note that the @Metric parameter will default to 'Time Between', the time in minutes between EventA→EventB.

```
--Markov Model created from the events listed above. Don't force refresh, so it
reads from MarkovEvents.
--Max, Avg, Min, StDev refer by default to the time between the events.
--@Metric (8th parameter) is NULL, which defaults to 'Time Between'.
SELECT
      ModelID,Event1A,EventB,[Max],[Avg],[Min],[StDev],CoefVar,
      [Sum],[Rows],Prob,IsEntry,IsExit
FROM dbo.[MarkovProcess](0,'restaurantguest',0, NULL,NULL,NULL,1,NULL,NULL,NULL,0)
```

Code 26: The Markov model with statistics-based columns.

Figure 32 is the result of executing Code 26.

ModelID	Event1A	EventB	Max	Avg	Min	StDev	CoefVar	Sum	Rows	Prob	IsEntry	IsExit
3	arrive	depart	5	5	5	NULL	NULL	5	1	0.1	1	1
3	arrive	greeted	15	6.13	3	3.68	0.6	49	8	0.8	1	0
3	arrive	seated	1	1	1	NULL	NULL	1	1	0.1	1	0
3	bigtip	depart	4.98	4.98	4.98	NULL	NULL	4.98	1	1	0	1
3	ccdeclined	charged	2	2	2	NULL	NULL	2	1	1	0	0
3	charged	bigtip	0.02	0.02	0.02	NULL	NULL	0.02	1	0.125	0	0
3	charged	ccdeclined	1	1	1	NULL	NULL	1	1	0.125	0	0
3	charged	depart	33	12.5	5	11.62	0.93	75	6	0.75	0	1
3	check	charged	15	6	2	4.12	0.69	42	7	1	0	0
3	drinks	order	5	3.86	1	1.95	0.51	27	7	1	0	0
3	greeted	seated	5.5	1.72	0.5	2.19	1.27	13.75	8	1	0	0
3	intro	drinks	7	3.61	3	1.5	0.42	25.25	7	0.875	0	0
3	intro	order	0.17	0.17	0.17	NULL	NULL	0.17	1	0.125	0	0
3	order	served	20	17.3	9	5	0.29	138.42	8	1	0	0
3	seated	depart	4	4	4	NULL	NULL	4	1	0.1111	0	1
3	seated	intro	3.5	1.43	0.25	0.98	0.69	11.42	8	0.8889	0	0
3	served	check	40	21.43	10	9	0.42	150	7	0.875	0	0
3	served	depart	20	20	20	NULL	NULL	20	1	0.125	0	1

Figure 32: The created Markov model.

Following is an explanation of each column in the MM shown in Figure 32, incorporating the details about the metrics:

- **ModelID**: This column identifies the specific Markov model used in the analysis. Here, 3 signifies that the transitions correspond to Model 3, which already existed.
- **Event1A**: This column represents the initial event in a sequence. It's the starting point of the transition. For example, arrive, charged, drinks, and served represent various events in the process.
- **EventB**: This column represents the event that occurs after Event1A (Event1A→EventB), indicating the next step or transition in the sequence. For example, after arrive, the next event could be greeted, departed, or seated.
- **Max**: This column represents the maximum time observed between Event1A→EventB the process across all cases. For example, for the transition from arrive to depart (first row of Figure 32), the max time recorded was 5 minutes.
- **Avg**: This column shows the average time between Event1A→EventB over all observations. It provides a measure of how long, on average, it takes to transition from one event to the next. For example, arrive to greeted takes an average of 6.13 minutes.
- **Min**: This column represents the minimum time observed between Event1A→EventB in the dataset. It gives the shortest observed transition time for each event pair.

- **StDev**: This column represents the standard deviation of the time between events, indicating how much the time varies between Event1A→EventB across different observations. A higher value shows more variability, while a lower value indicates more consistent timing between events.
- **CoefVar**: The coefficient of variation is a normalized measure of the dispersion of time between events. It's calculated as the ratio of the standard deviation to the mean (StDev/Avg) and gives insight into how much the time varies relative to the average time.
- **Sum**: This column shows the total time spent transitioning between Event1A→EventB across all observations. For example, the transition from "charged" to "depart" has a total of 75 minutes over 6 Rows (cases).
- **Rows**: This column indicates the number of observations of a particular transition. For example, "arrive" to "greeted" occurred 8 times in the data.
- **Prob**: This column provides the probability of transitioning from Event1A→EventB based on the number of observations. It reflects the likelihood of moving from one event to another in the process. For example, the transition from greeted to seated has a probability of 0.875, meaning it happens in 87.5% of cases where greeted occurs.
- **IsEntry**: This column indicates whether Event1A is an entry point in the process (i.e., whether the event starts a sequence). A value of 1 means it's an entry event, and 0 means it's not.
- **IsExit**: This column indicates whether EventB is an exit point in the process (i.e., whether the event ends the sequence). A value of 1 means it's an exit event, and 0 means it's not.

Fuel Metric as Opposed to Time Between

The previous demo used the default metric of Time Between. Let's do this again, but with a different use case and metric—the fuel consumption during commutes to work.

Code 27 will get the events involved with commutes. Note how the parameters of SelectedEvents have *commute* for the event set and *Fuel* as the metric.

```
--Display raw events related to commute.
SELECT CaseID, [Event], EventDate,[Rank],EventOccurence,MetricActualValue
FROM dbo.SelectedEvents('commute',0,NULL,NULL,NULL,1,'Fuel',NULL,NULL)
ORDER BY CaseID,[Rank]
```

Code 27: Look at raw events for commute.

Figure 33 is the partial result, the first few rows (out of 50) of commute events in the EventsFact table.

CaseID	Event	EventDate	Rank	EventOccurence	EventID	MetricActualValue
11	leavehome	2022-10-01 07:20:00.0000000	1	1	86	53
11	heavytraffic	2022-10-01 07:30:00.0000000	2	1	87	52
11	arrivework	2022-10-01 08:15:00.0000000	3	1	88	43
12	leavehome	2022-10-02 07:20:00.0000000	1	1	89	56
12	heavytraffic	2022-10-02 07:33:00.0000000	2	1	90	55
12	arrivework	2022-10-02 08:20:00.0000000	3	1	91	46
13	leavehome	2022-10-03 07:20:00.0000000	1	1	92	59
13	lighttraffic	2022-10-03 07:29:00.0000000	2	1	93	59.5
13	arrivework	2022-10-03 07:55:00.0000000	3	1	94	58
14	leavehome	2022-10-04 07:20:00.0000000	1	1	95	42
14	heavytraffic	2022-10-04 07:30:00.0000000	2	1	96	41
14	arrivework	2022-10-04 08:22:00.0000000	3	1	97	30
15	leavehome	2022-10-05 07:20:00.0000000	1	1	98	55
15	lighttraffic	2022-10-05 07:30:00.0000000	2	1	99	55.5

Figure 33: Raw commute facts.

Code 28 shows how we can create an MM for fuel consumption from the events we see in Figure 33.

```
SELECT
ModelID,Event1A,EventB,[Max],[Avg],[Min],[StDev],CoefVar,[Sum],[Rows],Prob,IsEntry,I
sExit
FROM dbo.[MarkovProcess](1,'commute',0,NULL,NULL,NULL,1,'Fuel',NULL,NULL,0)
```

Code 28: Markov model for the fuel metric of the commute event set.

Figure 34 shows the transitions between traffic conditions and arriving at work using the Fuel metric to evaluate fuel consumption. The highlighted rows indicate transitions for heavytraffic→arrivework and lighttraffic→arrivework. While both transitions have a probability of 1, the average fuel consumption (Avg) differs significantly.

Heavytraffic shows a much higher average fuel consumption (-10.5714) compared to lighttraffic (-2.625). Additionally, heavytraffic has a larger StDev, indicating greater variability in fuel usage. This emphasizes the impact of traffic conditions on fuel efficiency during commutes.

Event1A	EventB	Max	Avg	Min	StDev	CoefVar	Sum	Rows	Prob	IsEntry	IsExit
heavytraffic	arrivework	-8	-10.5714	-16	2.6367	-0.249	-74	7	1	0	1
leavehome	heavytraffic	-1	-1.125	-2	0.3536	-0.314	-9	8	0.4706	1	1
leavehome	lighttraffic	-0.5	-1.375	-2	0.75	-0.545	-5.5	4	0.2353	1	0
leavehome	moderatetraffic	-1	-1	-1	0	0	-5	5	0.2941	1	0
lighttraffic	arrivework	-2	-2.625	-3	0.4787	-0.182	-10.5	4	1	0	1
moderatetraffic	arrivework	-3	-4.4	-6	1.1402	-0.259	-22	5	1	0	1

Figure 34: Markov model for the fuel metric of the commute event set.

Figure 35 illustrates MMs in graph form for two different metrics for transitions between events in a system.

1. On the left side, it displays Fuel Consumption between events, where the numbers represent average fuel consumption during transitions. For example, leavehome→heavytraffic consumes -1.125 units of fuel.

2. On the right side, it presents the Coefficient of Variation for each transition, highlighting the relative variability in fuel usage. For example, leavehome→heavytraffic has a coefficient of 0.3143, indicating a moderate level of variability.

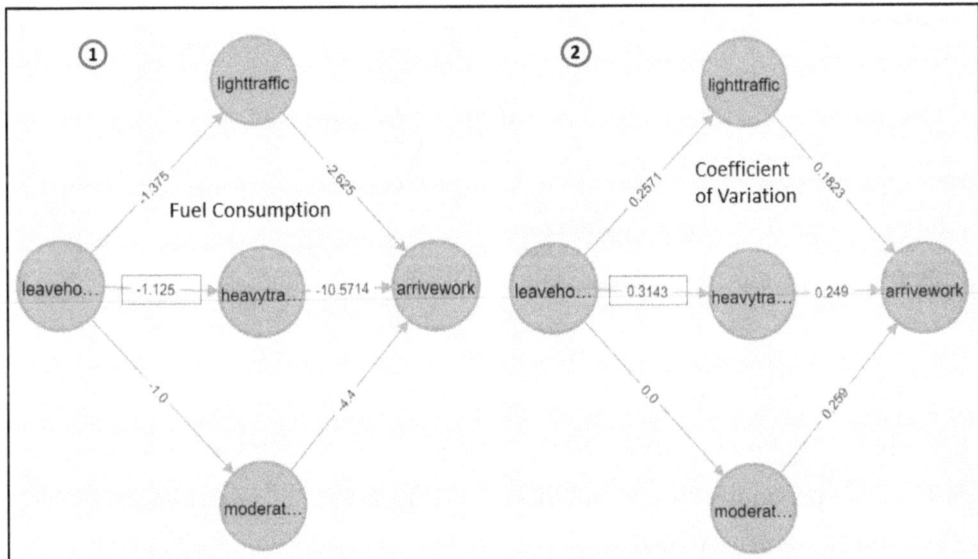

Figure 35: Markov model of Figure 34.

Compare Two Markov Models

Back in the section, Transforms, we looked through a simple example related to commute. In this section, we'll cover a more complicated example that has to do with website page views. This example will carry through to the next section, Caching Markov Models.

Markov with No Transforms

Code 29 will build an MM of website views.

```
SELECT
        ModelID, Event1A, EventB,
        [Max], [Avg], [Min], [StDev], CoefVar, [Sum],
        [Rows], Prob, IsEntry, IsExit
FROM dbo.[MarkovProcess](0,'websitepages',0,NULL,NULL,NULL,1,NULL,NULL,NULL,0)
```

Code 29: Markov Model of websitepages event set.

Figure 36 shows the results of Code 29.

ModelID	Event1A	EventB	Max	Avg	Min	StDev	CoefVar	Sum	Rows	Prob	IsEntry	IsExit	FromCache
NULL	arnold1	keto1	3	3	3	NULL	NULL	3	1	1	0	0	0
NULL	arnold2	keto1	3	3	3	NULL	NULL	3	1	0.5	0	0	0
NULL	arnold2	shoppmt	8.166666	8.1667	8.166666	NULL	NULL	8.166666	1	0.5	0	0	0
NULL	cart	shoppmt	0.166666	0.1667	0.166666	0	0	0.666664	4	1	0	0	0
NULL	chocprotein	arnold1	2	2	2	NULL	NULL	2	1	0.3333	0	0	0
NULL	chocprotein	arnold2	2	2	2	0	0	4	2	0.6667	0	0	0
NULL	chocproteinbars	cart	1	1	1	0	0	3	3	1	0	0	0
NULL	creditcard	keto1	2	2	2	NULL	NULL	2	1	0.25	0	0	0
NULL	creditcard	receipt	0.75	0.75	0.75	0	0	2.25	3	0.75	0	1	0
NULL	homepage	chocprotein	1	1	1	0	0	3	3	0.6	1	0	0
NULL	homepage	keto1	6	6	6	NULL	NULL	6	1	0.2	1	0	0
NULL	homepage	weightwatcher1	4	4	4	NULL	NULL	4	1	0.2	1	0	0
NULL	keto1	chocproteinbars	4	4	4	0	0	12	3	0.6	0	0	0
NULL	keto1	vanproteinbars	4	3	2	1.4142	0.471	6	2	0.4	0	0	0
NULL	shoppmt	abandonedcart	1.833333	1.8333	1.833333	NULL	NULL	1.833333	1	0.2	0	1	0
NULL	shoppmt	creditcard	1.833333	1.8333	1.833333	0	0	7.333332	4	0.8	0	0	0
NULL	vanproteinbars	cart	1	0.5417	0.083333	0.6482	1.197	1.083333	2	1	0	1	0
NULL	weightwatcher1	keto1	2	2	2	NULL	NULL	2	1	1	0	0	0

Figure 36: Markov model of website view event set.

Note that:

- The ModelID column values are NULL. That's because this MM is created in an ad-hoc fashion, not previously created and cached (using the CreateUpdateMarkovProcess TVF).
- There are 18 segments (rows).
- arnold1 and arnold2 under the Event1A column are considered separate event types.
- The values of the FromCache column is 0, which validates that this MM was computed on-the-fly and not a cached MM in the MME.

Markov with Transforms

With Code 30, we'll transform a few events as instructed with the @FM_Transforms JSON variable:

- arnold1 and arnold2 are mapped to arnold. This will merge arnold1 and arnold2 segments. This transform is due to data problems—arnold appearing differently.
- keto1 and weightwatchers1 are merged into dietpage. This is more of a business rule problem. We want to merge diet pages.

```
--Markov Model with transforms. Transform the two arnolds into a single one.
DECLARE @FM_Transforms NVARCHAR(1000)='{"arnold1":"arnold","arnold2":"arnold",
"keto1":"dietpage","weightwatcher1":"dietpage","vanproteinbars":"proteinbars","chocp
roteinbars":"proteinbars"}'

SELECT
	ModelID,Event1A,EventB,
	[Max],[Avg],[Min],[StDev],CoefVar,[Sum],
	[Rows],Prob,IsEntry,IsExit
FROM
dbo.[MarkovProcess](0,'websitepages',0,NULL,NULL,@FM_Transforms,1,NULL,NULL,NULL,0)
```

Code 30: Markov model using transforms that merges arnold1 and arnold2.

Figure 37 shows the segments of the MM created using Code 30.

ModelID	Event1A	EventB	Max	Avg	Min	StDev	CoefVar	Sum	Rows	Prob	IsEntry	IsExit	FromCache
NULL	arnold	dietpage	3	3	3	0	0	6	2	0.6667	0	0	0
NULL	arnold	shoppmt	8.166666	8.1667	8.166666	NULL	NULL	8.166666	1	0.3333	0	0	0
NULL	cart	shoppmt	0.166666	0.1667	0.166666	0	0	0.666664	4	1	0	0	0
NULL	chocprotein	arnold	2	2	2	0	0	6	3	1	0	0	0
NULL	creditcard	dietpage	2	2	2	NULL	NULL	2	1	0.25	0	0	0
NULL	creditcard	receipt	0.75	0.75	0.75	0	0	2.25	3	0.75	0	1	0
NULL	dietpage	dietpage	2	2	2	NULL	NULL	2	1	0.1667	0	0	0
NULL	dietpage	proteinbars	4	3.6	2	0.8944	0.248	18	5	0.8333	0	0	0
NULL	homepage	chocprotein	1	1	1	0	0	3	3	0.6	1	0	0
NULL	homepage	dietpage	6	5	4	1.4142	0.283	10	2	0.4	1	0	0
NULL	proteinbars	cart	1	0.8167	0.083333	0.4099	0.502	4.083333	5	1	0	1	0
NULL	shoppmt	abandonedcart	1.833333	1.8333	1.833333	NULL	NULL	1.833333	1	0.2	0	1	0
NULL	shoppmt	creditcard	1.833333	1.8333	1.833333	0	0	7.333332	4	0.8	0	0	0

Figure 37: Using transforms that convert all arnold1 and arnold2 events into arnold.

Note that:

- There are now only 13 rows compared to the 18 in Figure 37.
- arnold1 and arnold2 are no longer there—they are merged into arnold.
- keto1 and weightwatchers are no longer there—they are merged into dietpage.
- The values from the FromCache column are 0, indicating this MM is computed on the fly like the one in Figure 36.

Notice the first row of Figure 37, the segment arnold→dietpage with 2 Rows. This is the merging of the first two rows of Figure 36, the segments arnold1→keto1 and arnold2→keto1—as per the transforms that equates arnold1 and arnold2 to arnold and keto1 to dietpage.

Caching Markov Models into the Markov Model Ensemble

In the prior section, *Compare Two Markov Models*, the values for the ModelID columns for both figures (Figure 36 and Figure 37) were NULL, indicating that the models were computed on-the-fly during the query and were not saved. While generating models dynamically offers flexibility, it comes at a computational cost—especially when dealing with large datasets or performing high numbers of concurrent analytic queries.

We can significantly mitigate that challenge by saving them in the MME after computation. Much like caching sums and counts of billions to trillions of "facts" in traditional OLAP systems, storing computed MMs enables faster retrieval and analysis, significantly reducing the *average* query time, especially under high query concurrency. Once cached, these models can be queried repeatedly without recalculating the underlying probabilities and metrics. In other words, computing what would be millions to trillions of events in real time versus finding the cached model and returning its few dozen or so MM segments.

Additionally, much like OLAP, we can precompute sets of MMs—such as one for each county by product category by year—optimizing retrieval by leveraging user query patterns. This approach promotes the odds that frequently accessed models are readily available, further reducing average query latency and computational overhead.

Code 31 shows how to use the stored procedure, CreateUpdateMarkovProcess, which was introduced back in the section, Create Markov Process.

```
EXEC CreateUpdateMarkovProcess
     NULL,'websitepages',0,NULL,NULL,NULL,1,NULL,NULL,NULL
```

Code 31: Save the MM we looked at above in Figure 36.

Now, let's re-run the query shown in Figure 38 in Code 29 to query websitepages. The results shown in Figure 38 should look the same as Figure 36, but with two differences:

1. The values for the ModelID column are 27, unlike the NULL values as shown back in Figure 37.

2. The values for the FromCache column are 1. This means the query pulled the results from the cache we created with Code 32.

ModelID	Event1A	EventB	Max	Avg	Min	StDev	CoefVar	Sum	Rows	Prob	IsEntry	IsExit
27	arnold1	keto1	3	3	3	NULL	NULL	3	1	1	0	0
27	arnold2	keto1	3	3	3	NULL	NULL	3	1	0.5	0	0
27	arnold2	shoppmt	8.17	8.17	8.17	NULL	NULL	8.17	1	0.5	0	0
27	cart	shoppmt	0.17	0.17	0.17	0	0	0.67	4	1	0	0
27	chocprotein	arnold1	2	2	2	NULL	NULL	2	1	0.3333	0	0
27	chocprotein	arnold2	2	2	2	0	0	4	2	0.6667	0	0
27	chocproteinbars	cart	1	1	1	0	0	3	3	1	0	0
27	creditcard	keto1	2	2	2	NULL	NULL	2	1	0.25	0	0
27	creditcard	receipt	0.75	0.75	0.75	0	0	2.25	3	0.75	0	1
27	homepage	chocprotein	1	1	1	0	0	3	3	0.6	1	0
27	homepage	keto1	6	6	6	NULL	NULL	6	1	0.2	1	0
27	homepage	weightwatcher1	4	4	4	NULL	NULL	4	1	0.2	1	0
27	keto1	chocproteinbars	4	4	4	0	0	12	3	0.6	0	0
27	keto1	vanproteinbars	4	3	2	1.41	0.47	6	2	0.4	0	0
27	shoppmt	abandonedcart	1.83	1.83	1.83	NULL	NULL	1.83	1	0.2	0	1
27	shoppmt	creditcard	1.83	1.83	1.83	0	0	7.33	4	0.8	0	0
27	vanproteinbars	cart	1	0.54	0.08	0.65	1.2	1.08	2	1	0	1
27	weightwatcher1	keto1	2	2	2	NULL	NULL	2	1	1	0	0

Figure 38: Query pulled from cache.

To validate that the MM is really cached, run Code 32 with @Force_Refresh = 0. It will return very quickly, almost immediately, with the ModelID column filled as 27.

```
DECLARE @Force_Refresh BIT=0 --0=Will return model if it exists.
                             --1=Will recalculate the MM even if it exists.
SELECT
        ModelID,Event1A,EventB,
        [Max],[Avg],[Min],[StDev],CoefVar,[Sum],
        [Rows],Prob,IsEntry,IsExit
FROM dbo.[MarkovProcess](
        0,'websitepages',0,NULL,NULL,NULL,1,NULL,NULL,NULL, @Force_Refresh)
```

Code 32: Retrieve MM we hope is actually cached.

Next, try Code 32 again, but this time set @Force_Refresh=1. This flag will compute the MM even if it exists. This is helpful in case we suspect data has changed. It will take more time—from slightly longer to much longer, depending on the volume of events—and ModelID will be NULL again, indicating what is return is not re-computed MM.

Create a Code for the Transform

Now that we see how to create and cache a basic MM, let's utilize the next feature—a transform, which we saw a little earlier in "Markov with Transforms." In that example (Code 30), we set a variable, @FM_Transforms, to a rather verbose JSON of the set of transforms.

To avoid that verbose JSON each time we run a query, let's make life a little easier by creating a transform that we can use again and again.

Code 33 shows the code to do that. First, we see the JSON variable, @FM_transforms, set as before. We also define a code (a unique name, @Code='*arnold*') and a description.

```
DECLARE @FM_Transforms NVARCHAR(1000)='{"arnold1":"arnold","arnold2":"arnold",
"keto1":"dietpage","weightwatcher1":"dietpage","vanproteinbars":"proteinbars","chocp
roteinbars":"proteinbars"}'
DECLARE @Code NVARCHAR(20)='arnold' -- Code or name for the transform.
--@Description is a natural language description of the transform.
DECLARE @Description NVARCHAR(500)='merge different arnolds and combine keto,
weightwatchers to dietpage'
DECLARE @Transformskey VARBINARY(16)
EXEC [dbo].[UpdateTransform] @FM_Transforms, @Code,@Description, @Transformskey
OUTPUT

--Prints out: 0x903FBEFEFB94CFAD7968D8501583AFAC
PRINT @TransformsKey

--Display current transforms.
SELECT transformskey, transforms,Code, CreateDate FROM Transforms
```

Code 33: Create a transform name "arnold."

The last line of Code 33 displays the currently existing transforms. The first row of Figure 39 shows the transform we just created.

transformskey	transforms	Code	Description
0x903FBEFEFB94CFAD7968...	{"arnold1":"arnold","arnold2":"arnol...	arnold	merge different arnolds a...
0xC770BBCA21A3457DA37A9...	{"heavytraffic":"traffic","moderatetr...	NULL	NULL
0xCABA46EC39DAF9D421E4...	{"arnold1":"arnold","arnold2":"arnol...	NULL	NULL
0xCD3D15AFB1CCD3EAF4E7...	{"heavytraffic":"traffic", "moderatet...	merge-heavy-mod	NULL

Figure 39: Transforms.

Notes for the first row of Figure 39.

- The transformkey, 0x903FBEFEFB94CFAD7968..., is a hash for the transforms sorted by the elements key. That means the transforms can be in the JSON in any order, as a convenience for the user.

- The Description column could be vectorized and stored in a vector database to robustly find the transform, either using the vector database's capability or an LLM.

We can test that the transform key will be the same if we change the order of the transform elements—as shown in Figure 40. The variable, @FM_Transforms_1, is set to the same list, but in a different order.

```
--Switch the order of the transform elements.
SET @FM_Transforms_1 ='{"chocproteinbars":"proteinbars","arnold1":"arnold",
"keto1":"dietpage","weightwatcher1":"dietpage","vanproteinbars":"proteinbars",
"arnold2":"arnold"
}'
SELECT dbo.TransformsKey(@FM_Transforms_1)
--Prints out: 0x903FBEFEFB94CFAD7968D8501583AFAC
```

	(No column name)
1	0x903FBEFEFB94CFAD7968D8501583AFAC

Figure 40: Get the same transform key even if the order changes.

The JSON resolves to the same transform key as we saw back in Figure 39. This ensures that what is essentially the same set of elements is consistently recognized as the same set.

Cache the Markov Model with Transforms

With our arnold transform saved with simple code, let's see how it works. Code 34 will first create and save an MM for the websitepages set with the arnold transform. Then it will return the segments of the created MM.

```
--Cache the Markov Model with the arnold and dietpage transforms.
EXEC CreateUpdateMarkovProcess NULL,
'websitepages',0,NULL,NULL,'arnold',1,NULL,NULL,NULL
--Query the website pages event set with the arnold transform that we just created.
SELECT
	ModelID,Event1A,EventB,
	[Max],[Avg],[Min],[StDev],CoefVar,[Sum],
	[Rows],Prob,IsEntry,IsExit,FromCache
FROM dbo.[MarkovProcess](0,'websitepages',0,NULL,NULL,'arnold',1,NULL,NULL,NULL,0)
```

Code 34: Save the query with the transforms and requery.

Figure 41 shows the MM that has a ModelID of 28, which is different from the previous ModelID 27 (Figure 38) since this model applies the arnold transform. Additionally, the values for the FromCache column are 1, stating the result is not an on-the-fly computation of a MM.

ModelID	Event1A	EventB	Max	Avg	Min	StDev	CoefVar	Sum	Rows	Prob	IsEntry	IsExit	FromCache
28	arnold	dietpage	3	3	3	0	0	6	2	0.6667	0	0	1
28	arnold	shoppmt	8.17	8.17	8.17	NULL	NULL	8.17	1	0.3333	0	0	1
28	cart	shoppmt	0.17	0.17	0.17	0	0	0.67	4	1	0	0	1
28	chocprotein	arnold	2	2	2	0	0	6	3	1	0	0	1
28	creditcard	dietpage	2	2	2	NULL	NULL	2	1	0.25	0	0	1
28	creditcard	receipt	0.75	0.75	0.75	0	0	2.25	3	0.75	0	1	1
28	dietpage	dietpage	2	2	2	NULL	NULL	2	1	0.1667	0	0	1
28	dietpage	proteinbars	4	3.6	2	0.89	0.25	18	5	0.8333	0	0	1
28	homepage	chocprotein	1	1	1	0	0	3	3	0.6	1	0	1
28	homepage	dietpage	6	5	4	1.41	0.28	10	2	0.4	1	0	1
28	proteinbars	cart	1	0.82	0.08	0.41	0.5	4.08	5	1	0	1	1
28	shoppmt	abandon...	1.83	1.83	1.83	NULL	NULL	1.83	1	0.2	0	1	1
28	shoppmt	creditcard	1.83	1.83	1.83	0	0	7.33	4	0.8	0	0	1

Figure 41: Result from query with the arnold transforms. ModelID=28.

Create a Focused Model

In many analyses, we don't always need to account for every detail or intermediate step in a process. Sometimes, we might want a simplified view with just a few events included. This is what I call a "focused model." In other words, it's an MM created from a subset of an event set.

A focused model is a MM that focuses solely on selected events, omitting intermediate events. This allows us to simplify the analysis by reducing complexity and concentrating only on the key transitions we care about. One analogy might be the ability to zoom in and zoom out of the MM just as you would zoom in and out of a road map to look at higher or lower-level views.

For instance, when analyzing a restaurant customer service cycle, we might be interested in:

- The total time a customer spends at the restaurant, from arrival to departure.
- The length of time a diner is seated at a table until they leave.
- Just the times between when an order is placed, when it is served, and when the customer departs.

By creating focused models for each of these scenarios, we gain valuable insights into specific aspects of the process without being distracted by unnecessary details—either in between selected events and/or before or after certain events. The following section provides examples and results that illustrate how focused models streamline our understanding of key transitions.

For example, Code 35 shows three queries with different event sets related to serving guests at a restaurant. Note that we're specifying ad-hoc comma-separated lists of events.

```
--We're not interested in the details. We want to check the average of time
customers spend in the restaurant.

--1. Length of time, begin to end.
SELECT ModelID,Event1A,EventB,[Max],[Avg],[Min],[StDev],CoefVar,[Sum],
       [Rows],Prob,IsEntry,IsExit,FromCache
FROM dbo.[MarkovProcess](0, 'arrive,depart' ,1,NULL,NULL,NULL,1,NULL,NULL,NULL,1)

--2. From the time the party is seated until they depart.
SELECT ModelID,Event1A,EventB,[Max],[Avg],[Min],[StDev],CoefVar,[Sum],
       [Rows],Prob,IsEntry,IsExit,FromCache
FROM dbo.[MarkovProcess](0, 'seated,depart' ,1,NULL,NULL,NULL,1,NULL,NULL,NULL,1)

--3. From the time the party orders to the time they are served.
SELECT ModelID,Event1A,EventB,[Max],[Avg],[Min],[StDev],CoefVar,[Sum],
       [Rows],Prob,IsEntry,IsExit,FromCache
FROM dbo.[MarkovProcess](0, 'order,served' ,1,NULL,NULL,NULL,1,NULL,NULL,NULL,1)
```

Code 35: Three focused model results.

Figure 42 shows the results of the three queries:

1. **arrive->depart:** This measures how long a visit by diners lasts. In this case, an average visit lasts an average of 58.6 minutes with a standard deviation of 32.2256—meaning most visits last between roughly 30 to 90 minutes. A probability of 1 means, fortunately, every customer who arrived has departed.
2. **seated->depart:** This measures how long a diner typically occupies the table. In this case, they are seated for an average of about 56 minutes with a standard deviation of 26.9395—meaning most are seated for between about 30 to 90 minutes. This is just a little less than #1. The good news is that customers who arrive are generally seated pretty quickly.
3. **order->served:** This measures how long it takes for an order to arrive at the table. In this case, that's an average of about 19 minutes with a standard deviation of 8.0409—meaning most orders are processed between 11 to 27 minutes. That's not bad.

ModelID	Event1A	EventB	Max	Avg	Min	StDev	CoefVar	Sum	Rows	Prob	IsEntry	IsExit	FromCache
NULL	arrive	depart	110	58.6	5	32.2256	0.55	586	10	1	10	10	0

ModelID	Event1A	EventB	Max	Avg	Min	StDev	CoefVar	Sum	Rows	Prob	IsEntry	IsExit	FromCache
NULL	seated	depart	99.5	56.3611	4	26.9395	0.478	507.25	9	1	9	9	0

ModelID	Event1A	EventB	Max	Avg	Min	StDev	CoefVar	Sum	Rows	Prob	IsEntry	IsExit	FromCache
NULL	order	served	35	19.1771	9	8.0409	0.419	153.416666	8	1	8	8	0

Figure 42: Three focused model results.

Find Models by Selected Properties

Before analyzing MMs, we need the ability to search for models that meet specific criteria—like slicing and dicing OLAP cubes. For that, we have the *ModelsByParameters* TVF, which provides a way to programmatically search for models in the MME. By passing parameters such as event sets, date ranges, and filter properties, users can retrieve their desired models. For example, MMs can be filtered based on a variety of properties and characteristics, including:

- **Event Sets:** Specific sequences of events the model describes (leavehome, heavytraffic, arrivework).
- **Date Ranges:** Timeframes when the models were created or applicable.
- **Metrics:** The measurement used in the model, such as time between events or other metrics like fuel consumption.
- **Case-Level and Event-Level Properties:** Filters based on metadata about the cases or events the models represent (e.g., customer demographics or event-specific details).
- **Transforms and Model Types:** Additional configurations or types of models to match specific analytical goals.

Code 36 is an example. It finds all the saved MMs using the restaurantguest event set, and filters for cases with the property, EmployeeID=1—specified in the CaseProperties parameter as '{"EmployeeID":1}'

```
--Get models with the event set and CaseFilterProperties.
SELECT ModelID, CaseFilterProperties
FROM [dbo].[ModelsByParameters]
    ('restaurantguest', 0, NULL, NULL, NULL, 1, NULL,'{"EmployeeID":1}', NULL, NULL,
NULL)
```

Code 36: Find models by selected properties.

Figure 43 shows that three models exist for cases sliced by EmployeeID 1 in three different ways.

ModelID	CaseFilterProperties
5	{"EmployeeID":1,"LocationID":1}
6	{"EmployeeID":1,"CustomerID":2,"LocationID":1}
7	{"EmployeeID":1,"CustomerID":2}

Figure 43: Two models that were sliced by EmployeeID=1.

Alternatively, we could return the events of models using the *ModelEventsByProperty* TVF. Code 37 retrieves the events for models. Note that the parameters for the ModelEventsByProperty and ModelsByProperty TVFs are the same.

```
--Display Model details.
SELECT *
      FROM [dbo].[ModelEventsByProperty]('restaurantguest', 0, NULL, NULL, NULL, 1,
NULL,'{"EmployeeID":1}', NULL, NULL)
WHERE ModelID IN (5,7)
```

Code 37: Get model events for ModelIDs 5 and 7.

Figure 44 is a partial view of the event segments comprising ModelID 5 and the first few of ModelID 7.

ModelID	EventA	EventB	Max	Avg	Min	Sum	Rows	Prob	IsEntry	IsExit	Metric
5	arrive	greeted	16	10.5	5	21	2	1	1	0	Time Between
5	bigtip	depart	4.98	4.98	4.98	4.98	1	1	0	1	Time Between
5	charged	bigtip	0.02	0.02	0.02	0.02	1	0.5	0	0	Time Between
5	charged	depart	20	20	20	20	1	0.5	0	1	Time Between
5	check	charged	5	5	5	10	2	1	0	0	Time Between
5	drinks	order	5	3.5	2	7	2	1	0	0	Time Between
5	greeted	seated	0.75	0.63	0.5	1.25	2	1	0	0	Time Between
5	intro	drinks	3	2	1	4	2	1	0	0	Time Between
5	order	served	20	14.5	9	29	2	1	0	0	Time Between
5	seated	intro	1.5	1.38	1.25	2.75	2	1	0	0	Time Between
5	served	check	20	17.5	15	35	2	1	0	0	Time Between
7	arrive	greeted	5	5	5	5	1	1	1	0	Time Between
7	bigtip	depart	4.98	4.98	4.98	4.98	1	1	0	1	Time Between
7	charged	bigtip	0.02	0.02	0.02	0.02	1	1	0	0	Time Between
7	check	charged	5	5	5	5	1	1	0	0	Time Between
7	drinks	order	5	5	5	5	1	1	0	0	Time Between
7	greeted	seated	0.5	0.5	0.5	0.5	1	1	0	0	Time Between
7	intro	drinks	3	3	3	3	1	1	0	0	Time Between

Figure 44: Event segments for ModelID 5 and the first few of ModelID 7.

Figure 45 is a graphic view of ModelIDs 5 and 7, just to show how two models sliced differently might look.

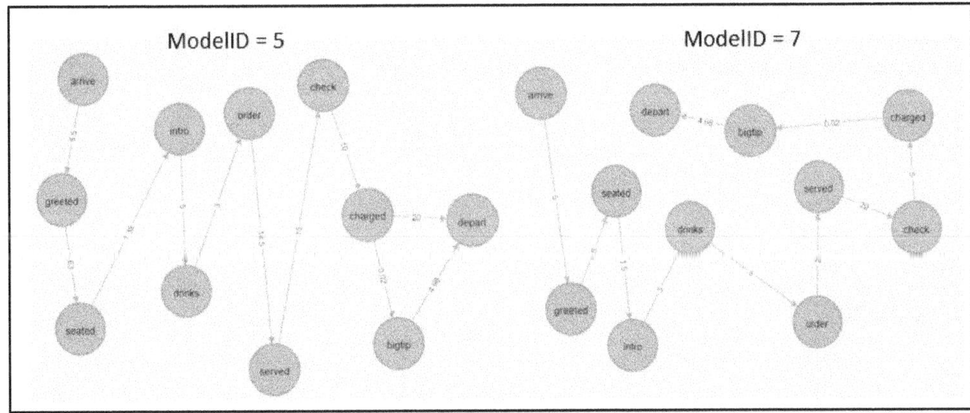

Figure 45: Graphic view of ModelID 5 and 7.

Find Models by Different Metric

We could also find MMs that are the same but for a different metric. Code 38 creates two models that only differ by metric—"Fuel" and "Time Between."

```
EXEC CreateUpdateMarkovProcess
        NULL,'leavehome,heavytraffic,lighttraffic,arrivework' ,
        0,NULL,NULL,NULL,1,'Fuel',NULL,NULL

EXEC CreateUpdateMarkovProcess
        NULL,'leavehome,heavytraffic,lighttraffic,arrivework' ,

        0,NULL,NULL,NULL,1,'Time Between',NULL,NULL
```

Code 38: Code that created two models only differing my metric.

Code 39 will find the two models with the event set specified Code 38, but all metrics.

```
DECLARE @Metric NVARCHAR(50)=NULL --NULL means all metrics.
SELECT *
FROM
        [dbo].[ModelEventsByProperty](
                'leavehome,heavytraffic,lighttraffic,arrivework', 0, NULL,
                NULL, NULL, 1, @Metric, NULL, NULL, NULL)
```

Code 39: Code that retrieves the two models created with Code 37.

Figure 46 shows events for both models we just created with Code 39.

ModelID	EventA	EventB	Max	Avg	Min	Sum	Rows	Prob	IsEntry	IsExit	Metric
12	heavytraffic	arrivework	-8	-10.57	-16	-74	7	1	0	1	Fuel
12	leavehome	arrivework	-4	-5.4	-7	-27	5	0.2941	1	1	Fuel
12	leavehome	heavytraffic	-1	-1.13	-2	-9	8	0.4706	1	1	Fuel
12	leavehome	lighttraffic	-0.5	-1.38	-2	-5.5	4	0.2353	1	0	Fuel
12	lighttraffic	arrivework	-2	-2.63	-3	-10.5	4	1	0	1	Fuel
13	heavytraffic	arrivework	52	45.86	41	321	7	1	0	1	Time Between
13	leavehome	arrivework	48	44.4	38	222	5	0.2941	1	1	Time Between
13	leavehome	heavytraffic	15	11	10	88	8	0.4706	1	1	Time Between
13	leavehome	lighttraffic	10	8	3	32	4	0.2353	1	0	Time Between
13	lighttraffic	arrivework	40	30.75	26	123	4	1	0	1	Time Between

Figure 46: Results from Code 39.

Alternatively, we could filter on a specific metric. Code 40 shows the code for finding just the model with the Fuel metric.

```
DECLARE @Metric NVARCHAR(50)='Fuel'
SELECT *
FROM
       [dbo].[ModelEventsByProperty](
              'leavehome,heavytraffic,lighttraffic,arrivework', 0, NULL,
              NULL, NULL, 1, @Metric, NULL, NULL, NULL)
```

Code 40: Code that retrieves only the model for Fuel.

Model Changes Across Dimensions

Dicing across dimensions is a fundamental BI concept, enabling the analysis of data from different perspectives to uncover trends, patterns, or anomalies. Arguably, the most basic yet most impactful application of this concept is dicing across the time dimension—which is great since this is, after all, *Time* Molecules. In the context of MMs, this involves comparing models generated for different time periods to understand how processes evolve over time.

By examining MMs across time dices—such as days, months, or years—we can capture changes in transition probabilities, uncover shifts in behavior, and identify periods of growing volatility or stability. This capability is especially powerful in complex domains like finance, where market dynamics can vary significantly across time, driven by factors such as economic trends, news events, or policy changes.

Code 41 demonstrates how MMs can be used to analyze changes in stock market behavior over time by examining daily transitions between different states of day-to-day stock price movements of MSFT. Each model represents a time period along the time dimension, capturing the probabilities of transitioning from one event to another, such as "Big Drop," "Big Jump," or "No Move."

These events are defined by thresholds for day-to-day changes in the stock price, with 3% serving as the cutoff for defining what “Big” means in terms of significant gains or losses. Anything below this threshold is categorized as "No Move." By comparing the probabilities across these time periods, shifts in market dynamics could surface to our attention.

```
DECLARE @StockEventSet NVARCHAR(50)='Big Drop-3%,No Move,Big Jump+3%'
DECLARE @Metric NVARCHAR(10)='Close'
DECLARE @Stock NVARCHAR(20)='{"Stock":"MSFT"}'
--Day to Day events for the year 2000.
SELECT Event1A,EventB,[Rows],[Prob],[Max] FROM dbo.[MarkovProcess](
   1, @StockEventSet,0,'01-01-2000','12-31-2000',NULL,1,@Metric,@Stock,NULL,0)
--Day to Day events for the year 2008.
SELECT Event1A,EventB,[Rows],[Prob],[Max]  FROM dbo.[MarkovProcess](
   1, @StockEventSet,0,'01-01-2008','12-31-2008',NULL,1,@Metric,@Stock,NULL,0)
```

Code 41: Analyze MSFT Close over two different years.

Figure 47 shows a comparison of the Markov models for 2000 and 2008.

MSFT Close - 2000

Event1A	EventB	Rows	Prob	Max
Big Drop-3%	Big Drop-3%	3	0.0789	-0.06
Big Drop-3%	Big Jump+3%	2	0.0526	0.05
Big Drop-3%	No Move	33	0.8684	0.03
Big Jump+3%	Big Drop-3%	6	0.2	-0.03
Big Jump+3%	Big Jump+3%	3	0.1	0.07
Big Jump+3%	No Move	21	0.7	0.03
No Move	Big Drop-3%	29	0.1585	-0.03
No Move	Big Jump+3%	25	0.1366	0.2
No Move	No Move	129	0.7049	0.03

MSFT Close - 2008

Event1A	EventB	Rows	Prob	Max
Big Drop-3%	Big Drop-3%	8	0.2581	-0.04
Big Drop-3%	Big Jump+3%	8	0.2581	0.19
Big Drop-3%	No Move	15	0.4839	0.03
Big Jump+3%	Big Drop-3%	6	0.2222	-0.03
Big Jump+3%	Big Jump+3%	4	0.1481	0.06
Big Jump+3%	No Move	17	0.6296	0.03
No Move	Big Drop-3%	17	0.0876	-0.03
No Move	Big Jump+3%	15	0.0773	0.06
No Move	No Move	162	0.8351	0.03

Figure 47: Markov models for MSFT day-to-day closing price changes for 2000 and 2008.

The transition probabilities in the 2000 period show different patterns compared to the latter 2008 period, likely reflecting variations in the market conditions, sentiment, or external factors influencing stock prices—i.e., the stock market crash around 2008.

Notably, the "No Move" to "No Move" day-to-day changes (bottom row) dominate in both periods, but other transitions exhibit changes in magnitude, suggesting shifts in the frequency and nature of large price swings. For example, the first row, Big Drop→Big Drop, moved from 0.0789 in 2000, tripling to 0.2581 in 2008—much more volatile.

Such insights can be critical for understanding how market behavior evolves over time, whether due to broader economic trends, company-specific events, or investor reactions. This type of analysis provides valuable information for traders, analysts, and researchers seeking to adapt strategies to changing market conditions or to forecast future behaviors.

Model Drillthrough

Drillthrough refers to the process of moving from summarized or aggregated results to the underlying detailed data—for Time Molecules, that means the events of the EventsFact table—from which the summary was calculated. In the context MMs, this means examining the individual events that contribute to a particular segment or transition.

To demonstrate drillthrough, we first need to find model event segments to drillthrough to. Code 42 creates a new MM for us to play with—*restaurantguest* event set, sliced by EmployeeID 1 and LocationID 1.

```
--This should be ModelID=5, which is referenced in the book.
DECLARE @ModelID INT
EXEC CreateUpdateMarkovProcess @ModelID OUTPUT,
      'restaurantguest',0,NULL,NULL,
      NULL,1,NULL,'{"EmployeeID":1,"LocationID":1}',NULL
--Display segments of the Markov Model we just created.
SELECT
      [ModelID],[EventA],[EventB]
      ,[Max],[Avg],[Min],[StDev],[CoefVar],[Sum]
      ,[Rows],[Prob],[IsEntry],[IsExit]
FROM [dbo].[ModelEvents]
                              WHERE Modelid=@ModelID
```

Code 42: Code that created ModelId=4.

Figure 48 shows the event segments of the MM we created with Code 42.

ModelID	EventA	EventB	Max	Avg	Min	StDev	CoefVar	Sum	Rows	Prob	IsEntry	IsExit
5	arrive	greeted	16	10.5	5	7.78	0.74	21	2	1	1	0
5	bigtip	depart	4.98	4.98	4.98	NULL	NULL	4.98	1	1	0	1
5	charged	bigtip	0.02	0.02	0.02	NULL	NULL	0.02	1	0.5	0	0
5	charged	depart	20	20	20	NULL	NULL	20	1	0.5	0	1
5	check	charged	5	5	5	0	0	10	2	1	0	0
5	drinks	order	5	3.5	2	2.12	0.61	7	2	1	0	0
5	greeted	seated	0.75	0.63	0.5	0.18	0.28	1.25	2	1	0	0
5	intro	drinks	3	2	1	1.41	0.71	4	2	1	0	0
5	order	served	20	14.5	9	7.78	0.54	29	2	1	0	0
5	seated	intro	1.5	1.38	1.25	0.18	0.13	2.75	2	1	0	0
5	served	check	20	17.5	15	3.54	0.2	35	2	1	0	0

Figure 48: Segments for ModelID=4 we just created

Looking at the first row of Figure 48, we see that the time between *arrive→greeted* averages 10.5 minutes. That's not good at all. We need to investigate by looking at the raw events that make up this segment.

Code 43 uses the ModelDrillThrough TVF to find all event facts that make up the arrive->greeted segment of ModelID 5.

```
--Retrieve events that make up the segment greeted->seated in ModelID=5.
SELECT CaseID,EventA,EventB,EventDate_A,EventDate_B,[Minutes],[Rank]
FROM ModelDrillThrough(5,'arrive','greeted')
```

Code 43: Events that make up the segment greeted->seated for ModelID 5.

Figure 49 shows two events from two different cases that make up *the arrive->greeted* segment of the ModelID 5. CaseID 2 takes 16 minutes to be greeted, drastically skewing the average in a terrible way. Something went wrong for the poor customer.

CaseID	EventA	EventB	EventDate_A	EventDate_B	Minutes	Rank
1	arrive	greeted	2023-01-01 17:00:00.000	2023-01-01 17:05:00.000	5	2
2	arrive	greeted	2023-01-01 17:00:00.000	2023-01-01 17:16:00.000	16	2

Figure 49: Two events from two cases make up segment greeted->seated in ModelID=5.

Lateral Intersegment Event Scan

As we just saw, when analyzing a segment of an MM, we may notice outlier time gaps between events that are significantly longer than expected. But what happened during that period between those events that aren't directly related to any of the cases? These are what I call "lateral intersegment events."

Lateral intersegment events are events outside of the MM cases that occurred between the times of a segment—even if they are not part of the MM. Understanding lateral intersegment events allows for a wider view for analysis by connecting MM insights with broader event context, offering clues to the causes of process inefficiencies or external influences.

For instance, let's say we've drilled through to the segment lv-csv1->homedepot1 for ModelID 29, we might discover a particular case where the transition took unexpectedly longer than others. That's what is causing the anomaly. But why? What other events occurred during this time that might explain the delay?

Let's start with the drill through. Code 44 returns the events that make up the segment lv-csv1->homedepot1 for ModelID 24.

```
SELECT * FROM ModelDrillThrough(24,'lv-csv1','homedepot1')
```

Code 44: Drillthrough to segment we wish to investigate.

Figure 50 shows that two rows make up that segment. Note that the minutes for the first row is more than the second row (50 vs 40).

CaseID	EventA	EventB	EventDate_A	EventDate_B	Minutes	Rank	EventOccurence	EventA_ID	EventB_ID
29	lv-csv1	homedepot1	2023-03-11 09:25:00.000	2023-03-11 10:15:00.000	50	8	1	158	160
30	lv-csv1	homedepot1	2023-03-12 09:35:00.000	2023-03-12 10:15:00.000	40	8	1	171	173

Figure 50: Two rows that make up the segment lv-csv1->homedepot1 for ModelID=29.

However, to investigate further, Code 45 retrieves all events that occurred during the time gap between the lv-csv1→homedepot1 segment for CaseID 24 (the offending segment). This includes any unrelated or unexpected events logged in the system, such as a heavytraffic event, which might explain why the transition took longer on a specific date.

```
SELECT CaseID, EventID, Event, EventDate
FROM dbo.[IntersegmentEvents](24,'lv-csv1','homedepot1')
```

Code 45: Return all events between 2023-03-11 9:25:00 and 2023-03-11 10:15,

Figure 51 shows that on 2023-03-11 between 9:25 and 10:15, an event of heavytraffic was logged around the location. It's an event completely unrelated to Model 24. That may or may not explain why it took 50 minutes on 2023-3-11, but it's at least a clue.

CaseID	EventID	Event	EventDate
-1	99021	heavytraffic	2023-03-11 09:26:00.000

Figure 51: Heavy traffic was logged, which lead to delays.

Note that the heavytraffic event is part of the commute event set, whereas Model 24 is part of the pickuproute event set.

Understanding lateral intersegment events connects the modeled process to the broader reality it lives in. Without them, we risk over-interpreting anomalies as internal failures, when they may actually be caused by external influences—like traffic, outages, or scheduled system events. These insights help bridge the gap between what the model sees and what actually happened, offering a more complete picture for diagnosing delays and improving processes.

Rare Events

Rare events in the context of MMs include extreme outlier transitions that exhibit behavior significantly different and infrequent from the norm, such as once unimaginable time gaps between expected events or metrics five or so standard deviations out. These anomalies bring unpredicted risks to light that were not captured within the defined event set of the model.

Rare events can sometimes align with the concept of Black Swan[5] events, popularized by Nassim Nicholas Taleb, which describe highly impactful, rare, and rather unpredictable occurrences. Even if we are aware of the possibility of such an event, they are so unlikely we don't include them in our plans. For example, a system designed to model delivery routes probably doesn't account for an earthquake shutting down critical infrastructure, resulting in unusually long delivery times at best to delivery being rendered impossible. Similarly, a factory process could be delayed by weeks from a sudden power outage caused by a regional grid failure—an event outside the scope of the expected or at least otherwise reasonable parameters of a workflow.

While Black Swan events are unpredictable and often beyond what systems are designed to handle, identifying intersegment events logged during these gaps can shed light on the context needed to understand their impact. These insights enrich the analysis, connecting MM outputs with broader real-world phenomena that drive deviations in process performance.

Model Event Anomalies – The EventPairAnomalies Table

As we saw in Model Drillthrough, identifying anomalies such as outlier values is a staple of analysis. However, instead of searching for these anomalies, we could automatically identify and store them.

The EventPairAnomalies table is designed to store and manage well-defined anomalies detected in transitions between events within MMs. These anomalies highlight unexpected or irregular behaviors in processes, such as transitions taking significantly longer than expected or occurring with unusually low probability. By analyzing these deviations, the table provides valuable insights into inefficiencies or potential issues within workflows.

---

[5] Taleb, N. N. (2007). The Black Swan: The Impact of the Highly Improbable. Random House.

This table captures detailed information about each anomaly, including the specific event pair (EventA→EventB), the associated MM, and the cases where the anomalies occurred. It also records statistical indicators, such as z-scores for metric deviations or unusually low transition probabilities, which quantify the extent of the anomaly. Metadata about the events, such as whether they are entry or exit points in a process, adds further context for interpretation.

The information stored in the EventPairAnomalies table is particularly useful for identifying root causes of inefficiencies and optimizing processes. By linking anomalies back to their contributing events, users can drill down to investigate patterns, make adjustments, and refine models. This makes the table a critical tool for ensuring the accuracy and reliability of TimeSolution's MMs while supporting continuous improvement in process analysis.

Code 46 retrieves anomalies for ModelID 1.

```
DECLARE @ModelID INT = 1
SELECT
      [CaseID], [AnomalyCode], [EventA], [EventB],
      MetricAvg, MetricStDev, metric_value, metric_zscore,
      [transistion_prob]
FROM
      ModelEventAnomalies(@ModelID)
```

Code 46: Anomalies for ModelID 1.

Figure 52 shows all the event segments across the cases involved with ModelID 1. We see two values under the AnomalyCode column:

1. **Metric Outlier:** This particular segment for the Case is an outlier. For example, Row 1, arrive->greeted for CaseID 2 is an outlier.
   - The metric_value of 16 means the customer waited for 16 minutes to be greeted, versus an average of 7.38 minutes.
   - The metric_zscore is the most informative column. In this case, the value of 16 is 1.7 standard deviations from the mean.

2. **Low Prob:** This is a segment that has a low probability for ModelID 1. For example, Row 3, arrive->seated (a customer seating himself directly) is a relatively rare occurrence. The transition_prob column shows it happens only 10% of the time.

	CaseID	AnomalyCode	EventA	EventB	MetricAvg	MetricStDev	metric_value	metric_zscore	transistion_prob
1	2	Metric Outlier	arrive	greeted	7.38	5.07	16	1.7015	NULL
2	4	Metric Outlier	order	served	19.18	8.04	35	1.9678	NULL
3	6	Low Prob	arrive	seated	1	NULL	1	NULL	0.1
4	7	Low Prob	arrive	depart	5	NULL	5	NULL	0.1
5	8	Metric Outlier	arrive	greeted	7.38	5.07	15	1.5042	NULL
6	8	Metric Outlier	greeted	seated	1.72	2.19	5	1.5015	NULL
7	9	Metric Outlier	charged	depart	13.2	13.01	33	1.5222	NULL
8	9	Metric Outlier	greeted	seated	1.72	2.19	5.5	1.7303	NULL
9	9	Metric Outlier	served	check	22.71	8.06	40	2.1456	NULL
10	10	Metric Outlier	seated	intro	1.43	0.98	3.5	2.11	NULL

Figure 52: Event Anomalies involved with ModelID=1.

It's interesting to note that in statistics, discarding outliers as "noise" is the typical practice. That's very valid since the models are intended to *generalize* the norm, whereas outliers skew what normally happens. However, because outliers are rare, we usually don't adequately prepare for them (as we discussed in Rare Events). Therefore, outliers are often associated with over-sized consequences—which could come with existential risks that must be directly addressed in an open-minded, logical, and data-driven manner.

Enumerate Multiple_Event Occurrences

The *@enumerate_mult_events* parameter addresses a common challenge in process modeling: differentiating events that occur multiple times within a single case. Typically, if an event happens repeatedly, in a MM it's treated as circling back to the same event. However, not all repeated events are equivalent—they may occur for different reasons, necessitating differentiation. This is particularly important when the context or handling of the repeated event changes over time.

For instance, in a restaurant scenario, a customer might have multiple credit card declines during their visit. Each declined attempt could be handled differently— the first attempt may lead to retrying with the same card, while the second attempt involves escalating to a different payment method (cash, someone else pays)—by the third, it's time to pay with dishwashing. By enumerating these occurrences, such as ccdeclined1 and ccdeclined2, the system can capture these distinctions and reflect them in the process model.

@enumerate_multiple_events is either a 0 or NULL, meaning not to enumerate, or a number from 1 through some max occurrences. If occurrences for an event exceed @enumerate_multiple_events, all subsequent events will be placed on the last one.

Code 47 is an example of the restaurantguest event set. We set @enumerate_mult_events to 3. That means any event that repeats in a case sequence will be renamed to xxx, xxx1, xxx2, and all repeats after that are xxx2 as well.

```
DECLARE @enumerate_mult_events INT=3
SELECT Event1A, EventB,[Rows],Prob,[IsEntry],[IsExit],[Max],[Min],[StDev],[Avg]
FROM dbo.[MarkovProcess](
   0,'restaurantguest',@enumerate_mult_events,NULL,NULL,NULL,1,NULL,NULL,NULL,0)
ORDER BY [OrdinalMean]
```

Code 47: Create Markov model, but enumerate multiple occurrences of events.

The results of Code 47 are shown in Figure 53.

	Event1A	EventB	Rows	Prob	IsEntry	IsExit	Max	Min	StDev	Avg
1	arrive	depart	1	0.1	1	1	5	5	NULL	5
2	arrive	greeted	8	0.8	1	0	16	3	5.07	7.38
3	arrive	seated	1	0.1	1	0	1	1	NULL	1
4	greeted	seated	8	1	0	0	5.5	0.5	2.19	1.72
5	seated	depart	1	0.1111	0	1	4	4	NULL	4
6	seated	intro	8	0.8889	0	0	3.5	0.25	0.98	1.43
7	intro	drinks	7	0.875	0	0	3.25	1	0.78	2.75
8	intro	order	1	0.125	0	0	0.17	0.17	NULL	0.17
9	drinks	order	7	1	0	0	5	1	1.73	4
10	order	served	8	1	0	0	35	9	8.04	19.18
11	served	depart	1	0.125	0	1	20	20	NULL	20
12	served	check	7	0.875	0	0	40	15	8.06	22.71
13	check	charged	7	1	0	0	5	2	1.13	4.43
14	charged	bigtip	1	0.1429	0	0	0.02	0.02	NULL	0.02
15	charged	ccdeclined	1	0.1429	0	0	1	1	NULL	1
16	charged	depart	5	0.7143	0	1	33	3	13.01	13.2
17	bigtip	depart	1	1	0	1	4.98	4.98	NULL	4.98
18	ccdeclined	charged1	1	1	0	0	2	2	NULL	2
19	charged1	depart	1	1	0	1	7	7	NULL	7

Figure 53: Markov model for enumeration of multiple event occurrences.

The highlighted line (15) in Figure 53 shows one row where the customer was charged and the credit card declined (see ccdeclined in line 18). The customer was given the opportunity to provide another credit card. That event was renamed to charged1. Apparently, that 2nd card went through since we don't see a charged2 event.

Figure 54 illustrates a graphical view of the MM for that restaurant guest process, emphasizing how multiple occurrences of events (like charged) are differentiated. This graphical representation provides insight into the flow of events and how unique transitions are handled when events repeat within a case:

1. **Initial Charging Attempt (charged):** After the customer is served and transitions to check, the process moves to an event labeled charged. This represents the first attempt to process the payment. We can see that most of the time (0.7143), the charge is successful and the customer departs.

2. **Credit Card Declined (ccdeclined):** Following the initial charge, the credit card is declined. This is logged as a separate event (ccdeclined), highlighting a failure in the transaction process.

3. **Second Charging Attempt (charged1):** After the card is declined, another charging attempt is made (charged1—with another credit card). This event is treated as distinct from the first charging attempt (charged) to reflect the unique circumstances of handling the declined payment and retrying. This situation accounts for a minority of the cases—0.1429 probability of the credit card being declined.

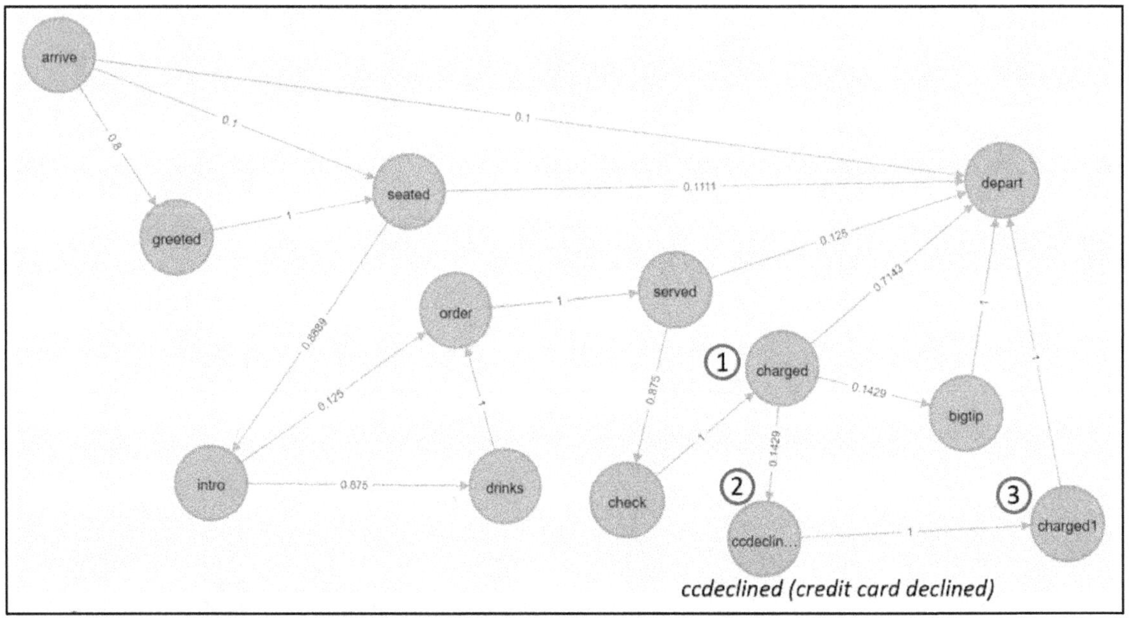

Figure 54: Markov model separating the initial charge with the 2nd charge.

Probabilities for all Sequences

The Sequences feature of Time Molecules complements MMs by capturing unique event paths. But not just full event paths, but every progressive segment from the start of each case through each new event. While MMs focus on state-to-state transitions and their probabilities, Sequences track the evolving path of events, allowing for analysis of how the history of a case influences what happens next. This creates a layered map of process behavior, revealing patterns that single-hop models might miss. However, calculating sequences in this way is usually much more computationally intensive than for MMs. The number of unique sequences grows exponentially with the number of events in the event set, especially when enumerating multiple occurrences of events within a case. For example, while the restaurantguest event set contains only 13 distinct events, the number of unique sequences across the cases can be much greater than that, particularly when accounting for repeated or reordered events. Code 48 shows how to use the Sequences TVF to analyze all sequences, across all cases, in the restaurantguest event set.

```
--Return all sequences CONTAINING the set of events in restaurantguest.
SELECT [Seq], lastEvent, nextEvent, SeqAvg, SeqStDev, [Rows], [Prob], ExitRows,
Cases
FROM dbo.[Sequences]('restaurantguest',1,NULL,NULL,NULL,1,NULL,NULL,NULL,1)
```

Code 48: Sequences of the restaurantguest event set.

Figure 55 shows the first few sequences returned by Code 48 starting from the beginning (arrive). Each line shows how each progressed.

- **Seq:** Comma-separated list of the sequence of events.
- **lastEvent:** Last event of the sequence.
- **nextEvent:** The event that comes after the last event of the sequence.
- **SeqAvg**: The time (in minutes) from the beginning of the sequence (arrive) through the nextEvent.
- **SeqStDev:** The standard deviation in minutes.
- **Rows:** The number of times this segment appears across cases.
- **Prob:** The probability of the lastEvent branching to the nextEvent. In this case, we see arrive branches to depart (1 time), greeted (8 times), and seated (1 time).
- **ExitRows:** For the restaurantguest event set, depart is the last event of the sequence.
- **Cases:** The number of cases that followed this sequence from the beginning to the last event (lastEvent).

Seq	lastEvent	nextEvent	SeqAvg	SeqStDev	Rows	Prob	ExitRows	Cases
arrive	arrive	depart	5	NULL	1	0.1	1	1
arrive	arrive	greeted	6.11666666666667	3.6815	8	0.8	NULL	8
arrive	arrive	seated	1	NULL	1	0.1	NULL	1
arrive,greeted	greeted	seated	7.83333333333333	5.3032	8	1	NULL	8
arrive,seated	seated	depart	5	NULL	1	1	1	1
arrive,greeted,seated	seated	intro	9.26666666666667	4.6876	8	1	NULL	8
arrive,greeted,seated,intro	intro	drinks	11.2833333333333	2.2147	7	0.875	NULL	7
arrive,greeted,seated,intro	intro	order	20.5833333333333	NULL	1	0.125	NULL	1
arrive,greeted,seated,intro,drinks	drinks	order	15.1333333333333	0.378	7	1	NULL	7
arrive,greeted,seated,intro,order	order	served	30	NULL	1	1	NULL	1
arrive,greeted,seated,intro,drinks,order	order	served	33.5666666666667	3.7796	7	1	NULL	7
arrive,greeted,seated,intro,order,served	served	depart	50	NULL	1	1	1	1

Figure 55: First few sequences for restaurantguest.

Things to note in Figure 55:

- The first row shows that, in one case, a guest arrived (lastEvent columns) but departed (nextEvent column) after five minutes.
- Three different things happened after the guests arrived:
  1. They departed (after five minutes).
  2. They were greeted after an average of about six minutes (2nd row). This happened in 8 cases.
  3. They just seated themselves. Their party was probably already seated, so they walked right in. Or perhaps there is a bar.
- The last row shows that in one case, the party was served, but departed without paying.

Whereas Code 48 above showed time spans from the beginning of the sequence through nextEvent, Code 49 shows the time spans from the last hop—lastEvent to nextEvent. Note that Code 48 and Code 49 are the same except for the selected list of columns.

```
SELECT [Seq], lastEvent, nextEvent,HopStDev, HopAvg, HopStDev/HopAvg AS
HopCoefVar,[Rows]
    FROM dbo.[Sequences]('restaurantguest',1,NULL,NULL,NULL,1,NULL,NULL,NULL,1)
```

Code 49: Timing for lastEvent to nextEvent. That is a hop.

Figure 56 shows the results. The highlighted row (6) shows statistics on the hop between the *seated* and *intro* events—at least when preceded by arrive, greeted, and seated. We can see that the average time across the eight rows is 1.4167 minutes with a standard deviation of 0.9824. The coefficient of variation for the hop is 0.69, which is a fairly wide range of times, indicating inconsistent service. In contrast to row 6, row 11 has a smaller value of 0.368 coefficient of variation, indicating more consistent service.

	Seq	lastEvent	nextEvent	HopStDev	HopAvg	HopCoefVar	Rows
1	arrive	arrive	depart	NULL	5	NULL	1
2	arrive	arrive	greeted	5.0692	7.3667	0.688123583151207	8
3	arrive	arrive	seated	NULL	1	NULL	1
4	arrive,greeted	greeted	seated	2.1853	1.7167	1.27296557348401	8
5	arrive,seated	seated	depart	NULL	4	NULL	1
6	arrive,greeted,seated	seated	intro	0.9824	1.4167	0.693442507235124	8
7	arrive,greeted,seated,intro	intro	drinks	0.7773	2.75	0.282654545454545	7
8	arrive,greeted,seated,intro	intro	order	NULL	0.1667	NULL	1
9	arrive,greeted,seated,intro,drinks	drinks	order	1.7321	4	0.433025	7
10	arrive,greeted,seated,intro,order	order	served	NULL	9.4167	NULL	1
11	arrive,greeted,seated,intro,drinks,order	order	served	7.5687	20.5667	0.368007507281188	7
12	arrive,greeted,seated,intro,order,served	served	depart	NULL	20	NULL	1
13	arrive,greeted,seated,intro,drinks,order,served	served	check	8.0563	22.7	0.354903083700441	7

Figure 56: Hop timing.

Predict Next Event

Predicting the next event in a real-time operational setting is the most conventional use case for MMs. It enables systems to anticipate actions based on current conditions, providing analytical insights for improving efficiency, optimizing processes, or mitigating potential issues.

In the TimeSolution, events and their associated probabilities are stored in such a way that they can be queried dynamically, allowing for rapid decision-making in an operational environment. To enable this, the system must ensure that every event can be reliably mapped to its source configured in DimEvents, providing a clear link between the operational data and the Time Molecules framework. Code 50 demonstrates how to predict what is likely to happen next after a specific event. In this case, it's a customer being served their meal. Using the MarkovProcess TVF with a WHERE clause, the system evaluates the possible outcomes for the given event, returning probabilities for each potential next event.

```
DECLARE @NextEvent_EventSet NVARCHAR(100)='restaurantguest'
DECLARE @CurrentEvent NVARCHAR(20)='served'

SELECT ModelID,Event1A,EventB,[Max],[Avg],[Min],[StDev],CoefVar,[Sum],[Rows],Prob
FROM dbo.[MarkovProcess](0,@NextEvent_EventSet,1,NULL,NULL,NULL,1,NULL,NULL,NULL,0)
WHERE
    Event1A=@CurrentEvent
```

Code 50: Predict the next event after being served their meal for operations.

The results, as shown in Figure 57, reveal a 0.125 probability that a customer will depart after being served—a scenario that might indicate dissatisfaction or other "operational issues". By measuring the risk of such outcomes in real time, businesses can intervene proactively.

ModelID	Event1A	EventB	Max	Avg	Min	StDev	CoefVar	Sum	Rows	Prob
1	served	check	40	22.71	15	8.06	0.35	159	7	0.875
1	served	depart	20	20	20	NULL	NULL	20	1	0.125

Figure 57: Predicted next events after being served their meal.

The MMs can be as specific as the case properties and event properties enable. For example, Code 50 shows how to return the probability for events after the served event for EmployeeID.

```
DECLARE @NextEvent_EventSet NVARCHAR(100)='restaurantguest'
DECLARE @CurrentEvent NVARCHAR(20)='served'
DECLARE @CaseFilterProperties NVARCHAR(100)='{"EmployeeID":1}'
SELECT
        ModelID,Event1A,EventB,[Max],[Avg],[Min],[StDev],CoefVar,[Sum],[Rows],Prob
FROM dbo.[MarkovProcess](
    0,@NextEvent_EventSet,1,NULL,NULL,NULL,1,NULL,@CaseFilterProperties,NULL,0)
WHERE
    Event1A=@CurrentEvent
```

Code 51: Predict next event after being served their meal for operations.

Figure 58 shows the results of Code 51. The data holds only one such occurrence. In this case, there is one event for EmployeeID 1, which transitioned from served→check. All is well for EmployeeID 1.

ModelID	Event1A	EventB	Max	Avg	Min	StDev	CoefVar	Sum	Rows	Prob
NULL	served	check	20	20	20	NULL	NULL	20	1	1

Figure 58: After a particular customer is served by a particular employee.

Advanced Time Molecules Analytics Topics

While basic use cases of MMs focus on straightforward transitions and metrics, such as time between events and probabilities from one event to the next, advanced use cases dive deeper into the nuances and complexities of process analytics. These advanced techniques extend beyond simple event-to-event relationships to include higher-order dependencies, changes across dimensions like time or location, and confidence metrics for model validation.

For instance, higher-order MMs consider the probability of a particular event, not just the previous event but a sequence of preceding events, capturing richer contextual information. Similarly, analyzing how MMs change across dimensions or periods allows for dynamic insights into evolving processes. This section explores these and other advanced use cases, offering tools and methodologies to refine and enhance the applicability of Time Molecules to intricate real-world scenarios.

Higher Order Markov Models

At a restaurant, once you've paid the bill, the next logical step is to leave. At that moment, your decision to leave depends only on the fact that you've paid the bill, not on everything that happened earlier, like what you ordered, how long you waited for your food, or whether you enjoyed the meal. These earlier events might have shaped how you got to the point of paying, but they usually no longer affect what happens next.

Now, in rare cases, something unusual might happen—maybe earlier, your waiter brought you the wrong meal. So, the next step isn't that you leave, but you're given a coupon and make happy talk with the waiter. In this case, the "exception" breaks the Markov property because the prior event of not paying reintroduces past context. However, in the vast majority of cases, the Markov property is held because the immediate past (paying the bill) contains all the relevant information needed to decide what happens next (leaving the restaurant).

In a standard 1st-order MM, the probability for the next event depends only on the current event. This is the essence of the Markov Property, where the future event is conditionally independent of events prior to the most recent one. However, in a higher-order MM, the next event depends on the previous t events, allowing the model to incorporate a longer sequence of past events for predicting future outcomes. Normally, t is set to 1—we consider only the last event. By increasing the value of t, the model adds more context to its predictions, capturing more nuanced relationships between events. For example, in a 2nd-order MM, the prediction of the next event is influenced by the last two events rather than just the most recent one.

MMs, by default, analyze transitions over a single time step to balance computational efficiency and generalizability. Extending the scope to higher orders or longer time spans significantly increases the complexity of the model, as the number of possible combinations of prior events quickly expands. This can lead to increased computational costs and the risk of overfitting, where the model becomes overly tailored (over trained) to specific sequences rather than capturing broader, generalizable patterns. The default one-prior-event transition thus provides a practical starting point, ensuring both efficiency and broad applicability, while higher-order models can be employed selectively to reveal richer insights where needed.

That said, higher-order MMs are best suited for processes with relatively short event sets, where a small number of events cycles repeated—usually over time, some period-to-period cycle, for example, hour-to-hour or day-to-day. For instance:

- A weather system with daily events like sunny, rainy, and cloudy weather benefits from higher-order modeling because the likelihood of future weather conditions is more plausibly dependent on patterns observed over the previous days.
- A business model with states like big sales, bad sales, and ok sales might similarly gain predictive power from incorporating recent trends (momentum from the past few days).

However, for processes with large event sets with irregular intervals between events, higher-order MMs are usually less practical. Processes tend to involve a larger number of distinct events, and the relationships between events are typically governed by rules or workflows rather than cyclic or recurring trends. For example, in our familiar restaurant process, the sequence *arrive → seated → order → served → check → depart* reflects a logical flow of events. A 1st-order MM can effectively capture the probability of each step in this flow without requiring the added complexity of higher orders.

In such cases, a 1st-order MM is sufficient to provide meaningful insights into transition probabilities while maintaining computational efficiency. Higher-order models may still have value in specialized scenarios, but their utility diminishes as the event set grows and the process becomes more linear or rule-driven.

Code 52 generates a first-order MM, followed by a 2nd-order MM of MSFT's day-to-day stock closing price movement for the year 2000.

```
DECLARE @StockEventSetHO NVARCHAR(50)='Big Drop-3%,No Move,Big Jump+3%'
DECLARE @MetricHO NVARCHAR(10)='Close'
DECLARE @StockHO NVARCHAR(20)='{"Stock":"MSFT"}'

DECLARE @level INT=1 --1st-order Markov model.
SELECT Event1A,EventB,[Rows],[Prob],round([Max],2) as [Max]
FROM dbo.[MarkovProcess](@level,
   @StockEventSetHO,0,'01-01-2000','12-31-2000',NULL,1,@MetricHO,@StockHO,NULL,0  )
ORDER BY Event2A,EventB

SET @level=2 --2nd-order Markov model.
SELECT Event1A,Event2A,EventB,[Rows],[Prob],round([Max],2) as [Max]
FROM dbo.[MarkovProcess](@level,
   @StockEventSetHO,0,'01-01-2000','12-31-2000',NULL,1,@MetricHO,@StockHO,NULL,0   )
ORDER BY Event2A,EventB
```

Code 52: High order Markov model comparison.

Figure 59 shows the results of the two queries in Code 52, comparing one-day and two-day MMs for MSFT's closing prices:

1. The table on the left illustrates the one-day model, where each row represents the probability of transitioning from Event1A→EventB on the following day. For instance, the first row shows that the probability of experiencing a "Big Drop" one day after a previous "Big Drop" is 0.0789.
2. The table on the right illustrates the partial results of a two-day MM, which accounts for both two days prior (Event1A→Event2A). Here, the probabilities for a "Big Drop" differ significantly depending on the combined context of the prior two days. For example, if two days ago there was a "Big Jump" (Event1A) and one day ago there was a "Big Drop" (Event2A), the probability of another "Big Drop" (EventB) is 0.1667, which is quite different from the single-day model's prediction.

MSFT Close – One Day (1)

	Event1A	EventB	Rows	Prob	Max
1	Big Drop-3%	Big Drop-3%	3	0.0789	-0.06
2	Big Jump+3%	Big Drop-3%	6	0.2	-0.03
3	No Move	Big Drop-3%	29	0.1585	-0.03
4	No Move	Big Jump+3%	25	0.1366	0.2
5	Big Jump+3%	Big Jump+3%	3	0.1	0.07
6	Big Drop-3%	Big Jump+3%	2	0.0526	0.05
7	Big Drop-3%	No Move	33	0.8684	0.03
8	Big Jump+3%	No Move	21	0.7	0.03
9	No Move	No Move	129	0.7049	0.03

MSFT Close – 2 Days (2)

	Event1A	Event2A	EventB	Rows	Prob	Max
1	Big Jump+3%	Big Drop-3%	Big Drop-3%	1	0.1667	-0.06
2	No Move	Big Drop-3%	Big Drop-3%	2	0.069	-0.07
3	No Move	Big Drop-3%	Big Jump+3%	1	0.0345	0.04
4	Big Drop-3%	Big Drop-3%	Big Jump+3%	1	0.3333	0.05
5	Big Drop-3%	Big Drop-3%	No Move	2	0.6667	0.02
6	Big Jump+3%	Big Drop-3%	No Move	5	0.8333	0.02
7	No Move	Big Drop-3%	No Move	26	0.8966	0.03
8	No Move	Big Jump+...	Big Drop-3%	5	0.2	-0.03
9	Big Jump+3%	Big Jump+...	Big Drop-3%	1	0.3333	-0.05
10	Big Drop-3%	Big Jump+...	Big Jump+3%	1	0.5	0.07
11	No Move	Big Jump+...	Big Jump+3%	2	0.08	0.05
12	No Move	Big Jump+...	No Move	18	0.72	0.03

Figure 59: Compare one-day Markov model versus 2nd-order 2-day.

Markov Models of Time-Based Cases

In the context of MMs, a "case" typically represents a specific instance (interval, cycle) of a process being analyzed. Examples include a visit to a website, a game of poker, or a hospital stay—each providing an event set that defines the case. However, in BI and many other analytics applications, time introduces a unique dimension: units of time, such as a day, month, or year, can themselves be treated as "cases". Each time unit is like a separate bucket of events.

Time-based cases enable us to analyze recurring patterns over time, such as day-to-day traffic trends, month-to-month sales, or year-to-year wildlife population fluctuations. These are what we familiarly refer to as time series. This approach is particularly valuable for processes that naturally reset or evolve from one unit of time to the next, helping identify trends, seasonality, or long-term changes. For instance, examining traffic conditions across consecutive days can reveal how today's traffic influences tomorrow's, offering valuable insights for planning and decision-making.

The ByCase parameter of the MarkovProcess TVF determines how cases are defined:

- **ByCase** = **1**: This is the default setting—the mode used by all examples until now. Each process, instance, or case is treated individually, based on the CaseID. For example, in a shipping study, each trip might be treated as a distinct case.
- **ByCase** = **0**: This mode ignores individual CaseID values and treats all events as part of a single, overarching case broken up by some unit of time (days, months, or years)—a time series.

Code 53 demonstrates how MMs can be applied to time-based cases, focusing on daily transitions between traffic conditions such as "heavytraffic," "moderatetraffic," and "lighttraffic." In this example, each day is treated as a distinct case, while transitions across days are analyzed to predict future traffic patterns.

```
--[START Time Period Case Markov Models]
DECLARE @DD_EventSet NVARCHAR(1000)='heavytraffic,moderatetraffic,lighttraffic'
DECLARE @DD_ByCase BIT=0 --This means we ignore the CaseID.
SELECT Event1A, EventB, Prob, [Rows]
FROM dbo.[MarkovProcess](1, @DD_EventSet ,0,NULL,NULL,NULL,
@DD_ByCase,NULL,NULL,NULL,1)
```

Code 53: Markov model for commute to work.

Code 53 provides a Markov Process analysis for predicting day-to-day traffic patterns. Here's the breakdown of the elements:

- **Purpose:** Day-to-Day Traffic Predictions. The goal is to predict the likelihood of different types of traffic on a day-to-day basis, using historical data about previous traffic patterns.
- **ByCase variable:** The ByCase parameter is set to 0 (@DD_ByCase), meaning that each day is treated as a "case" or sequence. It spans all cases, meaning it looks at traffic patterns across all days.
- **EventSet variable:** The event set (@DD_EventSet) contains three traffic events: heavytraffic, moderatetraffic, lighttraffic

Figure 60 shows the results of Code 53.

Event1A	EventB	Prob	Rows
heavytraffic	heavytraffic	0.375	3
heavytraffic	lighttraffic	0.5	4
heavytraffic	moderatetraffic	0.125	1
lighttraffic	heavytraffic	0.75	3
lighttraffic	moderatetraffic	0.25	1
moderatetraffic	heavytraffic	0.25	1
moderatetraffic	moderatetraffic	0.75	3

Figure 60: Result of Code 53.

Result columns:

- Event1A and EventB represent the traffic conditions on two consecutive days.
- Prob is the calculated probability of transitioning from Event1A to EventB from one day to the next day.
- Rows indicate how many occurrences of this transition were found in the dataset, giving additional insight into the reliability of the probability.

Figure 61 shows a graphic visualization of the MM with the transition probabilities.

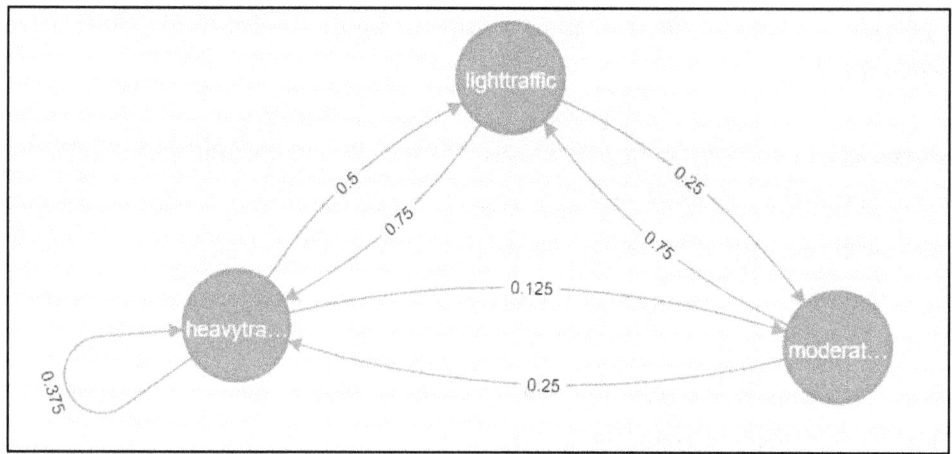

Figure 61: Graph view of the Markov model created from Code 53.

From the results, we can infer that:

- If today's traffic is heavytraffic, there is a:
    - 37.5% chance that tomorrow's traffic will also be heavytraffic.
    - 50% chance that tomorrow's traffic will be lighttraffic.
    - 12.5% chance that tomorrow's traffic will be moderatetraffic.
- If today's traffic is lighttraffic, there is a:
    - 75% chance of transitioning back to heavytraffic.
    - 25% chance of transitioning to moderatetraffic.

How do we determine the appropriate date interval to use? In the ETL process, events must be loaded into Time Molecules at the appropriate date granularity. For example, when analyzing events like traffic, weather, or stock prices with ByCase=0, it's important to decide how to calculate the value for each time period—whether it's an hour, day, month, or year. Consider the following examples:

- **Stock prices:** The closing price naturally represents the last non-empty value for the day.
- **Weather data:** The ETL process may need to aggregate observations at small intervals such as minute, 15-minute, or hour granularities. These readings must be interpreted into some representative value for each day—such as the mode (the most common weather condition) for the day.

- **Traffic data:** Since most people commute only once per day, one event should be submitted per day per commuter.
- **Monthly Wildlife Population:** One event loaded into Time Molecules holding the count of each species per month.

This ability to track metrics over time also supports a broader goal of bridging systems thinking with BI. When transition behavior begins to reinforce itself day over day or month over month—whether positively or negatively—we're no longer just observing processes, we could be observing a feedback loop. These dynamics are central to understanding how organizations behave and evolve at scale.

Markov Model Confidence and Support

Support and confidence are foundational metrics for evaluating the reliability and strength of any ML model, including MMs. These concepts, adapted from ML, help assess the frequency and predictability of transitions between events, providing decision-makers with robust insights for optimizing processes.

By integrating support and confidence into Time Molecules, businesses can gauge the reliability of predictions. Support is a metric of how often a transition occurs, while confidence assesses the likelihood of that transition given its context. Together, they offer a comprehensive understanding of process behavior, enabling more informed decisions.

Support

Support refers to the number of times a specific transition (EventA → EventB) occurs within the dataset. It's the difference between data of a few cases versus a more statistically reliable number of cases in the thousands to billions. We would think more of a statistic derived from millions of cases versus a few. It highlights the prevalence of transitions, helping analysts differentiate between frequent patterns and rare outliers.

For instance, in a sales cycle, a transition from inquiry to purchase might have high support, indicating it's a common part of the process, whereas a transition from complaint to lawsuit may have low support, marking it as a relatively rare occurrence.

In the SQL examples in this book, the Rows column represents support, capturing the count of occurrences for each transition. High support provides confidence that a transition reflects a meaningful pattern rather than an anomaly, making it a critical metric for assessing the relevance of MM insights.

Confidence

Confidence is the combination of several components. One of the primary components should be familiar by now. It's the probability of moving from EventA→EventB.

While probability is the key measure of confidence, its interpretation can be enriched by incorporating additional metrics, such as the Coefficient of Variation (CoefVar), to understand the consistency of associated metrics like time between events. For example, in customer service, if most customers transition from "issue reported" to "issue resolved" within a narrow time window, the confidence in this transition is kicked up a notch, indicating a high level of process optimization and/or automation efforts.

Additive Aspects of Markov Models

Additive metrics, such as rows and counts, play a very helpful role in the scalability and efficiency of MMs, particularly when dealing with distributed computation. Additive metrics allow for the aggregation of results from multiple MMs by simply adding the values—without requiring further detailed iteration through all individual event records. For example, if two separate datasets—say one MM sliced to Boise and another MM sliced to Honolulu—contain transitions between the same EventA→EventB pairs, the counts can simply be added together producing a consolidated view, bypassing the need to reprocess the superset of underlying events.

This property is especially valuable in a distributed computation platform similar to pre-aggregated OLAP cube environments, where data can be partitioned across multiple nodes or time slices for parallel processing. By relying on additive metrics, we can independently compute ranges of MMs and then simply combine the individual results to create a complete picture of the process. This not only saves significant computational resources, but also aligns with the principles of OLAP, where pre-aggregated sums and counts of data enables fast querying and analysis.

In the ModelEvents table, Sum and Rows are straightforwardly additive because they can be additively aggregated across multiple cases. Max and Min, aprinciplely additive, can be readily aggregated across MMs. For example, if two MMs have a Max value of 10, 15, we just take the greater (max) value of 15—we don't iterate through the entire data set.

Probability isn't directly additive, but it can be recomputed after additive metrics are combined. The probability of a given EventA→EventB transition is calculated as the count of that transition divided by the total number of transitions starting from EventA across all cases. If we add two MMs together, the new probability can be accurately recalculated using the aggregated row counts and sums for each EventA.

Figure 62 and Figure 63 provide an example. To combine insights across the Boise and Nampa restaurant locations, we can add the models in Figure 62 (sliced by Boise) and Figure 63 (sliced by Nampa). This additive property of MMs allows us to create a consolidated view of transitions across both locations without recalculating every individual event.

In Figure 62 (Boise), we observe the following:

- Total Rows = 10 (sum of transitions from arrive to depart, greeted, and seated).
- Probabilities reflect the distribution of transitions for the Boise location.

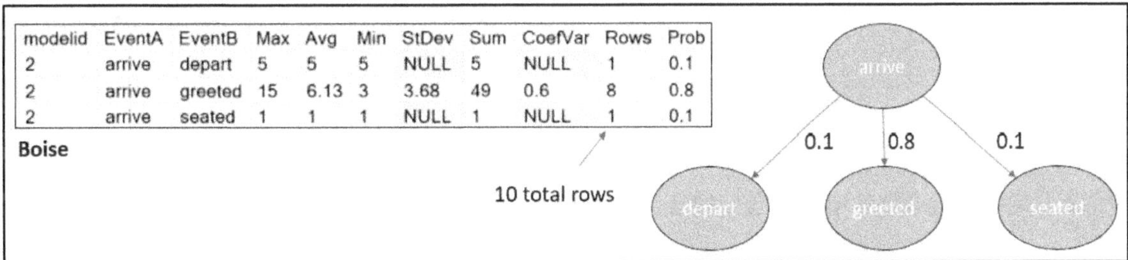

modelid	EventA	EventB	Max	Avg	Min	StDev	Sum	CoefVar	Rows	Prob
2	arrive	depart	5	5	5	NULL	5	NULL	1	0.1
2	arrive	greeted	15	6.13	3	3.68	49	0.6	8	0.8
2	arrive	seated	1	1	1	NULL	1	NULL	1	0.1

Figure 62: Probability for "arrive" event for a particular model. Let's say Boise.

Figure 63 (Nampa) introduces one additional row:

1. Total Rows = 11 after addition (10 from Boise + 1 from Nampa).
2. Transition counts for each event pair (arrive → greeted, etc.) are summed directly.
3. Added probabilities.

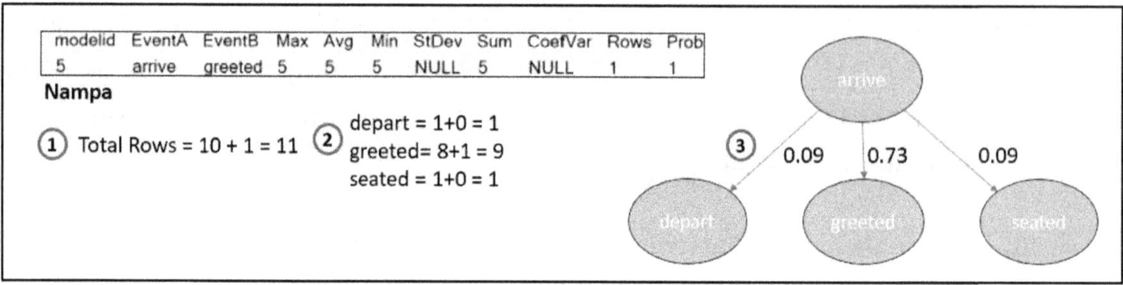

modelid	EventA	EventB	Max	Avg	Min	StDev	Sum	CoefVar	Rows	Prob
5	arrive	greeted	5	5	5	NULL	5	NULL	1	1

Figure 63: Add Model 5 (Nampa) to Model 2.

This ability to seamlessly aggregate MMs from different slices enables a unified analysis while maintaining computational efficiency.

However, it's important to note that when adding event pairs from different MMs, the underlying events should not overlap. Specifically, the cases used to compute each MM must be mutually exclusive. If any individual case appears in more than one MM, then the resulting metrics may be distorted. Additivity works when cases are cleanly separated by non-overlapping date ranges or by properties that uniquely partition the case population.

For example, if a model represents the year 2024 and another model represents November 2024, the events for November 2024 overlap with the MM for all of 2024. Adding the two models will result in November 2024 being double-counted. As the examples in Figures 62 and 63 show, case-level properties—in this case, cities, Boise and Nampa—effectively ensure mutual exclusiveness of the cases.

Non-Additive Metrics of Markov Models

While some MM metrics are additive and allow for simple aggregation across datasets, some metrics, such as standard deviation (StDev), are non-additive. This means that they cannot simply be combined from multiple models without re-iterating through the entire superset of events. Instead, MMs we wish to combine must be recomputed together to calculate an exact value. However, in some cases, the standard deviation, while very informative, isn't as critical for decision-making as sums and counts, which are additive, or probability, which can be readily calculated from counts.

StDev provides insight into the consistency or variability of the time between two events. A smaller StDev (or, better yet, a smaller Coefficient of Variation) indicates more reliability in the associated transition probabilities. For example, if the time between order_placed→order_fulfilled has a narrow StDev, we can trust the transition is fairly predictable—as opposed to wildly variable, which could indicate operational problems.

To address computational challenges, a weighted approximation of the standard deviation can be a reasonable stand-in for aggregated models. This enables high-level insights without requiring access to the raw event data, making it a practical, if not ideal, solution for scenarios where exact calculations are computationally prohibitive.

Details of this weighted standard deviation can be found in Appendix J – Weighted Standard Deviation Approximation.

Asynchronous Markov Model Creation

MM creation involves processing vast amounts of event data across multiple dimensions, time intervals, and filters. Generating models sequentially, one by one, for such datasets can quickly become time-prohibitive. By adopting an asynchronous approach, we can break this process into smaller, independent tasks that can run in parallel, significantly reducing the overall time required while ensuring optimal resource utilization.

The asynchronous method is particularly advantageous when working with distributed systems or analyzing data across different time periods (e.g., years, months, or days) and dimensions (e.g., product categories, regions, or customer segments). It allows the system to handle these tasks concurrently without waiting for one to finish before starting the next. This is essential for scenarios where both time efficiency and flexibility are critical.

Of course, with such compute distribution comes commensurate cost—but the option is there, especially on cloud platforms such as Snowflake.

This asynchronous approach on distributed databases brings several key benefits:

- **Scalability**: Models for different time intervals or dimensions can be generated independently, making the system adaptable to large datasets.
- **Efficiency**: By running tasks in parallel, computational and database resources are utilized to their full capacity, minimizing idle time.

- **Flexibility**: Users can tailor the analysis to specific time frames, dimensions, and filters without being constrained by sequential processing.

To dive deeper, the GitHub repository includes the Python script, tm_create_model_async.py. It's a simple but robust sample for handling asynchronous model creation and is an essential tool for scaling TimeSolution to real-world datasets.

CHAPTER 9

Bayesian Probabilities

Bayesian probability offers a structured approach to reasoning under uncertainty, making it a critical tool for businesses and analysts seeking actionable insights. Unlike conditional probability, which considers fixed probabilities, Bayesian probability incorporates prior knowledge (often subjective) or observations to continuously refine predictions based on new evidence. This dynamic updating makes it particularly relevant in analyzing processes where a situation evolves, such as customer journeys, financial trends, or operational workflows.

The value of Bayesian probability in the context of Time Molecules lies in its ability to evaluate the likelihood of one sequence of events occurring given the presence of another. For example, if customers typically go from arriving at a restaurant to being greeted by a friendly host, Bayesian methods can help determine the probability of them returning.

While this implementation focuses on calculating conditional probabilities rather than dynamically updating priors as in a truly Bayesian framework, it still provides essential insights for optimizing processes, predicting behaviors, and identifying key transition points. In practice, the relationships we model—whether using Bayesian, conditional, or statistical correlation measures like Pearson—ultimately produce a score between 0 and 1 (or -1 to 1), where values closer to 1 (or -1) represent stronger associations. For clarity and accessibility, this section refers to conditional probability, but the principles apply across methods.

The function described in this section exemplifies how Bayesian probability can be used to calculate conditional probabilities between event sequences, empowering users to measure the impact of one sequence on another and make data-driven improvements.

Later, we'll see how this Bayesian and/or conditional Probabilities feature connects with the Markov models, resulting in powerful Hidden Markov Models (HMM).

The BayesianProbability TVF encapsulates the logic for Bayesian probabilities. Code 54 is a sample that returns the probability of being offered drinks after arriving at the restaurant. In more "Bayesian" terms: Given that I arrive at the restaurant (Event A), what is the probability I will be offered drinks (Event B).

```
SELECT *
FROM
        dbo.BayesianProbability(
                'arrive', --Sequence 1 (sequence of 1 event).
                'drinks', --Sequence 2 (sequence of 1 event).
                'restaurantguest', --Event Set.
                NULL,NULL,NULL,NULL,NULL,NULL)
```

Code 54: What is the probability of customers ordering drinks?

Figure 64 shows the results of calculating the Bayesian probability of the event "arrive" (Event A) followed by "drinks" (Event B) within a set of events related to restaurant guests. The table indicates:

- Event A occurred 10 times (ACount), and Event B occurred 7 times (BCount).
- Both events occurred together 7 times (A_Int_BCount).
- Therefore, the conditional probability shows that Event B follows Event A with 70.0% likelihood (PA|B). In other words, customers arrived ten times—of those ten, seven had drinks.

ACount	BCount	A_Int_BCount	PB|A	PA|B	TotalCases	PA	PB
10	7	7	0.7	1	10	1	0.7

Figure 64: Result from Code 54.

However, notice that the first two parameters of the BayesianProbability TVF are referred to as "Sequence," not event. Code 55 shows that we can be more specific about the conditions, specifying sequences of events, not just one event. For this example, given that a customer was greeted by the host, seated by the host, and their server introduced himself, what is the probability of leaving a bigtip?

```
SELECT *
FROM
      dbo.BayesianProbability(
            'greeted,seated,intro', --Sequence 1 (sequence of three events)
            'bigtip', --Sequence 2 (sequence of 1 event)
            'restaurantguest', --Event Set.
            NULL,NULL,NULL,NULL,NULL,NULL)
```

Code 55: Probability of leaving a big tip.

Figure 65 shows the answer is 0.125 (one out of eight times). Given that a customer was greeted by the host and seated by the host, and their server introduced himself, what is the probability of leaving a bigtip?

ACount	BCount	A_Int_BCount	PB|A	PA|B	TotalCases	PA	PB
8	1	1	0.125	1	10	0.8	0.1

Figure 65: Probability of leaving a big tip.

BayesianProbabilities Table

The BayesianProbabilities table persists in the results generated by the BayesianProbability TVF, much like how MMs can persist in the MME. This table caches "sequence given another sequence" probabilities and related metrics, making them readily available for future analysis, reporting, or integration with other processes. As it is for caching MMs in the MME, by caching these probabilities, we avoid the need to repeatedly recompute Bayesian and/or conditional probabilities, saving computational resources and enabling seamless integration into workflows or dashboards.

This table is particularly useful in scenarios where understanding the relationship between sequences of events is crucial, such as identifying customer behavior patterns, diagnosing anomalies in processes, or predicting outcomes based on historical data. Each row in the table represents a comparison between two sequences (A and B) and includes key information such as the count of cases where these sequences occur, their intersection, and probabilities like P(B|A) and P(A|B)—the probability of EventB given EventB and the probability of EventA given EventB, respectively.

The BayesianProbabilities table supports different grouping type (GroupType column) types—CASEID, DAY, MONTH, YEAR—allowing for granular or aggregated analysis across various temporal dimensions. Additional metadata, such as CreateDate, LastUpdate, and anomaly categories

(AnomalyCategoryIDA and AnomalyCategoryIDB), provide context for when the probabilities were calculated and highlight potential issues or areas for further investigation.

We'll see how this table is populated later in the Tuple Correlation Web topic.

CHAPTER 10

Object Descriptions for LLM Integration

LLMs and Semantic Web technologies serve as versatile bridges from the Time Molecules world to the broader AI ecosystem. By integrating these advancements into the TimeSolution framework, we unlock new capabilities for interpreting, organizing, and enriching the data that drives MMs and other analytical processes. LLMs provide powerful contextual reasoning and natural language generation, while the Semantic Web offers structured, interoperable representations of knowledge—together forming a foundation for advanced system intelligence.

This section explores how LLMs and Semantic Web technologies enhance the TimeSolution by enabling richer insights and more effective interactions with its data. Specifically, we focus on two key areas where these technologies shine:

1. **Event Similarity Scoring**: Leveraging the natural language understanding of LLMs to evaluate semantic relationships between event types, revealing deeper connections that go beyond numerical analysis.
2. **Description Generation**: Utilizing LLMs to create meaningful metadata, summaries, and embeddings that enhance the searchability and utility of the complex TimeSolution objects, while aligning seamlessly with Semantic Web standards.

These integrations elevate Time Solution by:

- **Enhancing Metadata**: Automatically generated descriptions and similarity scores improve data organization and facilitate interoperability with tools like vector databases and Semantic Web technologies.

- **Providing Semantic Context**: LLM-driven insights into event relationships enable the ability to dig deeper for insights from process mining and systems thinking.
- **Streamlining Workflows**: Tailored metadata fine-tunes LLM capabilities, ensuring they can effectively analyze, interpret, and interact with your system.

At a conceptual level, MMs and LLMs share more in common than you might think. A higher-order MM, for example, resembles an *n*-gram model in NLP (predecessor of LLM), where the next word—or, in our case, event—depends on a short sequence of prior steps. And just as LLMs use transformer architectures to interpret tokens in context, TimeSolution slices event sets into context-specific MMs.

Generate Prompt for LLM Ratings of Events

The *PromptEventSimilarity* stored procedure generates a prompt for an LLM to score the semantic similarity between two events. By leveraging whatever information is available about the events in the TimeSolution, this procedure constructs a prompt that provides context and guides the LLM in evaluating their relationship. The similarity score can then be used in applications, such as a knowledge graph, to determine if the events can be equated—for example, through semantic web "is" or “sameAs” relationships.

In Code 56, we generate a prompt to evaluate the similarity between the events, “calls” and “checks.”

```
SELECT [dbo].[PromptEventSimilarity]('calls','checks',1,NULL,NULL,NULL)
```

Code 56: Generate an LLM prompt to test how similar two events are.

The result of Code 56 is shown in Code 57, which is a constructed LLM prompt to provide a similarity score between the two events.

```
On a scale of -1.0 to 1.0, -1.0 being perfect antonyms and 1.0 being the perfect synonyms,
how similar in semantics is “calls” (which often occurs with GameState-2, GameState-1,
SHOW DOWN, RIVER, TURN, FLOP, raises, small_blind, big_blind, NEW_GAME,
HOLE_CARDS) versus the word “checks” (which often occurrs with the words
GameState-2, GameState-1, SHOW DOWN, RIVER, TURN, raises, small_blind, big_blind,
HOLE_CARDS, NEW_GAME)? Return just the score with no explanation at all.
```

Code 57: Prompt to guess a similarity between calls and checks.

This prompt is a result of plugging in descriptions and other metadata in the TimeSolution into a template. We can see from the prompt that calls and checks seem to be in the context of poker. Note that the prompt in Code 57 includes:

- An explanation of the result.
- Context in the form of other event types it's often combined with.
- Instructions to just return the score. This way, you don't need to parse through all the explanations—even though those explanations would be valuable in certain contexts.

When I submitted the prompt to ChatGPT, it returned simply: *0.6*

I subsequently asked it to explain the score (which I think is fair):

*"The score of **0.6** reflects that **"calls"** and **"checks"** are **semantically similar** but not interchangeable. In poker, both actions are **non-aggressive ways to stay in the hand**, often occurring in similar game states (like RIVER, TURN, etc.), which explains their contextual closeness. However, "calls" typically responds to a **bet**, while "checks" means **no bet is made**—a subtle but important difference in intent and mechanics, which keeps them from being full synonyms."*

Let's do another example. Code 58 is very similar to Code 56. The difference is very subtle—we're referring to "check" (without an "s") versus "check*s*." "check" is an event in the context of our restaurantguest event set—the event of being given the bill for the meal. "calls" is the same, the event in the context of poker.

```
--checks versus check (no s), the latter being related to restaurants.
SELECT [dbo].[PromptEventSimilarity]('checks','check',1,NULL,NULL,NULL)
```

Code 58: Another attempt to rate similarity of two events using an LLM.

Code 59 is the prompt created by Code 58, which I will submit to ChatGPT.

The result from ChatGPT is *0.1*, a fair score—they are not in any way synonyms or antonyms, even though they are almost the same spelling. I validated this with ChatGPT, as shown in Figure 66.

```
On a scale of -1.0 to 1.0, -1.0 being perfect antonyms and 1.0 being the perfect synonyms,
how similar in semantics is "checks" (which often occurs with GameState-2, GameState-
1, SHOW DOWN, RIVER, TURN, raises, small_blind, big_blind, NEW_GAME,
HOLE_CARDS) versus the word "check" (which often occurrs with the words
order_queue, order_ready, order_received, order_start_prep, order_cook,
order_qlty_check, arrive, depart, drinks, greeted, intro, order, seated, served)? Return
just the score with no explanation at all.
```

Code 59: The prompt generated for us in response to Code 58.

please offer short explanation

The score of **0.1** reflects that "**checks**" (in the poker context) and "**check**" (in the restaurant or operations context) share the same root word but have **very different meanings** in practice. In poker, "checks" is a game action, while in a restaurant or workflow, "check" often refers to verification or a bill. They may both imply a kind of pause or evaluation, but their **semantic roles and usage contexts** are largely unrelated.

Figure 66: ChatGPT's explanation for the score.

Generate LLM Prompts for Generating Object Descriptions

The *Generate_LLM_Description_Prompts* stored procedure creates descriptive prompts for major objects in the TimeSolution framework that can be used with LLMs to generate detailed metadata. These descriptions enrich the system by providing meaningful context, which is useful for integration with Semantic Web technologies, robust vector databases querying, and LLM fine-tuning:

1. **Creates LLM Prompts**: Generates natural language prompts for LLMs to create concise and relevant descriptions for various objects within the TimeSolution framework.

2. **Includes Key TimeSolution Objects**: It supports the following TimeSolution entities:

    - **EventSets**: Groups of events that belong to specific processes or cases.
    - **Transforms**: Mappings of events to other events for better analysis and understanding.

- **Metrics**: Definitions of measurable values (time between events) with associated units.
- **Sources**: Information about data sources, including columns and properties.
- **SourceColumns**: Details about individual columns within a source, including their data type and role in a table.
- **Models**: Markov models with descriptions of transitions and properties for embedding or analysis.
- **CaseTypes**: Definitions of cases and their associated events.

3. **Enables Metadata Enhancement**: By generating and persisting descriptive LLM prompts, the procedure simplifies the enrichment of metadata with detailed object descriptions for searchability, analytics, and integrations in the TimeSolution.

The *Generate_LLM_Description_Prompts* procedure provides significant value by streamlining metadata creation, automating the generation of meaningful descriptions for system objects, and minimizing the manual effort needed to document and enhance metadata. Engaging with LLMs promotes the automation of maintaining consistent and high-quality descriptions across various entities, fostering greater system coherence.

The resultant LLM-generated descriptions can be embedded into a vector database for extremely versatile search or used to fine-tune LLMs with knowledge of the Time Solution. Additionally, the procedure supports Retrieval-Augmented Generation (RAG) by enriching datasets with structured metadata, making it easier for the RAG process to search for and retrieve insights, thereby enabling advanced AI-driven analytics and decision-making.

Code 60 begins a demonstration of how this works.

```
--The result of these prompts could be used as automatically-generated descriptions.
EXEC dbo.Generate_LLM_Description_Prompts
```

Code 60: Generate LLM prompts for the LLM to generate an object description.

Figure 67 is the partial result of Code 60.

Key	Table	Caption	Prompt
0x0888B97F18FEB280485557D2B0A778A6	EventSets	NULL	In 150 words or less, what is the context of leave...
0x0C9294682D92CC4CF747B36DE8AB499B	EventSets	NULL	In 150 words or less, what is the context of websi...
0x281CE40AD3A51DE5CAC588793498CBCA	EventSets	pokeractions	In 150 words or less, what is the context of raises...
0x384060D658FDAE2CB57186A008234AF6	EventSets	NULL	In 150 words or less, what is the context of arrive,...
0x510AB328E43FF6BA4BC5E6D10CD74AB2	EventSets	NULL	In 150 words or less, what is the context of arnold...
0x527C1854FE4C32C22484FAA8B87A7A10	EventSets	NULL	In 150 words or less, what is the context of restau...
0x5516AAD0BCE7F243D1ABA7374810FBB8	EventSets	poker	In 150 words or less, what is the context of NEW...
0x5D0816B650DD51E53E19B74C7771783F	EventSets	NULL	In 150 words or less, what is the context of poker...
0x6578313A71A8B642E194BEBA703F6AB9	EventSets	pokergamestates	In 150 words or less, what is the context of Game...
0x6CD99510BCA54729CBC41BBF6C6320C8	EventSets	NULL	In 150 words or less, what is the context of leave...
0x7447CED91DCCF7B553493E939027E522	EventSets	NULL	In 150 words or less, what is the context of heavy...
0x802DFFE5A341446AF7FD1E338FAFE937	EventSets	commute	In 150 words or less, what is the context of leave...
0x825604E51A843EE181BA50DC7DEDD5F8	EventSets	NULL	In 150 words or less, what is the context of arrive,...
0x8DCE23308B0F60FD22313BB8E0324D07	EventSets	pickuproute	In 150 words or less, what is the context of leave...

Figure 67: Partial result of the query in Code 60.

Note the highlighted line in Figure 67—an event set named pokeractions. Code 60 shows the automatically generated prompt (the Prompt column of the highlighted row in Figure 67). We will use this generated prompt to ask ChatGPT to generate a more "natural" summary-length description of the pokeractions event set.

```
In 150 words or less, please summarize raises,folds,calls,bets,checks Please omit any
alternatives and cautionary advice.
```

Code 61: Prompt to generate a good description of the pokeractions event set.

Code 62 is the result from ChatGPT to the prompt in Code 60. ChatGPT applied its innate knowledge of a massively broad range of topics—in this case, poker—to create a summary-length description of the event set that is readily comprehensible to a person.

```
In poker, raises increase the current bet, requiring other players to match or fold. A fold
occurs when a player exits the round and forfeits the pot. Calls match the current bet to
stay in the round. Bets place a new wager to initiate action. Checks allow passing the turn
without betting, only if no previous bets were made. These actions shape each round and
influence strategies, leading to the outcome of the hand.
```

Code 62: Summary of the pokeractions event set generated by ChatGPT.

Code 63 shows how we can update the description column of the EventSets table with the description created by ChatGpt.

```
UPDATE dbo.EventSets
SET
    [Description] = 'In poker, raises increase the current bet, requiring other
players to match or fold. A fold occurs when a player exits the round and forfeits
the pot. Calls match the current bet to stay in the round. Bets place a new wager to
initiate action. Checks allow passing the turn without betting, only if no previous
bets were made. These actions shape each round and influence strategies, leading to
the outcome of the hand.'
WHERE
    EventSetKey = 0x281CE40AD3A51DE5CAC588793498CBCA;
```

Code 63: Update the description.

The generated descriptions are directly helpful in enhancing RAG workflows and enabling advanced search capabilities when transformed into embeddings and stored in a vector database or fine-tuned into an LLM.

See *time_solution_generate_description_prompts.py* in the GitHub repository, which automates this process.

Model Descriptions

Let's go through the same exercise but for an MM instead of an event set. Prompts for MMs are also included in the results in Figure 67 above, even though we can't see them because Figure 67 shows just the first few rows. Figure 68 shows some of the rows for MMs—from the Models table.

	ID	HashKey	Table	Caption	Prompt
40	2	NULL	Models	NULL	In 150 words or less, for the purpose of creating useful embe...
41	3	NULL	Models	NULL	In 150 words or less, for the purpose of creating useful embe...
42	4	NULL	Models	NULL	In 150 words or less, for the purpose of creating useful embe...
43	5	NULL	Models	NULL	In 150 words or less, for the purpose of creating useful embe...
44	6	NULL	Models	NULL	In 150 words or less, for the purpose of creating useful embe...
45	7	NULL	Models	NULL	In 150 words or less, for the purpose of creating useful embe...
46	8	NULL	Models	NULL	In 150 words or less, for the purpose of creating useful embe...
47	9	NULL	Models	NULL	In 150 words or less, for the purpose of creating useful embe...
48	10	NULL	Models	NULL	In 150 words or less, for the purpose of creating useful embe...
49	11	NULL	Models	NULL	In 150 words or less, for the purpose of creating useful embe...
50	12	NULL	Models	NULL	In 150 words or less, for the purpose of creating useful embe...

Figure 68: LLM prompts to generate descriptions for models.

Note Row 33 (ModelID 5). The generated LLM prompt for that MM is shown in Code 64. The segments for the model are serialized as a string separated by vertical bars.

```
In 150 words or less, for the purpose of creating useful embeddings, what is this Markov model, properties (EmployeeID:1|LocationID:1) about: arrive-(1)->greeted|bigtip-(1)->depart|charged-(0.5)->bigtip|charged-(0.5)->depart|check-(1)->charged|drinks-(1)->order|greeted-(1)->seated|intro-(1)->drinks|order-(1)->served|seated-(1)->intro|served-(1)->check
```

Code 64: LLM prompts to generate a description for ModelID 5.

Code 65 shows ChatGPT's response to the prompt shown in Code 64. It is an automatically generated description for ModelID 5.

```
This Markov model outlines a typical restaurant service process, where an employee
(EmployeeID:1) serves a customer at a specific location (LocationID:1). Each state
represents a step in the dining experience, from arriving at the restaurant to departure.
Key transitions include being greeted upon arrival, ordering drinks, and eventually being
served. After being served, the customer moves to the payment stage, which can result in
being charged and either leaving a tip or departing. All transitions have probabilities of 1,
except for being charged, where there's a 50% chance the customer leaves a big tip or
departs. This model reflects a standard service workflow and can be embedded to
analyze employee-customer interactions, service efficiency, or tipping patterns based on
the observed events and their transitions.
```

Code 65: The description for ModelID 5 generated by ChatGPT.

Get Semantic Web and LLM Descriptions

Once you have descriptions set up for the TimeSolution objects, we can now create a consolidated file of those descriptions to feed into a vector database, incorporate into a knowledge graph, or fine-tune into an LLM.

The *get_semantic_web_llm_values* stored procedure complements the *Generate_LLM_Description_Prompts* by retrieving existing metadata and descriptions from the TimeSolution system. This procedure dynamically scans the database to identify tables, views, stored procedures, and other objects that contain descriptive metadata such as "Description" and "IRI" columns. It consolidates this information into a single, unified result set, making it easier to access, review, and use structured metadata.

This procedure is particularly valuable in scenarios where metadata plays a central role in system intelligence, such as integrating TimeSolution with Semantic Web technologies or vector databases for advanced analytics. In short, *get_semantic_web_llm_values* ensures that all relevant descriptive data from TimeSolution objects is centrally accessible, structured, and ready to be leveraged for downstream tasks like search, retrieval, and semantic analysis. Code 66 shows how to run this stored procedure.

```
EXEC get_semantic_web_llm_values
```

Code 66: Retrieve all descriptions for integration with Semantic Web or LLMs.

Figure 69 is a partial result from Code 66. Notice the description for the pokeractions event set we created earlier in the highlighted row. These results should be saved to a CSV file.

TableName	CodeColumn	Code	Description	IRI
DimEvents	Event	vanproteinbars	Vanilla protein bars product	NULL
DimEvents	Event	walmart1	Walmart event 1	NULL
DimEvents	Event	walmart2	Walmart event 2	NULL
DimEvents	Event	walmart3	Walmart event 3	NULL
DimEvents	Event	weightwatcher1	Weight Watcher event 1	NULL
EventSets	EventSetCode	pokeractions	In poker, raises increase the current bet, requiring other players to match or fold. A fold occurs when a p...	NULL
Sources	Name	PokerStars	PokerStars	NULL
Sources	Name	EventHub	Consolidated Event Hub	NULL
CaseTypes	Name	Meal	The process of serving a customer in a typical sit-down restarurant.	NULL
CaseTypes	Name	Truck Trip	A route of some delivery or pickup vehicle, such as a package delivery or a garbage truck pickup.	NULL
CaseTypes	Name	Commute to Work	Commute to Work	NULL
CaseTypes	Name	PokerGame	PokerGame	NULL

Figure 69: Descriptions of entities in the TimeSolution.

Encoding System Enterprise Data-Driven Information into LLMs

The examples in this chapter show how LLMs can describe metadata objects like event sets and models—but a broader possibility emerges when we look at the entire network of Time Molecules. Across the enterprise, millions of MMs and the relationships between tuples in the TCW represent an evolving map of how events and things relate. These individual structures—each a compressed summary of many cases or correlations—can be serialized into sequences suitable for fine-tuning or adapting a language model.

Just as LLMs "learn" language (at least the appearance of learning) by compressing the relationships between words and phrases across many documents into a dense, high-dimensional space, MMs compress relationships between events across many cases (examples of a process). Both are, in essence, sequence compression systems. These MMs can be easily transformed into natural-language statements or graph constructs (e.g., RDF/OWN, DOT Language), which become high-value fine-tuning material—embedding process logic and causal relationships—for LLMs.

CHAPTER 11

The Event Correlation Trio

Understanding complex systems requires a cohesive framework for reasoning that bridges inductive insights and deductive reasoning. Markov models, Bayesian probabilities, and correlations together provide such a framework, a tool for us to observe, infer, and predict with precision. These tools collectively navigate the spectrum of reasoning (inductive, deductive, and abductive), allowing us to uncover patterns and model processes and relationships, potentially performing abductive reasoning—the kind of reasoning Sherlock Holmes actually performs (it's incorrectly referred to in his books as deductive) about our complex world of imperfect and uncertain data.

In this chapter, the focus is more on inductive and deductive reasoning. However, we will lightly cover abductive reasoning in *Time Molecules in an Adversarial World.*

Inductive Reasoning - Correlations

Correlations are the bonds of inductive reasoning. It's about drawing general conclusions from a historic log of observations of some phenomenon—looking at how variables co-vary to infer patterns and relationships. For example, my cat learned over the course of days that when the coffee machine beeps that it's done, I'm pouring a cup and going back to my office.

By noticing these correlations, we move from the specific (data) to the generalized (a model capable of prediction). This inductive process underpins much of ML, whether it's in regression, classification, clustering, or association rules.

But when we start stitching together models that use probabilities to infer deeper structures, like with Markov models and Bayesian/Conditional probabilities, we get something richer than just inductive reasoning—we get the building blocks of deductive reasoning—and, as mentioned, the "creative" inference of abductive reasoning.

Markov Models - Inductive by Nature

MMs provide a form of inductive reasoning. They are built from observations of event or state transitions over time—they infer transition probabilities from logs of event data. As we mentioned about the Markov Property: the next event depends only on the last event, not the full sequence of past events. From this specific historical data, the MM generalizes how likely one event is to follow another.

For example, we can induce from events over our many days of living at our house that if we hear loud yelling from our neighbor, he's probably yelling at his dog to stop barking—which is usually even more disturbing than the barking. It's important to note that the MM does not explain *why* the owner yells after the dog barks—it just states that's a high probability.

Bayesian and Conditional Probabilities - A Hybrid Approach

Bayesian and conditional probabilities span inductive and deductive reasoning. On the inductive side, Bayesian inference updates our belief about an event as new evidence comes in. For example, if past weather data suggests that sunny days follow certain conditions and we observe those conditions, we may induce a high probability that tomorrow will be sunny. This process generalizes from past observations, continuously refining our understanding.

On the deductive side, once we have an updated belief (that tomorrow will be sunny), we can apply that information to make logical conclusions. If we accept the premise that a sunny day means the patio at our favorite restaurant will be open, we can deduce that we can wisely plan for an outdoor meal. This duality—learning inductively and applying deductively—is what makes Bayesian reasoning so powerful.

Hidden Markov Models - The Deductive Leap

When we combine Markov models and Bayesian or conditional probabilities (in this case, conditional probabilities), we get a Hidden Markov Model (HMM). The inductive side is still present because the transition probabilities in the MM and the emission probabilities (observing events emitted from hidden states—like the signals from a person's body language or facial expressions—are learned from data. But HMMs also introduce an element of deductive reasoning—once the model is trained, it's used to deduce the most likely sequence of hidden states given a sequence of observations.

Think of it like trying to infer someone's mood based on their text messages. The mood (Happy, Neutral, or Sad) is the hidden state, while the text messages you read are the observable emissions. A message like "I'm feeling great!" is likely emitted by the Happy state, whereas "Not a good day" likely comes from the Sad state. But we don't know—some people are more open than others.

Over a day, you might receive a series of messages like "I'm feeling great!" followed by "I'm doing fine." Using a trained HMM, you could infer that the person was likely in a Happy state and then transitioned to a Neutral state. The model doesn't directly see the mood—it deduces the most likely sequence of moods based on observed clues and learned probabilities.

In essence, an HMM uses inductive reasoning to infer the transition probabilities and emission probabilities, but the process of decoding hidden states from observed data is deductive. It's like solving a puzzle where the clues are probabilistic, and the solution requires piecing together both what you believe and what you observe.

Piecing It All Together: A Spectrum of Reasoning

With some background on inductive and deductive reasoning and HHMs, let's look at an example. Let's use a common example of Lulu attempting to predict Sadie's mood. Lulu realizes Sadie's mood is strongly influenced by the weather. Because Sadie calls Lulu every day, and it can be a short and pleasant or a long and troublesome one, it would help Lulu to figure out how much time to allocate to Sadie's call the next day.

Figure 70 illustrates a simple HMM that Lulu developed to solve her problem. The top part represents an MM—the black box part hidden from the Lulu—that shows the probabilities of transitioning between weather states (Sunny, Cloudy, or Rainy) where Sadie lives from one day to the next. The bottom part includes two nodes that represent the emotional states of Sadie—Happy or Sad—which are conditional on the weather for that day.

The connections between the weather nodes (top part) and the emotional state nodes (bottom part) show the conditional probability of Sadie being Happy or Sad, given the current weather.

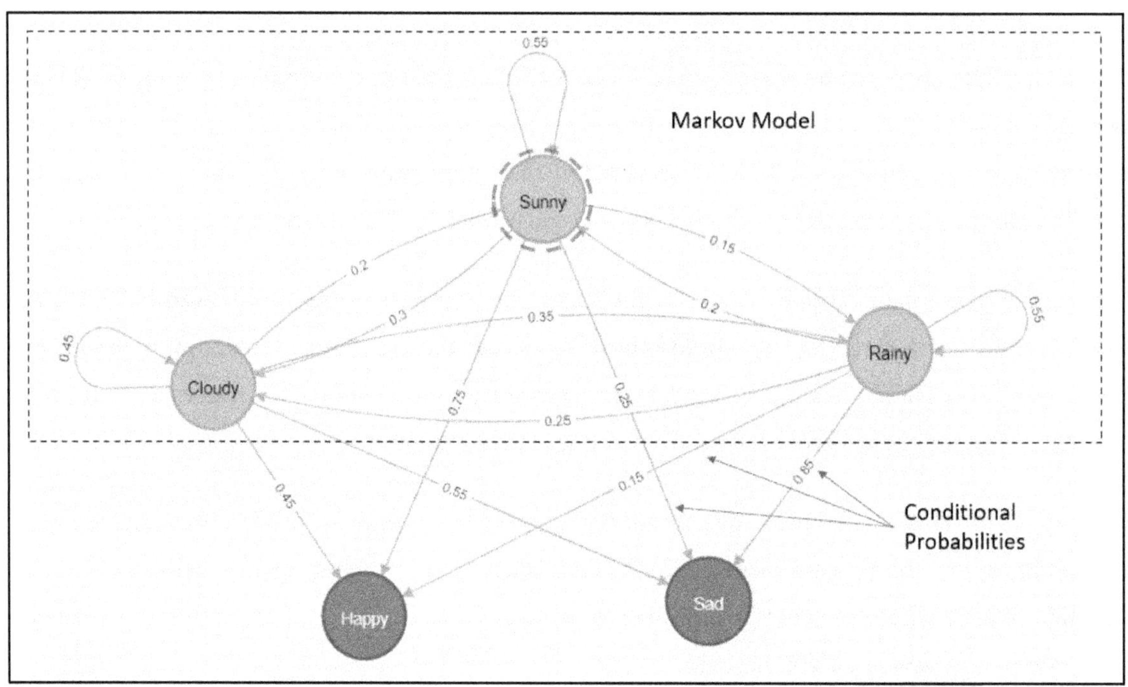

Figure 70: Hidden Markov Model.

Suppose it's Sunny where Sadie lives today (red circle in Figure 70). The probabilities for *tomorrow's* weather are as follows:

- There is a 0.55 probability that tomorrow will also be Sunny. If tomorrow is Sunny, there is a 0.75 probability that Sadie will be Happy tomorrow and a 0.25 probability he will be sad.
- There is a 0.20 probability that tomorrow will be Cloudy. If it's Cloudy, there is a 0.45 probability that Sadie will be Happy.
- There is a 0.25 probability that tomorrow will be Rainy. If it's Rainy, there is a 0.15 probability that Sadie will be Happy.

Once we have the probabilities for tomorrow's weather and the corresponding conditional probabilities for Sadie's mood, we can calculate the total probability of Sadie being Happy or Sad by summing over all possible weather conditions. The total probability for Sadie being Happy is calculated as:

1. Multiply the probability of each weather condition by the conditional probability of Sadie being Happy given that weather.
2. Add these products together.

For Sadie being Happy:

- If it's Sunny: 0.55×0.75=**0.4125**
- If it's Cloudy: 0.20×0.45=**0.09**
- If it's Rainy: 0.25×0.15=**0.0375**

Adding these together:

- 0.4125+0.09+0.0375=**0.54**

So, the probability of Sadie being Happy tomorrow is 54%.

For Sadie being Sad, we follow the same process:

- If it's Sunny: 0.55×0.25=0.1375
- If it's Cloudy: 0.20×0.55=0.11
- If it's Rainy: 0.25×0.85=0.21250

Adding these together:

- 0.1375+0.11+0.2125=**0.46**

So, the probability of Sadie being Sad tomorrow is 46%. It's a toss-up for poor Lulu.

Let's Try that Again with Another Example

The combination of MMs and Bayesian-inspired conditional probabilities accounts for two of the three parts of the structure we need for *abductive* reasoning—that Sherlock Holme's or House (the

TV character) type of problem—the most sophisticated form of reasoning. That's a big deal, so let's go through another simple example of an HMM to help drive this home.

Think of the probability of leaving a big tip at our next meal at our favorite restaurant. Of course, the size of the tip depends a lot on the quality of service. Being such regular customers, we have daily data that helps us predict the quality of service tomorrow based on today's quality.

Here are the pieces we need:

- Hidden States (Markov Model): Friendly Service, Average Service, Poor Service
- Observations (Emissions): Big Tip, Small Tip, No Tip

The transition matrix (a Markov model) for hidden states might look like what appears in Table 24.

From / To	Friendly Service	Average Service	Poor Service
Friendly Service	0.7	0.2	0.1
Average Service	0.3	0.5	0.2
Poor Service	0.1	0.4	0.5

Table 24: Markov model of probabilities for day-to-day service quality.

The first row of Table 24 is read: if the current state is "Friendly Service," there's a 70% chance the service quality remains friendly the next day, a 20% chance it becomes average, and a 10% chance it becomes poor.

At this point, we have a way to predict the service for tomorrow. Now, given some level of service, how are the tips? Friendly service doesn't guarantee a big tip—maybe the food was awful, maybe we're only allowed a maximum amount for business meals.

Table 25 is a table of the probability for a tip size given some level of service. This is the emission probability table—given some event (row), the probabilities are distributed.

Hidden State	Big Tip	Small Tip	No Tip
Friendly Service	0.6	0.3	0.1
Average Service	0.2	0.5	0.3
Poor Service	0.1	0.2	0.7

Table 25: Hidden Markov model of probabilities for day-to-day service quality.

This means that if the hidden state is "Friendly Service" (the first line), there's a 60% chance a customer will leave a big tip, a 30% chance they'll leave a small tip, and a 10% chance they won't tip at all.

Figure 71 shows the hidden Markov model combining the transition probabilities (Table 24) and the Emission probabilities (Table 25). As an example of how this works, consider the following question: What is the probability of getting a big tip tomorrow if today's service is average and tomorrow is friendly?

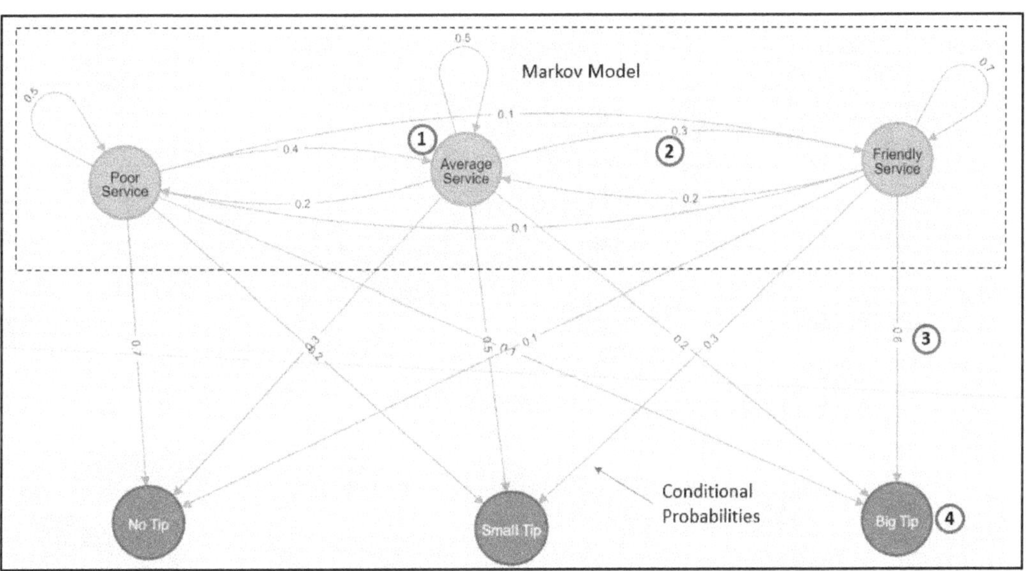

Figure 71: Hidden Markov Model for our tip probability.

From Figure 71, the calculation is as follows:

1. Today's service was average.
2. **Transition Probabilities (from Average Service):** There is a *0.3* probability of transitioning to **Friendly Service** tomorrow.
3. **Emission Probabilities (Big Tip):** If tomorrow's state is Friendly Service, the probability of a Big Tip is 0.6.
4. **Combined Probability for a Big Tip given today's service is average:** Transitioning to Friendly Service: ***030 * 0.60 = 0.18.***

Deductive Reasoning with Prolog

To demonstrate how HHMs are deductive, we'll convert the HHM shown back in Figure 71 into the coding language built for deductive reasoning: Prolog, the old AI staple of the 1980s. If something can be encoded in Prolog, it is an example of deductive reasoning.

The idea is that Prolog is the best way to express deductive reasoning and RDF is the best way to express semantics.

The relationships from Figure 71 are all represented in Code 67.

```
% transition(FromState, ToState, Probability)
transition(poor_service, poor_service, 0.5).
transition(poor_service, average_service, 0.4).
transition(poor_service, friendly_service, 0.1).

transition(average_service, poor_service, 0.1).
transition(average_service, average_service, 0.5).
transition(average_service, friendly_service, 0.4).

transition(friendly_service, poor_service, 0.2).
transition(friendly_service, average_service, 0.3).
transition(friendly_service, friendly_service, 0.5).

% emission(State, Observation, Probability)
emission(poor_service, no_tip, 0.7).
emission(poor_service, small_tip, 0.2).
emission(poor_service, big_tip, 0.1).

emission(average_service, no_tip, 0.3).
emission(average_service, small_tip, 0.5).
emission(average_service, big_tip, 0.2).

emission(friendly_service, no_tip, 0.1).
emission(friendly_service, small_tip, 0.3).
emission(friendly_service, big_tip, 0.6).
```

Code 67: Hidden Markov Model translated to Prolog facts.

Don't worry about the Prolog. It's easy to see the relationships above transformed into Prolog facts. For example, the 3rd line, *transition(poor_service, average_service,0.4)*, means that given today is poor_service, there is a 0.4 probability tomorrow will be average_service.

From those facts in Code 67, we can again deduce the service level tomorrow based on today's service level. Code 68 is the Prolog rule for that query.

```
% Calculate the probability of a tip given today's service quality
tip_probability(TodayService, Tip, Probability) :-
   transition(TodayService, TomorrowService, TransitionProb),
   emission(TomorrowService, Tip, EmissionProb),
   Probability is TransitionProb * EmissionProb.
```

Code 68: Prolog rule for determining the service level tomorrow based on today.

In regular English, Code 68 states If you want to calculate the probability that a customer leaves a certain tip tomorrow based on today's service level, here's how:

1. Look at all possible ways today's service could lead to tomorrow's service level.
2. For each possible tomorrow service level, find:
    - The transition probability from today's service to tomorrow's service.
    - The emission probability of tomorrow's service results in the specific tip you're interested in.
3. Multiply the two probabilities together to find the chance of *that* path resulting in the tip.

Code 69 is an example of how to query the Prolog snippet.

```
% Query: What is the probability of receiving a big tip tomorrow if today's service is average?
?- total_tip_probability(average_service, big_tip, Probability).
```

Code 69: Prolog query for determining person's mood based on tomorrow's weather.

The results are shown in Table 26.

Service Tomorrow given Average today	*Probability of Tomorrow Service*	*Big Tip Given the Service*	*Probability*
Poor	*0.10*	*0.10*	*0.01*
Average	*0.50*	*0.20*	*0.10*
Friendly	*0.40*	*0.60*	*0.24*
Total	***1.00***		***0.35***

Table 26: Probability for being happy if today is sunny.

In English terms, Table 26 could be stated:

- There's a 10% chance tomorrow's service will be poor, and a 10% chance of getting a big tip in that case: **0.01**
- There's a 50% chance of remaining at average service, and a 20% chance of getting a big tip there: **0.10**
- There's a 40% chance of tomorrow being friendly service, and a 60% chance of getting a big tip in that case: **0.24**
- So the *total* chance of getting a big tip tomorrow is **0.35**.

CHAPTER 12

Enterprise Intelligence

In my previous book, *Enterprise Intelligence*, the protagonist of the story is the Enterprise Knowledge Graph (EKG)—a "knowledge graph plus," a comprehensive framework designed to unify the enterprise's understanding of its data, processes, and relationships. The goal is for the EKG to be a wide and deeply scoped map of charted enterprise relationships. The EKG is a sophisticated structure that requires the methodical integration of many intricate disciplines, including AI (particularly LLMs as the glue to all the moving parts), BI, data mesh, metadata management, and the Semantic Web. *Enterprise intelligence* is about how to build the EKG.

Although the Time Molecules framework can stand independently, a richer potential is realized when integrated into the EKG. In that way, *Time Molecules* is a natural follow-up to *Enterprise Intelligence*. Expanding on the introduction of the event ensembles and conditional probabilities discussed in *Enterprise Intelligence*, *Time Molecules* dives deeper into process-centric modeling using MMs, Bayesian and conditional probabilities, and HMMs. This further enriches the EKG by providing a detailed, probabilistic view of enterprise processes, creating a seamless bridge between traditional BI and advanced analytics.

It is important to emphasize that this new approach builds on—rather than replaces—the existing BI infrastructures that have been painstakingly developed by human teams over the past few decades. These systems encompasses not just data, but a deep understanding of business logic, process flow, and institutional memory. Even a hypothetical artificial superintelligence (ASI), no matter how advanced, is more effective when it treats this structured history and state as an external foundation, rather than attempting to absorb and internalize it entirely.

Incorporating can mean using BI data. I mean more like if an ASI digested the data. Assimilating this structured BI into a purely neural or probabilistic reasoning process risks re-deriving—or worse, distorting—what was already explicitly and carefully modeled. Logic, reasoning, and inference is less complex when decoupled from the mechanics of data storage and structure. By maintaining that separation, we allow a super-intelligent AI to focus on what it will do best: interpreting, hypothesizing, and acting. By folding Time Molecules into the EKG, we preserve the hard-won foundations of traditional BI while equipping them with a reasoning layer optimized for intelligence.

This chapter kicks off the "3rd Act" of this book, where we combine Time Molecules with Enterprise Intelligence. The result is a more holistic framework that benefits from the synergy of solid, existing BI and leading-edge AI, ultimately empowering organizations to uncover deeper insights and optimize processes more effectively.

The EKG consists of three core components: a Knowledge Graph (KG) to capture semantic relationships, a Data Catalog (DC) to organize and index data source metadata from across the enterprise, and a structure composed of two sub-structures derived from BI activity—the Tuple Correlation Web (TCW) and the Insight Space Graph (ISG). Together, these components provide a powerful foundation for integrating and contextualizing data across the enterprise.

Figure 72 is a diagram of the EKG:

1. **Enterprise Knowledge Graph (EKG):** The EKG, the compound object consisting of the KG, DC, and ISG/TCW, is the brain of the enterprise, the conglomeration of the structured relationships between entities, departments, and processes. It captures semantic connections, offering an integrated and detailed view of how different parts of the business work together.

2. **Knowledge Graph (KG):** The KG is an ontological and taxonomic store of enterprise entities and concepts such as people, departments, or products and how their attributes are interconnected within the enterprise. It captures semantic descriptions and relationships between entities, which adds a contextual layer of understanding to how different parts of the business interact.

3. **Data Catalog (DC):** This is the centralized metadata system that captures the structure and lineage of all enterprise databases. While its foundation is schema metadata—tables, columns, data types—it also encompasses business definitions, lineage, usage patterns, and governance rules. Within the EKG, the DC acts as the hub that links the KG, TCW, and

ISG. It ensures that all insights and relationships ultimately anchor back to something concrete: the enterprise's curated and well-governed data assets.

4. **Insight Space Graph (ISG):** The ISG collects and charts relevant insights derived from the normal BI queries from analysts and managers. Whatever trained analysts see in various BI visualizations can be automatically captured and recorded using an array of functions called The Insight Function Array.

5. **Tuple Correlation Web (TCW):** The TCW is where correlations between BI data sliced in various ways (tuples) are captured. The TCW stores Pearson correlations between countless tuples that are involved with normal BI activity by analysts.

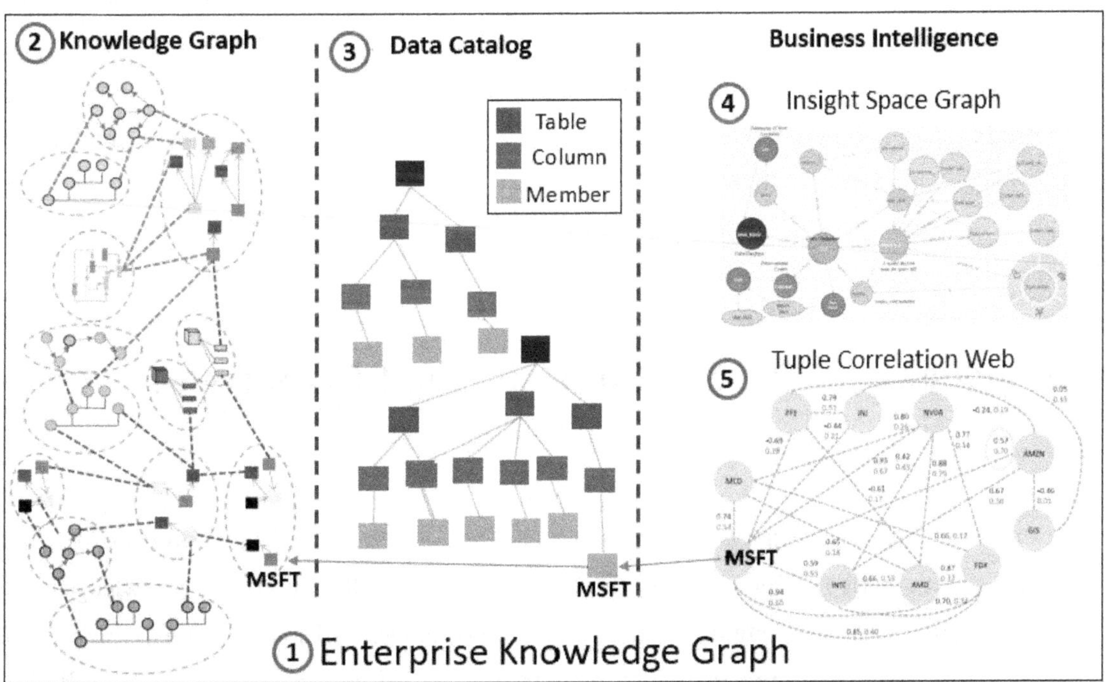

Figure 72: Enterprise knowledge graph.

The concepts in *Time Molecules* extend the scope of the EKG by introducing at-scale process-centric analytics that allows enterprises to move from discovering "what happened" to modeling "what will happen." MMs in the ISG enable analysts to compress processes into an analyzable form, while Bayesian and conditional probabilities in the TCW provide complementary likelihoods –which together form HMMs.

For example, an MM as a type of model in the ISG would illuminate insights within the sequence of customer touchpoints of a sales cycle, while the TCW quantifies the correlation between each touchpoint and eventual purchase behavior. By tying these models together through HMMs, the enterprise gains not only a detailed map of its processes but also the ability to predict outcomes and adjust strategies dynamically.

Ultimately, *Time Molecules* builds on the foundation of *Enterprise Intelligence* by focusing on the dynamic, evolving nature of processes within the enterprise. Combining event sequences, conditional probabilities, and process-centric models shifts the focus from static data analysis to a fluid, interconnected view of the intelligence of a business.

For readers unfamiliar with *Enterprise Intelligence*, Appendix A provides a concise overview of its concepts, introducing the EKG framework enough so you can see how *Time Molecules* complements and extends the ideas introduced in my earlier work. Additionally, there are extensive follow-ups to *Enterprise Intelligence* on my blog site: https://eugeneasahara.com/category/enterprise-intelligence-book/.

Knowledge Graph Beyond Ontologies and Taxonomies

While the term *knowledge graph* is usually associated with ontologies and taxonomies—structured vocabularies that describe entities and how they relate—what I call the Enterprise Knowledge Graph (EKG) is designed to incorporate other structures of knowledge. As I just described, in *Enterprise Intelligence*, the EKG is a composite of not just a traditional Knowledge Graph, but also the Data Catalog, and the two BI-derived structures I call the Insight Space Graph and Tuple Correlation Web. Of course, this book is mainly about the Markov model and Hidden Markov Model structures.

Beyond those structures, the EKG might also support goal-driven reasoning and rule-based awareness. In the chapters ahead, I'll introduce two additional structure types—strategy maps, which express how competing goals and trade-offs are managed, and non-deterministic finite automata (NFAs), which formalize the idea that many outcomes can arise from the same initial state depending on shifting conditions. These structures complement the probabilistic logic of Markov models introduced in this book, and extend the EKG into the domain of strategy and intent.

Together, these elements form a more complete substrate for enterprise reasoning—one that incorporates not just what is but what might be, what should be, and how we might get there. This reflects the foundational belief behind both *Enterprise Intelligence* and *Time Molecules*. That is, knowledge is cache—the caching of substantial energy invested in discovery and effective application.

Set up the Environment

To work with the EKG—a large enterprise knowledge graph—you'll need a graph database in addition to the local SQL Server instance we set up back in the TimeSolution Architecture chapter.

For this walkthrough, we'll use **Neo4j**, a powerful enterprise-class graph database. Fortunately, Neo4j offers a free desktop version. Neo4j Desktop, available for download at neo4j.com, provides a local development environment. It's free for developers and small teams, making it ideal for this project. Additional licensing options are available for commercial use or larger teams.

Full setup instructions, including how to load the EKG, can be found in the GitHub repository in *Time_molecules_book_tutorial.pdf*. At a high level, the process involves:

1. **Loading the Data Catalog**: Use the sql_server_entire_data_catalog.sql T-SQL script to extract database metadata from a SQL Server instance you're allowed to use for the walkthroughs.
2. **Initializing the EKG in Neo4j**: Run the Cypher script load_data_catalog_into_neo4j.cyp in the Neo4j Browser.

In this book, my goal is to convey the concepts of how the TimeSolution integrates with the EKG. Fully documenting the tutorial would add a lot of bulk to this book. Again, please refer to *Time_molecules_book_tutorial.pdf* in the GitHub repository for more comprehensive coverage of the tutorial.

Insight Space Graph Markov Models

This exercise will create a few MMs that we will load into the ISG. Following are the high-level steps:

1. **Generate Event Data**: Use *Create_markov_data*.py in VS Code to generate a CSV file named *sales_event_data.csv*.
2. **Import the Data**: Import sales_event_data.csv into the TimeSolution.STAGE.sales_event_data table in SQL Server using the "Import Flat Data" tool.
3. **Insert Events and Create a Markov Model**: Run the SQL script save_case_from_create_markov_py.sql in SQL Server to insert the events into the TimeSolution database and create a Markov model.
4. **Prepare Data for Neo4j**: Run the Python script markov_to_ISG.py to create a dataset suitable for Neo4j import.
5. **Load Data into the ISG**: Run the Cypher statement, load_markov_to_isg.cql, in Neo4j to load the prepared data into the ISG.

With these steps completed, Figure 73 illustrates how TimeSolution fits into the broader framework of the EKG. It shows how a query definition (QueryDef—the metadata of a query to a BI data source) in the EKG links to an MM derived from the resultant dataset. This highlights the integration of advanced analytics into business processes, illustrating how insights are structured to be more readily insightful. This is an explanation of Figure 73:

1. **QueryDef Node:** Represents a specific query that aggregates data from an enterprise data warehouse. This is a typical BI slice-and-dice query resulting from the normal BI activities of analysts. This example retrieves the sum of sales by date (sale_dollars by datekey), filtered by a store's name, zip code, and product class (various alcoholic beverages). This query forms the starting point for extracting the dataset upon which analytics will be performed.
2. **Model Node:** Acts as a metadata hub connecting the query definition (QueryDef) to various ML models derived from it—in this case, an MM. This node formalizes the relationship between the query and the MM, enabling traceability and reuse of both the query and the derived insights.

3. **Markov Model:** Encodes the probabilities of transitioning between different states, in this case, "Big Sales Day," "Normal Sales Day," and "Bad Sales Day." The relationships between these states are annotated with probabilities computed from event transition counts. For instance, Transition from "Normal Sales Day" to "Big Sales Day" has a probability of 0.6612. Transition from "Normal Sales Day" to "Bad Sales Day" has a probability of 0.224. These probabilities help analyze patterns and forecast behaviors, making the Markov model an essential tool for dynamic decision-making.

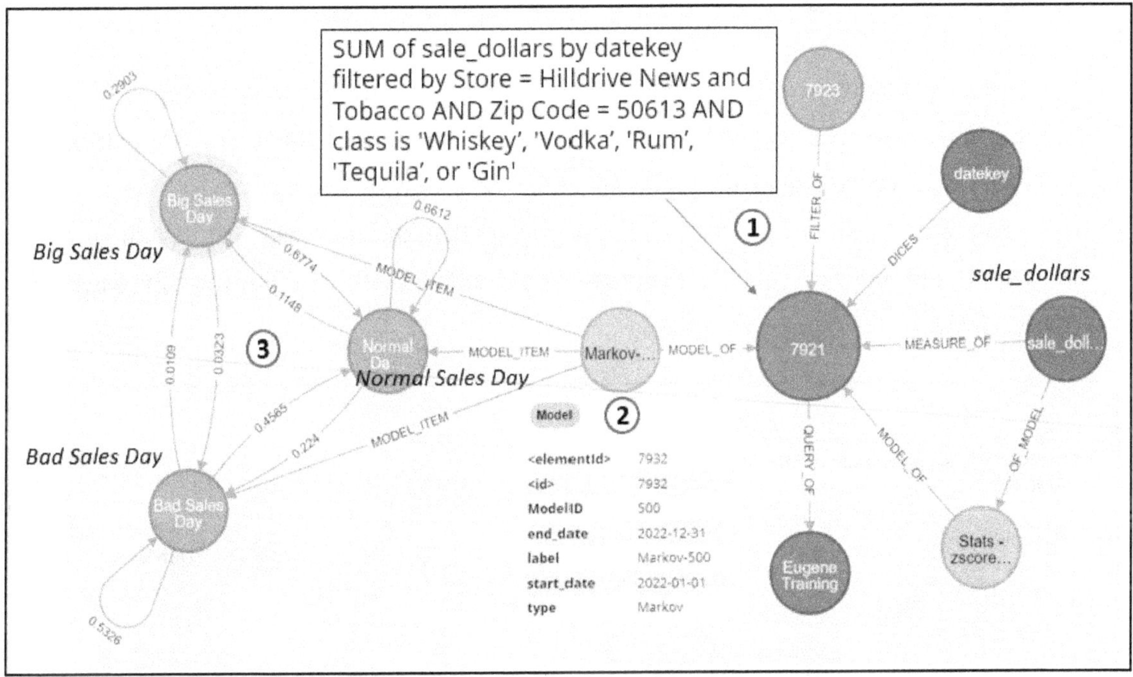

Figure 73: Markov model associated with query that retrieved the data upon which it was computed.

This visualization encapsulates the fusion of the TimeSolution with enterprise knowledge, illustrating how MMs derived from event data contribute to analytical insights within the broader framework presented in Enterprise Intelligence. It underscores the bidirectional relationship between advanced analytics and the structured, curated data that powers modern BI implementations.

Figure 74 illustrates an example of multiple slices of MMs (three QueryDefs). In this example, we'll look at a store, Hilldrive News and Tobacco, sliced by product category—resulting in multiple MMs that capture the sales dynamics between "Normal Sales Day," "Bad Sales Day," and "Big Sales Day" of their respective category:

1. This is a member node signifying that the MM is sliced by a store named "Hilldrive News and Tobacco."
2. This represents a dataset of sales (sales_dollars) for Hilldrive News and Tobacco filtered to a select set of product categories: whiskey, vodka, tequila, gin, and rum.
3. This represents a dataset of sales (sales_dollars) for Hilldrive News and Tobacco filtered to just the rum category.
4. This represents a dataset of sales (sales_dollars) for Hilldrive News and Tobacco filtered to a smaller set of categories: tequila, gin, and rum—much smaller categories than whiskey and vodka.
5. This is the hub of an MM implemented into the EKG for the dataset described in item 4. In fact there is one of these MM hubs for items 2 and 3 as well. Each of these MM hub nodes connects to an MM, showing probabilities for the quality of the next day.
6. As an example of the MM, this relationship states that for the dataset that includes just tequila, gin, and rum (item 4), the probability of a Bad Sales Day following a Big Sales Day is 0.0968.

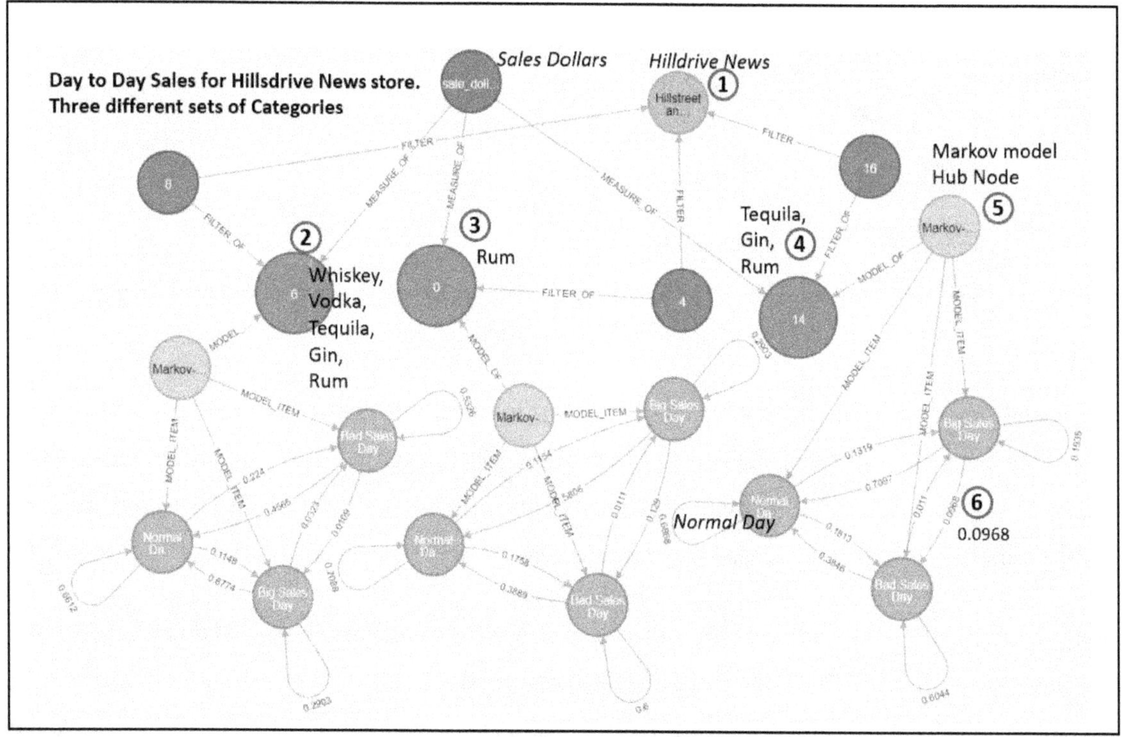

Figure 74: Three models for sales at Hilldrive News store.

MMs aren't the only "insights" that can be derived from a dataset. There are many other ML models, such as linear regressions, clusters, and even plain old standard statistics—for example, mean, standard deviation, skew, coefficient of variation, etc.

Figure 74 showcases the power of the TimeSolution to create targeted, category-specific MMs that help businesses analyze and understand sales-related processes at a granular level. By generating separate MMs for each slice of the data, enterprises can uncover unique process dynamics for each category, enabling tailored strategies for inventory, marketing, and resource allocation. This process seamlessly integrates with the EKG, providing traceability and context for every model and decision.

We can retrieve MM information from the EKG using a Cypher query (Neo4j's graph query language) like the one shown in Code 70. This Cypher will return the "Big Sales Day" to "Normal Sales Day" segments from the three MMs.

```
MATCH (s:Column{label:"sale_dollars"})--(q:QueryDef)--(m:Model{type:"Markov"})
--(mi:ModelItem)-[r]->(m2:ModelItem)
WHERE mi.label='Big Sales Day' AND m2.label='Normal Sales Day'
return m.ModelID,mi.label,m2.label,r.Rows,r.Prob,r.StDev,r.CoefVar
```

Code 70: Retrieve Markov models from EKG.

The results of Code 70 are shown in Figure 75.

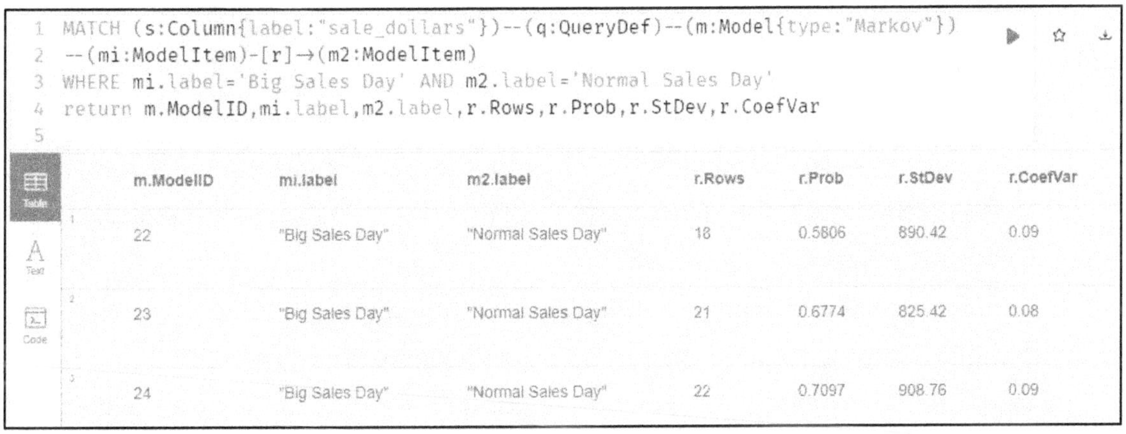

```
MATCH (s:Column{label:"sale_dollars"})--(q:QueryDef)--(m:Model{type:"Markov"})
--(mi:ModelItem)-[r]→(m2:ModelItem)
WHERE mi.label='Big Sales Day' AND m2.label='Normal Sales Day'
return m.ModelID,mi.label,m2.label,r.Rows,r.Prob,r.StDev,r.CoefVar
```

Table | Text | Code

	m.ModelID	mi.label	m2.label	r.Rows	r.Prob	r.StDev	r.CoefVar
1	22	"Big Sales Day"	"Normal Sales Day"	18	0.5806	890.42	0.09
2	23	"Big Sales Day"	"Normal Sales Day"	21	0.6774	825.42	0.08
3	24	"Big Sales Day"	"Normal Sales Day"	22	0.7097	908.76	0.09

Figure 75: Compare the Big Sales Day to Normal Sales Day transitions across the three product category sets.

We can see from the result that ModelID 24 has the highest probability for a "Normal Sales Day" following a "Big Sales Day" (0.7097).

Tuple Correlation Web

The TCW is a web of correlations—primarily easily computed Pearson correlations (explained in Enterprise Intelligence) and conditional probabilities between tuples. It is the third part I hinted at back in "Hidden Markov Models" that will facilitate abductive reasoning. The correlations of the TCW combined with MMs of Time Molecules are connected through the common elements of conditional probabilities.

First, an elevator pitch understanding of the TCW. It's a web of Pearson correlations and conditional probabilities between values of "qualified somethings" (tuples) over a period of time. In other words, the measure (-1 to 1) of how closely the two values go up and down together. Figure 76 shows a very simplified TCW of fictional tuples (circles):

1. All of the tuples are qualified by daily data (counts or sums of metrics) from January 2000 through December 2005, for NYC.
2. This tuple is a count of major sports events for each day.
3. This tuple is a count of spikes in pizza orders over the days.
4. This conditional probability states that given a spike in pizza orders, there is a 0.96 probability that there was a major sporting event.
5. This is the converse of 4. Given a major sporting event, there is a 0.75 probability of a spike in pizza orders.
6. Another probability—given a major sporting event, there is a 0.73 probability for a spike in sports viewership.
7. This is a Pearson correlation between Pizza sales and counts of spikes in sports viewership. Spikes in sports viewership go up and down together with pizza sales with a Pearson correlation of 0.80.
8. Additionally, spikes in sports viewership go up and down with ad prices.
9. The Pizza Sales tuple and the Spike in Pizza Sales tuple are related through data catalog members, Pizza (a product in a Products dimension table), and Sales (a metric in the fact table of metrics).

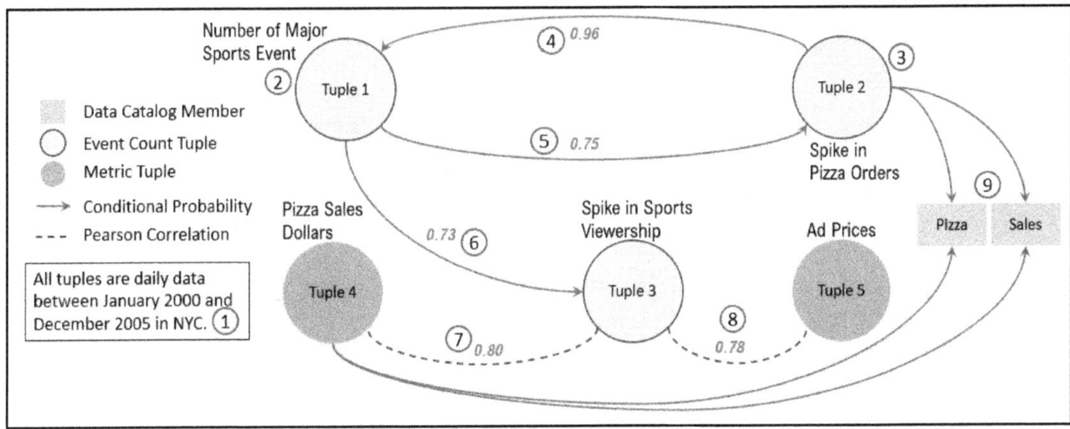

Figure 76: Sample TCW—Pearson correlations and conditional probabilities between tuples.

With this basic idea of what the TCW of *Enterprise Intelligence* is, let's focus on how the TCW links into Time Molecules. Again, that link is via the shared concept of conditional probability.

Conditional Probabilities in the TCW

The following exercise shows how conditional probabilities created in Time Molecules can be created and optionally linked into the TCW, enriching the web of correlations and probabilities.

Code 71 shows how to create a conditional probability in Time Molecules. Reminder: Although "Bayesian" is in the name of the stored procedure, the calculation could be probabilities of the Bayesian or conditional (frequentist) type.

```
--Given the arrive event, what is the probability of leaving a big tip?
EXEC [dbo].[CreateUpdateBayesianProbabilities]
     'arrive', 'bigtip', 'restaurantguest',NULL,NULL,NULL,NULL,NULL,'CASEID'
--Given the customer arrived and was greeted, what is the prob of leaving a big tip?
EXEC [dbo].[CreateUpdateBayesianProbabilities]
     'arrive,greeted','bigtip','restaurantguest',NULL,NULL,NULL,NULL,NULL,'CASEID'
--Given the truck arrived at walmart2, what is the probability of going to walmart3?
EXEC [dbo].[CreateUpdateBayesianProbabilities]
     'walmart2','walmart3','pickuproute',NULL,NULL,NULL,NULL,NULL,'DAY'
```

Code 71: Created two conditional probabilities to store in the BayesianProbabilities table.

After executing Code 71 above, Code 72 will display the new probabilities in the *BayesianProbabilities* table using the *vwBayesianProbabilities*_TCW view.

```
--Run this SQL in SSMS.
--Save results to bayesian_tm_prob.csv. Remember to replace NULL with blanks.
--From Neo4j browser, run load_tm_bayesian_prob.cql.
SELECT [ModelID],[CaseType]
      ,EventSetA], EventSetB]
      ,[ACount],[BCount],[A_Int_BCount],[PB_A],[PA_B]
      ,[TotalCases],[PA],[PB],[EventA_Description],[EventB_Description]
      ,[CaseFilterProperties],[EventFilterProperties],[StartDateTime],[EndDateTime]

,[Server],[Database],[EventSetTable],[EventSetColumn],[EventA_Hash],[EventB_Hash]
  FROM
      [dbo].[vwBayesianProbabilities_TCW]
```

Code 72: Retrieve Bayesian probabilities for import into TCW.

ModelID	CaseType	EventSetA	EventSetB	ACount	BCount	A_Int_BCount	PB_A	PA_B	TotalCases	PA	PB
21	CASEID	arrive	bigtip	10	1	1	0.1	1	10	1	0.1
21	CASEID	arrive,greeted	bigtip	8	1	1	0.125	1	10	0.8	0.1
22	DAY	walmart2	walmart3	2	1	1	0.5	1	3	0.66...	0.333...
2	ModelProp	greeted,seated	charged,depart	2	1	1	0.5	1	9	0.22...	0.111...
2	ModelProp	greeted,seated	served,check	2	1	1	0.5	1	9	0.22...	0.111...

Figure 77: Results of Code 72.

Figure 77 shows the results of Code 72. Note the two highlighted rows in Figure 77, which are the two tuple subjects of Figure 78. Figure 78 shows how the conditional probabilities look in the TCW. Here is the description:

1. The nodes with the dashed outline are tuples. The relationship to the nodes on the lower level indicates the composition of the tuple. In this case, the tuple represents the respective node below it. For example, node 3380 could be expressed in tuple nomenclature as: (arrive), 3383 as (bigtip), etc.
2. **arrive,greeted->bigtip**: The highlighted relationship between "arrive,greeted" and "bigtip" shows a conditional probability of 0.125 (12.5%). This means given a customer has arrived and been greeted, there is a 12.5% chance they will leave a big tip.
3. **ACount**: The value used to compute the probability mentioned in line 2 of Figure 77. It's the number of cases where the "arrive,greeted" event set occurred.
4. **A_Int_BCount**: Indicates that the "arrive,greeted" and "bigtip" event sets co-occurred in one case.
5. **PB_A and PA**: The calculated probability of arrive,greeted->bigtip: *A_Int_BCount / ACount (1.0 /8).*
6. **arrive->bigtip**: This is the probability between arrive (but not necessarily properly greeted) and bigtip (line 1 in Figure 77). The probability is 0.10 versus 0.125.

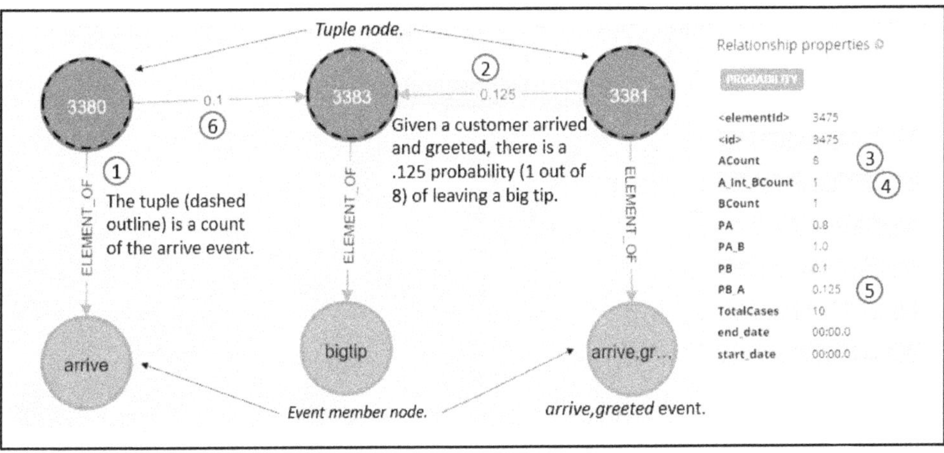

Figure 78: Conditional probability of a big tip.

Custom Correlation Scores

While we've previously explored Pearson correlations, Bayesian probabilities, and Markov model probabilities, it's important to recognize that there are countless ways to measure correlations. This topic provides an example of a custom correlation score. It assesses the similarity of liquor sales profiles across a set of stores. For this example, you can refer to this code in the GitHub repository:

1. stacked_bar_chart.py
2. load_stacked_bar_chart_similarities.cql

Figure 79 illustrates a network of tuples (dashed nodes)—in graph form. Each node represents the tuple of a store (1,2) and sale_dollars (3). The relationships between the tuples are the similarity score based on a custom algorithm derived from the compositions of whiskey, vodka, rum, tequila, and gin sales for each store. The relationship values indicate the degree of similarity in their sales profiles—0.0 through 1.0—with higher values reflecting closer alignment in the composition of the product categories.

A particularly notable insight is the highlighted connection (4) between nodes 1613 (2) and 1614 (1), which demonstrates a strong similarity in sales composition between these two locations. This visualization provides a concrete example of how correlations within the TCW can help uncover patterns, alignments, and potential opportunities across entities, driven by domain-specific metrics and features.

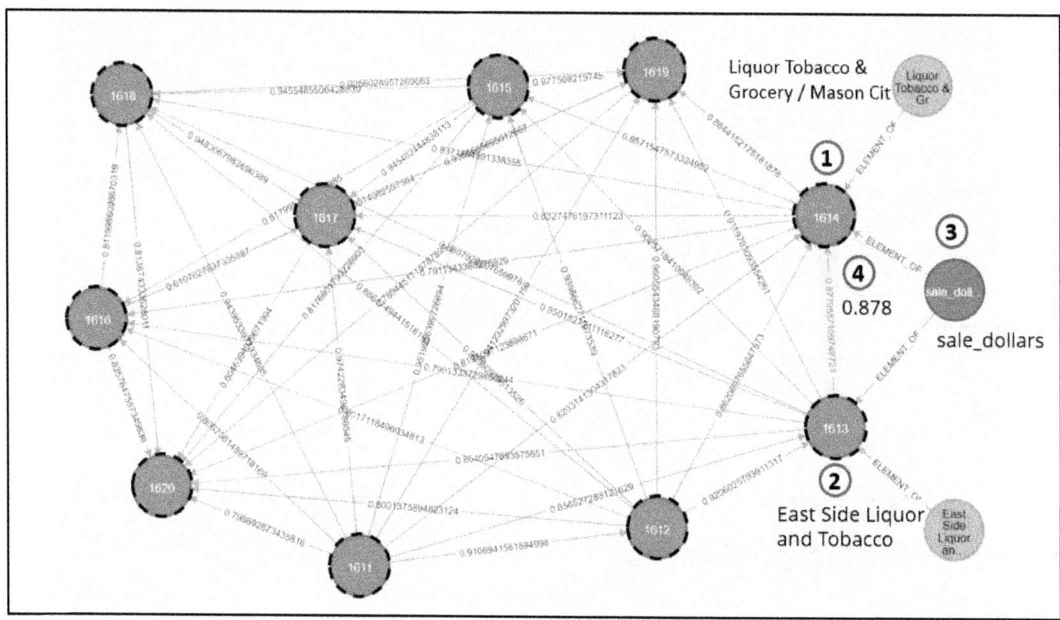

Figure 79: Custom correlation score. Similarity score.

Figure 80 shows an example of a Cypher query that returns these similarities in a table form. The last line of Figure 80 is the correlation represented by item 4 in Figure 79.

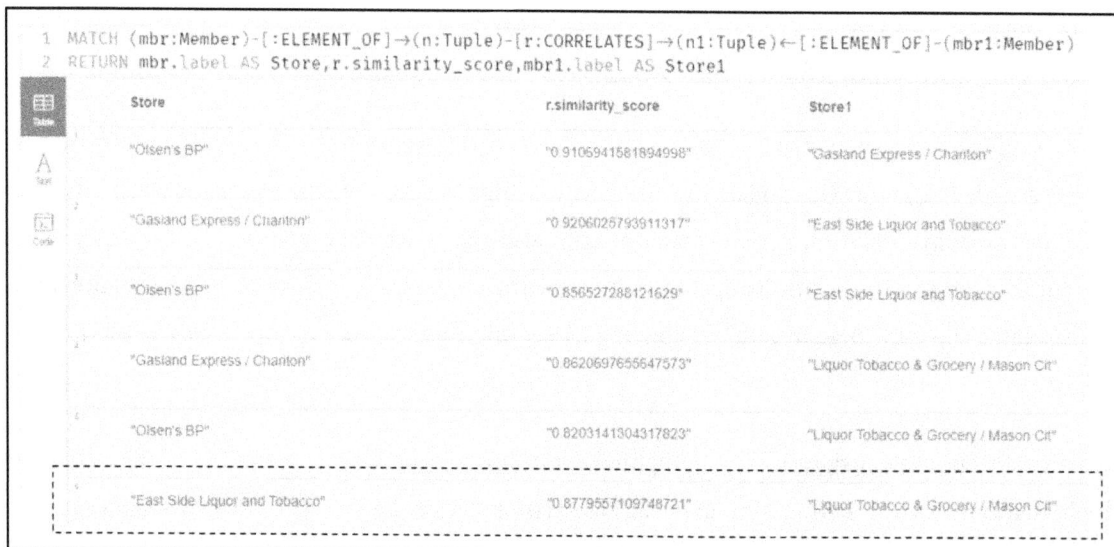

```
MATCH (mbr:Member)-[:ELEMENT_OF]→(n:Tuple)-[r:CORRELATES]→(n1:Tuple)←[:ELEMENT_OF]-(mbr1:Member)
RETURN mbr.label AS Store,r.similarity_score,mbr1.label AS Store1
```

Store	r.similarity_score	Store1
"Olsen's BP"	"0.9106941581894998"	"Gasland Express / Chariton"
"Gasland Express / Chariton"	"0.9206026793911317"	"East Side Liquor and Tobacco"
"Olsen's BP"	"0.856527288121629"	"East Side Liquor and Tobacco"
"Gasland Express / Chariton"	"0.8620697655647573"	"Liquor Tobacco & Grocery / Mason Cit"
"Olsen's BP"	"0.8203141304317823"	"Liquor Tobacco & Grocery / Mason Cit"
"East Side Liquor and Tobacco"	"0.8779557109748721"	"Liquor Tobacco & Grocery / Mason Cit"

Figure 80: Dataset of Store Similarity queried from Neo4j.

Time Molecules and the Data Catalog

The TimeSolution includes a mechanism that maps event codes, case properties, and event properties to its source data. In the context of this book, that is the data catalog (DC) part of the EKG.

We'll demonstrate the connection through the event properties of a particular event. Code 73 retrieves a little information on a particular event (EventID 435820).

```
DECLARE @EventID BIGINT=435820
--Retrieve basic information and case-level properties of eventid 435820.
SELECT f.CaseID, [EventID], [Event], EventDate, SourceID,cp.Properties
FROM EventsFact f
JOIN CaseProperties cp ON cp.CaseID=f.CaseID
WHERE EventID=@EventID
```

Code 73: Metadata tying Case and Event data to the DC and KG.

Figure 81 shows the result of Code 73. EventID 435820 indicates that YUM jumped 3% or more on 09/18/1997 from the prior trading day.

CaseID	EventID	Event	EventDate	SourceID	Properties
944	435820	Big Jump+3%	1997-09-18 00:00:00.0000000	6	{"Stock":"YUM"}

Figure 81: EventID 435820.

We'll now retrieve the event property metadata for EventID 435820 using the *EventPropertiesSource* TVF, as shown in Code 74.

```
--TVF EventPropertiesSource(@EventID) collects data source metadata.
--Get the case and event property sources related to the EventID=435820
DECLARE @EventID BIGINT=435820

SELECT
  PropertyName, PropertyValueNumeric,[Property_Table_Name],[Property_Column],
  Property_DBName, [Case_NaturalKey], [Property_ServerName],
  [NaturalKey_Table_Name], [NaturalKey_Column], NaturalKey_DBName,
  [NaturalKey_ServerName], [Date_Column]
FROM EventPropertiesSource(@EventID)
```

Code 74: Metadata tying Case and Event data to the DC and KG.

The two figures below, Figure 82 and Figure 83, represent the results of executing the query in Code 74. The two figures are left-right continuations of the same dataset—breaking the columns into two parts for clarity.

The highlighted row (for both figures) represents the property, "Low" (low price for YUM on 9/18/1997). The source of this value is:

- From in the "Low" column of the DailyFigures table.
- Located in the Stocks database on the specified server.
- Tied to the case for YUM Brands using the natural key "YUM," with the "Stock" column providing the case-level linkage.

Figure 82 shows the first six columns of the result:

- **PropertyName**: The name of the property, such as "Low" (low stock price for the day), "AdjustedClose," or "Volume."
- **PropertyValueNumeric**: The numerical value of the property, like the stock price or volume. In this case, 29.25, the low stock price for the day of EventID 435820
- **Property_Table_Name**: The source table where the property is stored, in this case, "DailyFigures."
- **Property_Column**: The column in the source table containing the value, such as "Low" or "Close."
- **Property_DBName**: The database name where the table resides, "Stocks."
- **Case_NaturalKey**: The unique natural key associated with the case, here "YUM"—from the case properties.

PropertyName	PropertyValueNumeric	Property_Table_Name	Property_Column	Property_DBName	Case_NaturalKey
Low	29.25	DailyFigures	Low	Stocks	YUM
AdjustedClose	7.09	DailyFigures	AdjustedClose	Stocks	YUM
High	30.12	DailyFigures	High	Stocks	YUM
Close	30.12	DailyFigures	Close	Stocks	YUM
Volume	4862000	DailyFigures	Volume	Stocks	YUM
Open	29.5	DailyFigures	Open	Stocks	YUM

Figure 82: First six columns of the result.

Figure 83 continues with additional metadata columns:

- **Property_ServerName**: The server hosting the database.
- **NaturalKey_Table_Name**: The table name associated with the case's natural key, which remains "DailyFigures."
- **NaturalKey_Column**: The column containing the natural key, which is "Stock."
- **NaturalKey_DBName**: The database name for the natural key, "Stocks."

- **NaturalKey_ServerName**: The server where the natural key data is located.
- **Date_Column**: The column identifying the date dimension, "DateID."

Property_ServerName	NaturalKey_Table_Name	NaturalKey_Column	NaturalKey_DBName	NaturalKey_ServerName	Date_Column
DESKTOP-N5ISJJF\MS...	DailyFigures	Stock	Stocks	DESKTOP-N5ISJJF\MSS...	DateID
DESKTOP-N5ISJJF\MS...	DailyFigures	Stock	Stocks	DESKTOP-N5ISJJF\MSS...	DateID
DESKTOP-N5ISJJF\MS...	DailyFigures	Stock	Stocks	DESKTOP-N5ISJJF\MSS...	DateID
DESKTOP-N5ISJJF\MS...	DailyFigures	Stock	Stocks	DESKTOP-N5ISJJF\MSS...	DateID
DESKTOP-N5ISJJF\MS...	DailyFigures	Stock	Stocks	DESKTOP-N5ISJJF\MSS...	DateID
DESKTOP-N5ISJJF\MS...	DailyFigures	Stock	Stocks	DESKTOP-N5ISJJF\MSS...	DateID

Figure 83: Next set of columns after the first six in Figure 82.

This metadata establishes how event properties like stock prices are mapped to their data sources, tying case-level and event-level data to the broader data catalog and knowledge graph components of the EKG. Code 75 is a SQL that will retrieve the event properties shown in Figures 82 and 83.

```
DECLARE @EventID BIGINT=435820
SELECT
   ep.[PropertyValueNumeric],
   ep.SourceColumnID,
   ep.EventID,
   sc.ColumnName,
   sc.TableName
FROM
   [TimeSolution].[dbo].[EventPropertiesParsed] ep
   JOIN [dbo].[SourceColumns] sc ON sc.SourceColumnID=ep.SourceColumnID
WHERE
   ep.eventid=@EventID
```

Code 75: Retrieve properties for an event.

Figure 84 illustrates how the Data Catalog (DC) of the Enterprise Knowledge Graph (EKG) connects to the Time Solution Mechanism. On the left, the DC serves as a metadata layer that captures the enterprise structure—databases, tables, columns, and values—standardizing how source data is referenced. On the right, the Time Solution mechanism uses two tables—close to what Code 75 above would return:

- **SourceColumns**: records table and column metadata, mapping back to the DC via SourceColumnID.
- **EventProperties**: stores the actual values from the event stream and links each value to its source column and event ID.

Together, this structure allows Time Molecules to interpret raw event data in the context of its enterprise origin, linking every event value to its source and meaning within the EKG.

Data Catalog—DC of the EKG				Time Solution Mechanism						
				Event Properties			Sources and SourceColumns Table			
Database	Table	Column	Member	Prop Value	SourceColumnID	EventID	Column	SourceID	TableName	SourceColumnID
EAA_Desktop	DailyFigures	DateID	09/18/1997	09/18/1997	38	435820	DateID	6	DailyFigures	38
EAA_Desktop	DailyFigures	Stock	YUM	YUM	37	435820	Stock	6	DailyFigures	37
EAA_Desktop	DailyFigures	Close	30.12	30.12	40	435820	Close	6	DailyFigures	40
EAA_Desktop	DailyFigures	Low	29.25	29.25	42	435820	Low	6	DailyFigures	42
EAA_Desktop	DailyFigures	High	30.12	30.12	41	435820	High	6	DailyFigures	41

Figure 84: Time Molecules event metadata linked to sources via the EKG Data Catalog.

Leveraging the Knowledge Graph

Incorporating the KG component of the EKG into the TimeSolution provides powerful flexibility when analyzing hierarchical or equivalence relationships. Consider an MM representing business events tied to employees and customers. The cases and events that will be distilled down to the MM have properties associated with it.

For example, a feature of TimeSolution is the *Models.CaseFilterProperties* column, which stores properties (in JSON) by which we will filter (slice) cases involved in the MM. For example, *{"EmployeeID":2,"CustomerID":2}*, will include only the cases with these two properties.

In turn, EmployeeID 2 and CustomerID 2, each might be associated with semantic KG data such as their names, address, role, how they relate to other entities, etc. In fact the very concepts of "Employee" and "Customer" are classes of objects with attributes in the KG.

Earlier, I referred to a Markov Model Manifold, a system of MMs linked through a knowledge graph. Here, we'll cover the basics of how MMs link through the glue of the EKG's KG component.

Drilling Up for Hierarchical Aggregation

With a KG connected to the semantic data of objects, such as employees, we can attempt drill-up (a.k.a. roll-up, and different from drill-through) operations. For example, through the KG, we would find that EmployeeID:2, is a paralegal. The KG can then return all employees with the same or even similar roles, allowing us to aggregate cases across all employees in that role. For example, we could create a Markov model representing an aggregation across all paralegals using a CaseFilter such as *{"EmployeeID":[2,3,4],"CustomerID":2}*

This approach enables real-time adjustments to the analysis, aggregating to higher-level insights, much like drill-down and drill-up processes in traditional OLAP systems. By embedding the KG into this workflow, users can gain a broader context for analysis and decision-making, enabling analysts to study transitions not only at an individual level but across defined groups in the organization.

Figure 85 shows an example of a drill-up. It is a graph representation of a table named Employees, with two columns (EmployeeID and Role), with four rows (a row for EmployeeID 1, 2, 3, and 4). In addition to the Employees table is a partial view of an ontology describing the structure:

1. Paralegal is a role with two employees.
2. Employee 2 (and 3) are Paralegals.
3. Employee 4 is a Legal Assistant.
4. The knowledge graph shows that the Roles, Legal Assistant and Paralegals, are the same thing. Therefore, we could roll up EmployeeID 2, 3, and 4, to analyze all "Paralegals".

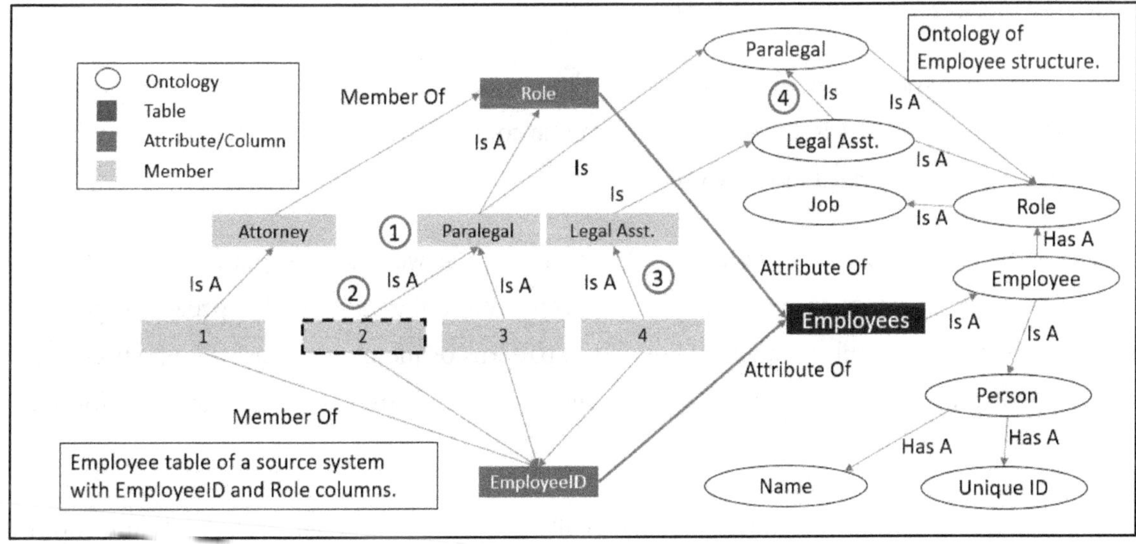

Figure 85: Drill Up using the EKG Data Catalog.

Code 76 is an example of a SPARQL query that can aggregate employees by role—in this case, the role of EmployeeID 2. *Note that this is not a SQL statement—I only show this SPARQL query as an example since we haven't covered SPARQL, a query language for retrieving and manipulating data stored in RDF format.*

```
PREFIX ex: <http://example.org/schema#>
PREFIX rdfs: <http://www.w3.org/2000/01/rdf-schema#>

SELECT ?employee ?employeeID ?role
WHERE {
 # Step 1: Find the role of the employee with EmployeeID = 2
 ?employee2 ex:EmployeeID 2 ;
        ex:hasRole ?targetRole .

 # Step 2: Get all roles that are the same as or subclass of that role
 ?role rdfs:subClassOf* ?targetRole .

 # Step 3: Find all employees with one of those roles
 ?employee ex:hasRole ?role ;
        ex:EmployeeID ?employeeID .
}
```

Code 76: Query to retrieve list of EmployeeID who have the same role as EmployeeID:2.

Semantic Context for Transforms

In any complex system, the ability to group (loosely speaking: abstract, generalize, categorize, aggregate, roll-up) entities is key to reducing analytic complexity. That's crucial since everything in the world can be categorized in many ways by various subsets of their properties.

Large datasets contain numerous granular elements—such as web pages, products, or events—that represent variations of the same overarching concept. Without a structured approach to grouping these elements, it's difficult to identify meaningful patterns or measure system-wide metrics due to the noise of unnecessary differentiation between entities that are essentially the same for some purposes.

The KG serves as a tool for addressing this challenge. By linking related elements into unified categories or concepts, the KG reduces the number of paths and entities requiring analysis, enabling a more focused and efficient exploration of data. This aggregation process is not just about simplifying the dataset, but also about providing a semantic structure that aligns with the underlying relationships between entities.

The drill-up example of Employees 2, 3, and 4 rolling up to Paralegals is a kind of aggregation. As another example, in the domain of e-commerce, the KG might group multiple web pages about the same product or topic into a single entity, allowing for an aggregated view of metrics like page views or sales attributed to a page. However, this principle extends far beyond e-commerce. In any domain, the ability to semantically group and transform entities—whether events, records, or objects—enhances our ability to track trends, identify spikes in activity, and predict future behavior.

Figure 86 illustrates how the KG and DC components of the EKG and the TimeSolution framework work together to provide this semantic context. Structuring and aggregating data through semantic relationships creates a foundation for deeper insights and more effective decision-making.

Here are details of the numbered items in Figure 86.

1. **Time Molecules:** This is the overarching framework where events are logged and analyzed. It captures significant patterns or jumps in events, like a spike in page views, as part of the Time Molecules system.

2. **Ontology:** The ontology (domain-specific part of the KG) structures semantic relationships between entities, such as connecting arnold1 and arnold2 as web pages that are about Arnold. The KG enables aggregation by linking these entities and simplifying analysis.

3. **Data Catalog:** The Data Catalog is where schema information about source data is stored—such as key attributes like DateID, Web Page, and Sales. These attributes are essential for tracking and analyzing event data over time, with DateIDs used to align with the Time Molecules framework for more detailed analysis of events like page clicks.

4. **Event Tuple (Arnold Pages):** This is the tuple that combines different interactions or events related to Arnold web pages. It captures key metrics, such as page views and clicks, from both arnold1 and arnold2 and aggregates them based on their relationship with Arnold in the KG.

5. **Big Views Jump**: This specifies that the Arnold tuple (4) relates to an event signifying a big jump in views for some period. This refers to a significant increase in page views or activity across the related Arnold web pages. By aggregating arnold1 and arnold2, the Knowledge Graph allows for the tracking of a Big Views Jump as a unified metric, simplifying the analysis of the spike in views.

6. **Date (Crucial to Markov Models):** The DateID represents the dates (and time) when events occur (Q1-2020). In the context of MMs, dates are fundamental because they allow the system to track how events, such as page clicks or views, transition over time. This helps in building predictive models based on time-series data, allowing the system to map out potential future jumps or shifts in user behavior.

7. **Arnold1 (Web Page):** Arnold1 is a specific web page about Arnold. The KG shows it's related to his biography.

8. **Arnold2 (Web Page):** Arnold2 is another related web page about Arnold. The KG shows it's a web page about his movies.

9. **Aggregation of Arnold1 and Arnold2 (Both Web Pages):** The KG shows that arnold1 and arnold2 are both web pages about Arnold. This enables their aggregation into a single entity for metrics like page clicks, views, and sales. By doing this, analysis across the two pages becomes more streamlined, and we can analyze the combined impact of all Arnold-related pages.

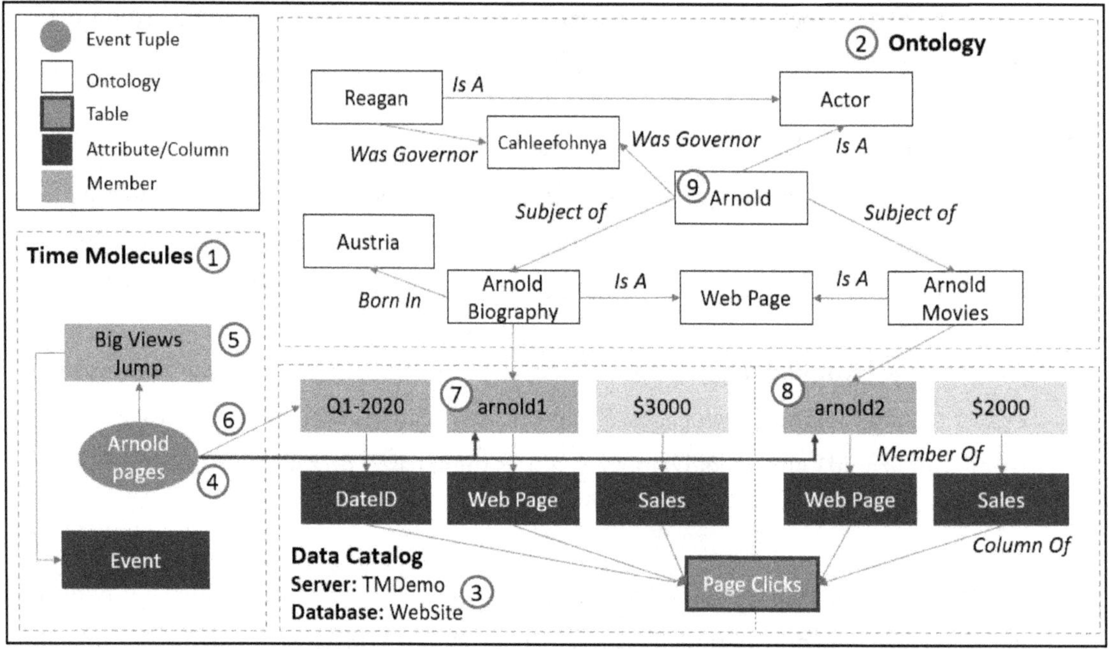

Figure 86: Aggregating the page views of two web pages related to Arnold.

Linking Markov Models Across Domains with the Knowledge Graph

MMs are invaluable tools for understanding transitions within processes. However, in complex systems, processes never operate in a vacuum. Much like proteins in a biological system bind together, creating a macro-structure that performs intricate functions, MMs interconnect to form a cohesive macro process. The ability to link MMs provides a richer understanding of how different processes interact and influence one another. At the center of this integration is once again the KG, which serves as the binding framework, enabling MMs from different domains to align and be viewed together.

Consider our example of a restaurant. Each part of the restaurant—front room, kitchen, and billing—represents a separate process, and each can be modeled as an independent MM:

- **Front Room Process MM**: Captures transitions such as Customer Arrival → Seated → Order Placed → Order Served → Check Delivered → Bill Paid → Depart.
- **Kitchen Process MM**: Focuses on transitions like Order Received → Cooking Started → Cooking Completed → Dish Delivered.
- **Billing Process MM**: Models events such as Bill Generated → Payment Processed → Receipt Delivered.

Figure 87 illustrates how these three very different processes link through KG objects.

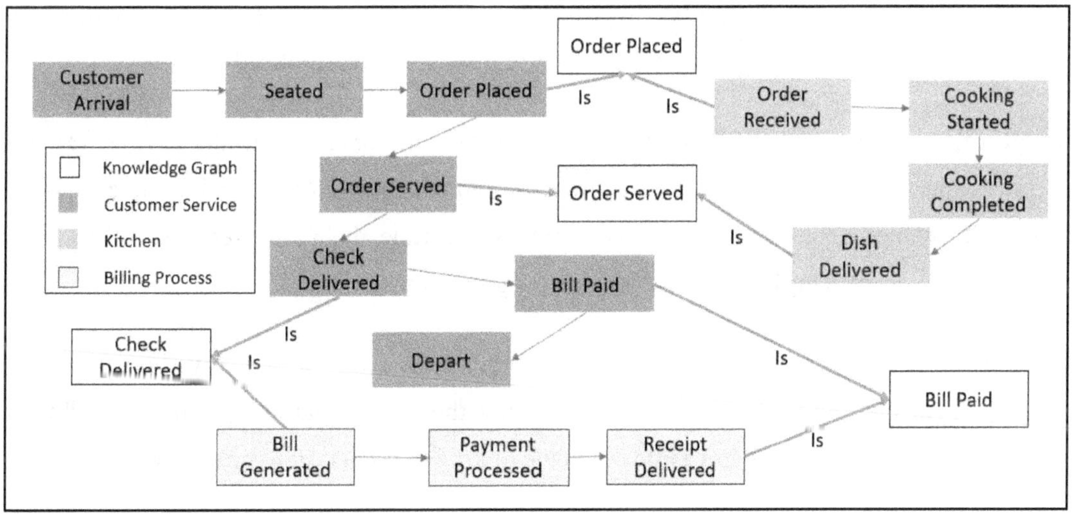

Figure 87: MMs linked through KG definitions.

Each of the three models provides useful insights within its domain, but these processes are interconnected. For example, the *Order Placed* event in the customer service process corresponds to *Order Received* in the kitchen, and the *Bill Paid* event in the customer service process corresponds to *Receipt Delivered Processed* in billing. Without an explicit mechanism to connect these events, the insights from each model remain siloed.

The KG provides the semantic structure to unify these models. It maps relationships such as *"Order Placed is equivalent to Order Received"* or *"Bill Paid is equivalent to Payment Processed,"* creating shared reference points across domains. These reference points act as "binding sites," allowing the individual MMs to link together into a cohesive web of transitions.

By linking MMs through the KG, a tapestry of MMs emerges, what I referred to earlier as the Markov Model Manifold. It enables cross-domain analysis and holistic insights. For example, a delay identified in the kitchen process—such as a longer-than-expected transition from *Cooking Started* to *Cooking Completed*—can now be analyzed in terms of its ripple effects on the front room process, such as increased wait times or decreased customer satisfaction. Similarly, inefficiencies in billing might surface in upstream processes, revealing patterns that would otherwise remain hidden.

This interconnected system of MMs resembles the behavior of proteins in biological systems. Proteins interact and bind through shared structures or signals, forming networks essential for life. Similarly, the KG binds MMs across domains, transforming isolated process models into a broadly connected system. The KG doesn't just aggregate data—it provides the semantic clarity needed to align processes and uncover relationships that might otherwise go unnoticed.

Through this integration, the KG expands into a crucial component of an intelligence framework that transforms the Time Molecules into a powerful web of adaptive MMs. By linking events across domains, it enables organizations to break down silos, scale their analyses, and reveal the full complexity of their systems in a way that is both insightful and actionable.

Of course, even our relatively simple restaurant enterprise consists of many more processes—procuring food, planning the menu, communicating the menu, marketing, hiring, dealing with government agencies, etc. Each is a Time Molecule linking to others yet to be discovered.

CHAPTER 13

Composite Cases

Each event we observe in a business system—whether it's a purchase, an invoice being processed, or a product being shipped—rarely, if ever, tells the full story. Instead, as we just discussed, it is the culmination of a chain of interconnected sub-processes, each contributing to the completion of the larger event. These sub-processes form a web of interrelated actions, each with its own sequence of events, dependencies, and outcomes.

Take the example of a shipping event. While "shipped" may appear to be a single event in our data—which began with some sort of initial contact of a customer to a business—it is actually the endpoint of an intricate series of sub-processes, such as:

- **Sales cycle execution:** Before an order is ready for shipping, it often passes through a sales cycle that can include customer outreach, needs assessment, proposal generation, pricing negotiations, contract signing, and possibly credit checks or financing approval—all of which must be completed before fulfillment can begin.
- **Processing invoices**: This involves verifying the purchase, reconciling payment details, and ensuring compliance with financial or regulatory requirements.
- **Inventory management and packaging**: Before shipping, inventory must be checked, the product retrieved from the warehouse, and prepared for delivery, often including packaging and labeling.
- **Logistics coordination**: The product is assigned to a carrier, routes are planned, and schedules are aligned to ensure timely delivery.

Similarly, a purchase event might represent the culmination of customer browsing, product selection, payment processing, and fraud detection checks. An event signifying receipt by the customer could signify the end of another sub-process involving tracking, confirmation of delivery, and receipt validation.

What makes this even more complex is that many of these sub-processes can occur in parallel. For example, while the inventory is being updated, packaging may be underway, and at the same time, the invoice might be in the final stages of approval. Events from these parallel sub-processes can appear in the system asynchronously, creating what seems like a muddied order of events.

This complexity has profound implications for modeling and analysis. Instead of treating events as isolated points in time, we must view them as nodes in a larger network of causality and dependencies. By identifying and mapping these underlying webs of sub-processes, we can better understand the true nature of each event, uncover patterns, and optimize the system as a whole.

For instance, by mapping the full sub-process behind a shipping event, we can identify bottlenecks in packaging or delays in logistics. Similarly, tracing the sub-process of a purchase event might reveal issues in payment processing or inventory stockouts. This level of insight enables businesses to not only react to events but to anticipate them and target the root cause (with a lower risk of adverse side effects from the "cure"), ensuring smoother operations and a more cohesive understanding of how interconnected systems function.

Event sets are the primary mechanism for addressing this. The events for each sub-process are segregated into separate event sets.

Case Entry and Exit Points

An important early step in working with composite cases is to identify where cases of processes and sub-processes begin and end. These are the handoff points where they link.

The example we're using here is essentially the same one that we just went over in "Linking Markov Models Across Domains with the Knowledge Graph." There, the domain models were linked through "Is" relationships defined between events in the context of the KG component of the EKG. However, Time Molecules doesn't necessarily involve the concepts of Enterprise Intelligence. So, we're looking at this from an angle of "composite cases"—cases made up of sub-cases, whether linked or nested.

Figure 88 is the flow of the restaurantguest event set we've used in this book:

1. **arrive** is the start of the main restaurantguest model.
2. **depart** is the end of the restaurantguest model. The weak link between 1 and 2 illustrates that once in a while, someone just arrives and leaves.
3. In the course of serving a guest, the guest places their order and is later served the food. But of course, preparing the order is a process in itself. It's a process that occurs in the kitchen and is usually opaque to the customer.
4. When the order is completed, the server is notified, and the order is served to the customer. The "order processed" node (dashed outline) represents the entire process of what happens between placing the order (3) and serving it to the customer (4).

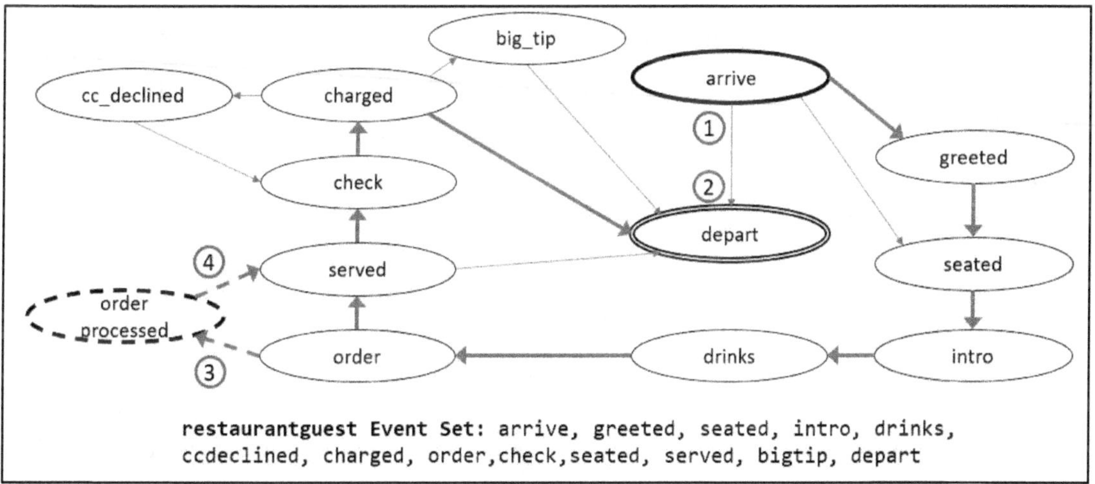

Figure 88: Restaurant guess process. order processing is a sub process.

Figure 89 is the inverse of Figure 88, where we focus on the kitchen process. This time, the nodes with dashed lines represent the nodes of the front-room customer service process, while the solid lines represent the events in the kitchen:

1. The customer places the order with their front-room server and it's received by the kitchen.
2. When the order prepared by the kitchen is ready, the server is notified, and the order is delivered to the customer. From there, the customer service process continues on.

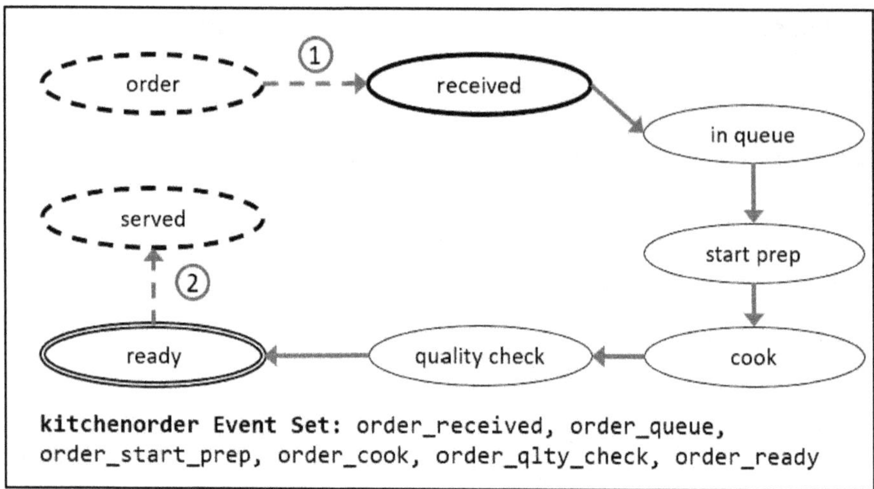

Figure 89: Kitchen order processed.

Code 77 shows how to find the entry and exit points of an event set—kitchenorder, which includes *order_received, order_queue, order_start_prep, order_cook, order_qlty_check, and order_ready.* Remember, an event set only defines the events in the process—the probable order in which they happen is what creating MMs determines. The TVF, *EntryAndExitPoints*, analyzes cases depending on its parameters and finds which events happen first and last for each case.

```
--Find the entry and exit points of the kitchen order event set.
SELECT *
FROM
      [dbo].[EntryAndExitPoints]('kitchenorder', 0, NULL, NULL, NULL,1,NULL, NULL,
NULL)
```

Code 77: Find the entry and exit points of the kitchenorder sub-process.

Figure 90 shows the results. The events, order, and order_ready appear first and last, respectively, for two cases.

EventA	EventB	Description	CaseCount
order	order_received	The order event hands off to theorder_receivedev...	2
order_ready	served	The order_readyevent exits the kitchenorder proc...	2

The **order** event hands off to the **order_received** event as entry INTO the *kitchenorder* process.

The **order_ready** event exits the *kitchenorder* process, handing off to the **served** event.

Figure 90: The entry and exit points for the kitchenorder event set.

Code 78 is an example of how to find event sets that contain one or more specified event. The TVF, *EventSetInclusion*, looks for all event sets that contain the specified subset of events—in this case, event sets that include order or served.

```
SELECT * FROM [EventSetInclusion]('order,served')
```

Code 78: List all event sets that include the list of events.

Figure 91 shows the result of Code 78. It found four event sets that include order and served. We now know that the kitchenorder event set is related to the restaurantguest event set.

EventSetKey	EventSet	EventSetCode
0x384060D658FDAE2CB57186A008234AF6	arrive,bigtip,drinks,greeted,order,check,...	NULL
0x3FD43F954A562D38585B31DF4FC2E45D	arrive,greeted,seated,intro,drinks,ccdecli...	restaurantguest_full
0x527C1854FE4C32C22484FAA8B87A7A10	restaurantguest	NULL
0xF55D96AAC5C1BB4F0DF26587CD8CC1C2	arrive,greeted,seated,intro,drinks,ccdecli...	restaurantguest

Figure 91: Result of Code 78.

Open Events Onboarding

Deciding which facts to load from very many event sources into the EventsFact table should be the easy part. By "easy", I don't mean in the sentiment of simply dumping all sorts of files into cloud storage. Rather, in the sentiment of, "We don't know if this data is important now, but at least we have it somewhere readily accessible." We want to encourage facts from as many corners of the world as possible in order to paint a bigger and more detailed picture—or at least enable the ability to do that given the proper compute and storage resources. But there's a fine line that crosses into the data equivalent of hoarders.

What is great about being liberal regarding the events that go into the EventsFact table is that we don't "censor" events based on what we think defines processes. For example, most systems will "cleanse" data before it hits a data warehouse. That means removing or confirming data that doesn't meet strict criteria or beliefs. Process Mining, Business Intelligence, and Time Molecules are most valuable when it's about the discovery of the unknown, not just computing and monitoring metrics.

By loosely collecting events, we have a chance to study the changes that are going on. We can also observe clever, resourceful workarounds that the front-line workers have devised to resolve problems that can't wait for formal implementations from HQ.

Discovering Processes

A prime concept of Time Molecules is the discovery of processes or sequences we aren't aware of—emergent patterns hidden within a mountain-sized muddy ball of events. For example, employee turnover can be linked to subtle and surprising precursors like increased use of sick days or declining engagement in meetings. These behaviors may not seem directly related to resignation at first, but over time, patterns emerge. While sick days may not cause turnover, identifying such trends enables early, preventive intervention—a concept well-aligned with the Triple Aim in healthcare, which emphasizes proactive measures to improve outcomes and reduce downstream costs. Similarly, other business issues like customer churn, equipment failure, or supply chain disruptions often have telltale early signals. When observed through process discovery, these signals surface as valuable correlations, empowering teams to act before problems escalate.

Let's assume that it hasn't occurred to anyone that increased utilization of sick days could be an indicator of the impending departure of an employee. The normal expectation is that an employee utilizes sick days for a relatively brief illness. Here are several possible reasons for the increased utilization of sick days leading to the employee departing:

- The employee might be seriously ill and possibly may not be able to work.
- The employee is traveling to interviews with other companies.
- The employee is disengaging and using time to get away from work.

Those are real scenarios, as I'm aware of more than a few situations where sick time was used in that manner.

Figure 92 illustrates a causal or predictive relationship between increased use of sick days and the likelihood of resignation, based on past patterns or probabilities in the data. The system tracks and links these events as tuples associated with the employee ID, helping to model such relationships for future analysis or decision-making.

1. **BI Dev**: This represents an attribute or column, likely coming from a database or an event log. The specific Role, "BI Dev", is the focus, and it connects the employee to events and actions that are tracked, such as increased sick days and resignations.

2. **Tuple of Employee and Increased Sick Days Event**: This refers to a specific event tuple linking the BI Dev role to the event "Increased Sick Days." In a system that tracks employee events, this tuple captures the employee's increased use of sick days and associates it with the individual in question.

3. **Tuple of Employee and Resignation Event**: Similar to the previous tuple, this one connects the same BI Dev role to the event of "Employee Resigns." It's another event being tracked, which provides critical information for analysis.

4. **Synthetic Event of Unusual Sick Days Utilization**: This synthetic event represents a calculated or derived event based on the employee's behavior. "Unusual utilization of sick days" likely refers to an anomaly detection or pattern recognition that suggests the employee's sick day usage has deviated from the norm.

5. **Conditional Probability ("Often Follows")**: This arrow suggests a relationship between the events. The model indicates that when a BI dev shows unusual utilization of sick days (Event A), there is often a subsequent event where the employee resigns (Event B). This Bayesian link helps indicate potential predictive behavior, where unusual sick days might be a precursor to resignation.

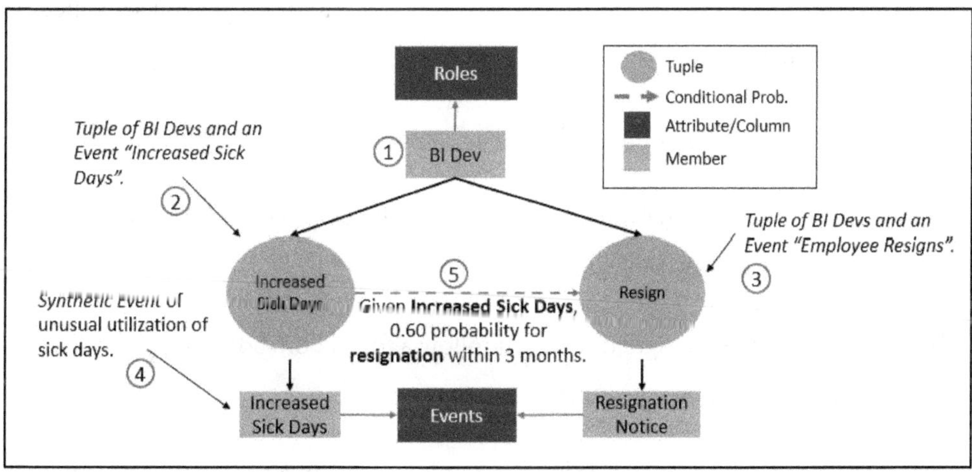

Figure 92: Custom Event leading to surprising event.

Event Sets to Parse Cases

Although the entire history of an employee with an employer is a single, long-running case, there are so many types of events that we can't build a comprehensible MM for the life of employees as a cohort. So, we need to discover event sets that parse out sub-processes for complicated cases.

Figure 93 shows a far from exhaustive set of event examples logged by HR during the duration of an employee's employment.

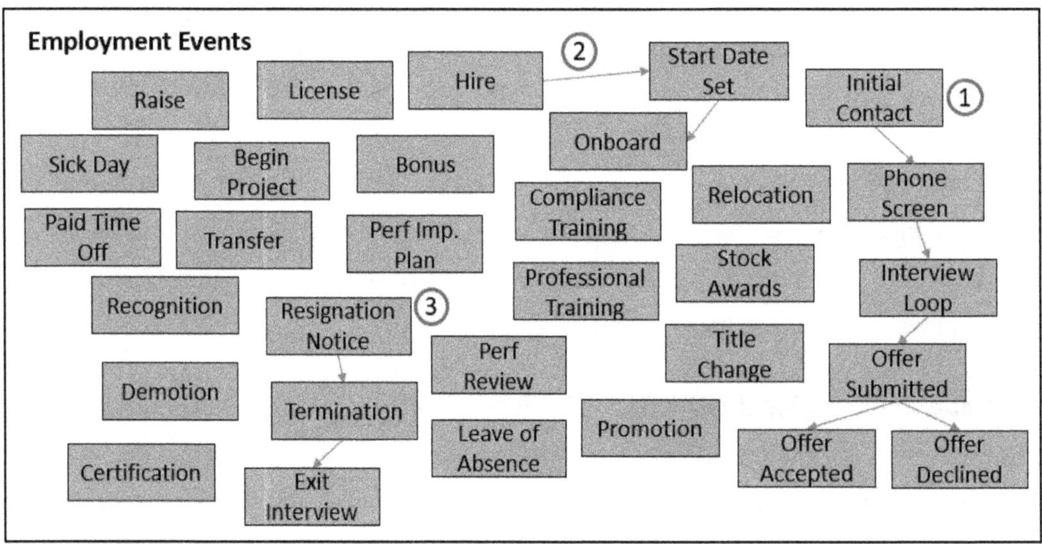

Figure 93: Examples of the many event types during an employment.

Note that among that zoo of events, there are some events that follow a general sequence. Those are indicated by events linked by arrows:

1. **The hiring process:** Beginning with Initial Contact follows a set sequence.
2. **Onboarding Process:** After the offer is accepted, the employee is hired, a start date is set, and the onboarding process begins.
3. **Resignation Process:** Resignation might follow a formal off-boarding process, including exit interviews and a goodbye lunch.

But for most other events, the sequence is kind of random. This means that most events can happen at any time in any order or even in parallel.

Parallel Sub-Processes

We already discussed how processes within complex systems are linked and layered into hierarchies. Serving a customer at a restaurant is centered around the dining room (front-end) service process along with adjoining kitchen (back-end) and billing processes. They are layered so that we can drill into deeper layers for each event transition. For example, the transition of *served_food→charged* is a high-level transition that ignores all the conversations, spilled glasses of wine, and agendas that took place during the meal.

By parallel, I mean that there are sub-processes pertaining to a case that occur concurrently. For example, think about a hospital diagnosing a patient with a transient ischemic attack (TIA). This case might include multiple sub-processes happening simultaneously—for example, blood work, a Holter monitor, an echocardiogram, ENT tests, and, of course, obtaining insurance approval. Each sub-process operates mostly independently, with its own sequence of events. However, when recording these events related to a single patient in an integrated system such as the TimeSolution—without grouping them into processes and looking at that historical whole purely chronologically—it will look as though steps from one sub-process follow or precede steps from another. This misrepresentation will be confusing.

Parallel processes are the bane of many engineering disciplines, including my discipline of software development. Parallelism is a primary factor in what makes systems complex.

To address this, we again engage the concept of event sets, allowing us to accurately isolate and represent parallel sub-processes. Each parallel sub-process for a patient visit (case), like the blood work or Holter monitor, can be assigned into separate event sets. This ensures that the events within one sub-process are not incorrectly intermingled with those of another.

Here are a few notes on the process:

- **Event Sets as Filters**: Each sub-process is defined as an event set, acting as a filter to partition events within the wider-scoped case. For example:
    - The blood work process might include events like blood_drawn, sample_processed, and results_reviewed.

    - The Holter monitor process might include events like monitor_applied, monitor_removed, and data_analyzed. By associating these events with distinct event sets, the system can accurately represent their independence.

- **Human Guidance in Event Set Definition**: While some event sets are straightforward to define, others will require human expertise to sort out which events belong to which sub-process. For example, medical professionals could sort out overlapping events or dependencies that require nuanced categorization. This is actually one of the primary tasks for process mining, especially in the data prep and discovery phases.

- **Role of LLMs in Automation**: LLMs can assist in automating this process. Given a comprehensive dataset of events and their contexts, an LLM, based on its incredible breadth of knowledge, would construct a draft (meaning, at best, people should use it only as a starting point) of identifying patterns, relationships, and clusters that suggest how events should be grouped into event sets. This can significantly reduce the manual effort required to define sub-process boundaries starting completely from a blank page. It won't be perfect, but the LLM's output should at least be a reasonable place to start.

Benefits of isolated sub-processes:

1. **Accurate Representation**: By isolating events into their respective event sets, the system prevents erroneous assumptions about the order or dependencies of events across sub-processes.

2. **Enhanced Analysis**: Isolated sub-processes enable precise analysis of each workflow, making it easier to identify inefficiencies, bottlenecks, or anomalies.

3. **Better Markov Model Construction**: With sub-processes clearly defined, the Markov models generated for each process are more coherent and, therefore, easier to understand. They represent the true transitions and probabilities within a single sub-process, rather than a muddy amalgamation of multiple workflows.

4. **Scalability**: In massive complex systems with hundreds of concurrent sub-processes, event sets enable the system to better scale in a loosely-coupled system by keeping MMs restricted to a tight, coherent set of events.

CHAPTER 14

Non-Deterministic Finite Automata

The Theory of Computation explores how problems can be solved using different types of computational systems, organized as a stack of capabilities, starting with the simplest at the bottom, Finite State Automata (FSA), and each layer above more complicated with added powers. At the top of this stack is the Universal Turing Machine (UTM), a model capable of performing any computation that can be described algorithmically. In fact, the familiar CPU and RAM-based architecture we've lived with for decades is an implementation of the UTM. The most familiar level is probably Regular Expressions (RegEx), particularly to programmers.

While the Theory of Computation describes systems that grow in *complication*—with each level adding more capabilities and formal structure—it doesn't describe *complexity* in the sense used to study dynamic, emergent systems. A UTM is more powerful than a Finite State Automaton, but it is not more *complex* in the systems sense. The stack moves from simple to more elaborate, but each layer remains fully understandable and predictable within its formal logic. Complexity, by contrast, arises from interactions between components in ways that are not easily decomposed or reduced.

Non-Deterministic Finite Automata (NFA) sits near the bottom of this stack, just above FSA. FSAs recognize basic patterns, while NFAs add flexibility by allowing multiple pathways for a given input. This makes them slightly more powerful and useful for tasks requiring simultaneous evaluation of possibilities.

Unlike FSAs, which follow a single deterministic path, NFAs branch into multiple potential states in parallel, making them akin to a computational multiverse where multiple possibilities unfold at once. This parallel exploration of states is what makes NFAs "non-deterministic"—they don't commit to a single path until a final acceptance state is determined, whereas FSAs process inputs in a strictly sequential manner. While NFAs lack the versatility of higher models like UTMs, they provide an essential stepping stone in understanding the capabilities of computational systems.

Figure 94 is a fun and simple NFA for recognizing phonetically valid spellings of Eugene. Can you see all the ways? Eugene, Ugeen, Ewejeane ...

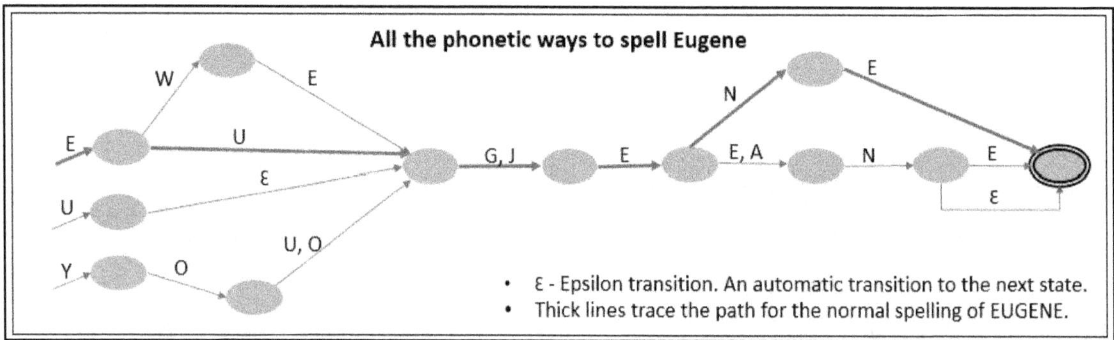

Figure 94: Fun NFA that recognizes all ways to spell Eugene.

While we could simply list all the ways to phonetically spell Eugene in a brute-force manner (like in a SQL IN clause), the NFA carries much more information than a simple list. It expresses the rules for spelling Eugene. This is like answering with the word, "buoyancy," to the question of why an egg floats in water when salt is added versus conveying an understanding of why the egg floats with the salt added to the water.

NFAs excel at tasks that require recognizing patterns or validating sequences across multiple paths simultaneously. They are particularly effective in real-time applications like rule validation in event processing systems, where there could be thousands of rules that might be interested in a particular sequence of events. NFAs present the simplicity afforded by a single algorithm that is conducive to processing very many rules in parallel.

The fact that NFAs are rules makes them a powerful structure that could be merged into enterprise-wide KGs. That is, in a manner similar to our earlier discussion of how MMs could be incorporated into KGs.

NFAs are primarily about recognizing valid sequences of symbols—most relevant to this book are event sequences. They don't provide a probability of what the next event will be—that's the role of MMs. For example:

- An MM might predict that after "Loan Reviewed," there is a 30% chance of "Loan Approved," a 50% probability of being denied, and a 20% chance of requiring further review.
- An NFA would recognize whether the sequence "Loan Reviewed → Loan Approved" is a valid step within a workflow towards some outcome (approved, denied, more info).

MMs are Like Hypotheses and NFAs are Like Theories

MMs and NFAs serve complementary roles in process modeling, each addressing different aspects of how processes unfold. In the context of Time Molecules, MMs take the lead in exploring massive and highly-diverse event logs, uncovering probabilities and transitions that bring to light patterns that may be subtle, obscured, or easily overlooked amid noise and variation. This makes MMs ideal for hypothesis generation—identifying potential structures or workflows within a dataset. NFAs, on the other hand, represent the "theory" derived and cemented from these hypotheses. They validate and formalize workflows, transforming discovered patterns into rules or grammars that can be rigorously tested and applied.

For instance, an MM might reveal that "Customer Browses → Adds to Cart → Makes Purchase" occurs with high frequency and high probability between steps, suggesting an underlying process pattern. We have a hypothesis for a workflow that is occurring. We could transform the MM into deployable rules, such as an NFA that recognizes valid sequences and reports unexpected sequences. While today, this transformation from MM to NFA often requires manual intervention, automating this process holds immense potential, bridging exploratory insights with structured process modeling.

Figure 95 compares an MM generated from hypothetical sleep data. It just reflects the order of the raw events for monitoring sleep over many different patients over many nights. The NFA is the rules of possible accepted event sequences.

Possible NFA sequence of events include:

- Wake →Light → Deep → REM→Wake up
- Wake →Light → REM→Wake up
- Wake→ Light →Wake up

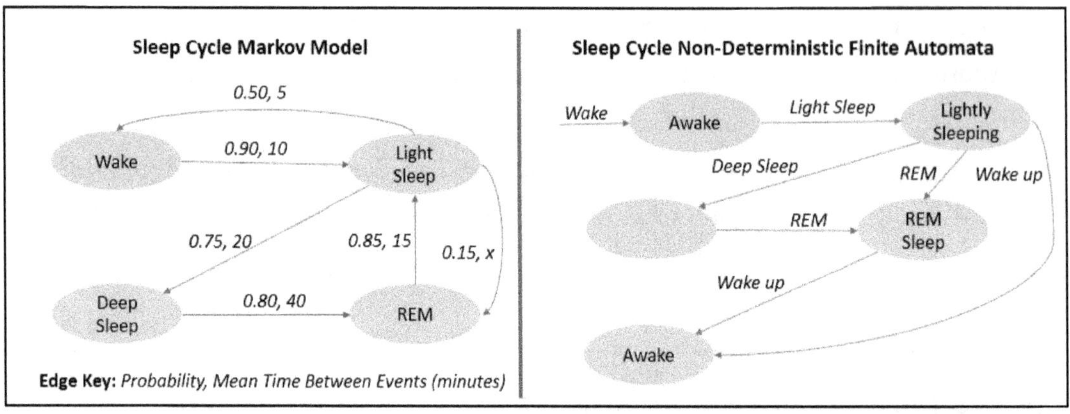

Figure 95: Comparison of a Markov model theory versus NFA rules.

Let's compare the practical differences between MMs and NFAs. MMs focus on transitions between events, with nodes representing events (actions or occurrences) and edges capturing probabilities of the next event. NFAs, in contrast, center on states—conditions or configurations a system can occupy—and transitions between these states are triggered by specific events. This makes automata ideal for scenarios where processes are well understood and the rules governing transitions can and should be explicitly spelled out. NFA, in essence, are "machines" (FSAs are a.k.a. Finite State *Machines*) that respond predictably to inputs, moving from one state to another according to predefined rules. The term "machine" is, in fact, synonymous with "automata" in this context. MMs, however, are about discovering and analyzing data to reveal patterns and relationships in processes that may not yet be understood.

Ultimately, while the elements that go into the creation of MMs and NFAs might appear similar, the constructions are fundamentally different. MMs are tools for discovery, helping us uncover latent structures in processes that are not fully known—or reconnecting with known processes that have deviated/evolved from what we last knew about them. NFAs, in contrast, codify and enforce what is understood. This complementary dynamic deepens our understanding of process modeling, whether we aim to explore the unknown or formalize the known.

Workflow Machines

It might intuitively feel "familiarly comfortable" to think of Time Molecules as just a way to monitor operational work processes. That makes sense since the collection of events has generally been used for that purpose—noticing when something goes wrong or is about to go wrong. However, the rise of process mining is about a recognition that a whole lot goes on in ways that don't match what we think is happening or that we never noticed.

Work processes are really machines—optimized through consistent tweaking throughout its life. They have measurable metrics that are emitted from them and are captured for observation and study. MMs forged from events emitted from work processes hopefully have low coefficients of variance—which suggests the process is running smoothly.

In a workflow, metrics should fall within a range of acceptability. If it doesn't, that should be revealed in a "current Markov model"—an MM created from recent events, say the last 24 hours, to study against acceptable ranges (or an older window of events to detect a trend).

That is certainly one of the primary use cases. But the world is relentlessly stochastic. This means that things change beyond anyone's ability to control and/or comprehend them. Things change and we don't know what possible delayed cascading effects await the system as a whole. This wasn't nearly the problem years ago when the world moved much more slowly, operated more locally, and requirements and systems were magnitudes simpler. But we've sped the merry-go-round of progress to dangerous levels, where things will start flying off the ride.

Today, the word "complex" is an understatement. The wise approach to wrangling complexity is to embrace it and look more towards how to evolve the system more readily as opposed to dragging it kicking and screaming back to within normal operating parameters.

For example, if an MM reveals that the time between ordering food and leaving the restaurant is highly variable, don't just give the waitstaff instructions for encouraging a time limit on the diners. Dig deeper. Ask, what is it about the diners who stay for very long periods or even very short periods? And customize to those segmented needs.

Probabilities to Workflow: Markov to NFA

The motivation for converting MMs into NFAs stems from the progression of understanding processes. While MMs are powerful tools for discovering patterns and sequences within event-driven data, they function primarily as probabilistic representations. These models are ideal for uncovering the likelihood of transitions between events, providing a starting point to map processes based on observed behavior.

However, once the MM has sufficiently captured and illuminated the dynamics of a process, it becomes valuable to shift from probabilistic representation to deterministic structure—i.e., NFAs. NFAs represent a bridge between discovery and operationalization, turning probabilistic insights into well-defined workflows. By defining states and transitions explicitly, an NFA is a deterministic perspective on a process, enabling direct application in systems or workflows.

The real power of NFAs lies in their ability to validate sequences—essentially answering whether a particular "word" (sequence of events, same as a word is a strict sequence of letters) belongs to the "language" (valid event set) that defines the scope of the NFA. This is conceptually similar to how regular expressions validate patterns in text. For example, in a restaurant process, an NFA can validate whether a sequence like *arrive → seated → order → served → depart* is a valid execution of the process. While that sequence might happen in real life, it should *not* happen since it doesn't mention the bill being paid—without which, it defeats the purpose of a business. This validation capability makes NFAs essential for recognizing and structuring observed sequences into deterministic workflows. Moreover, NFAs align closely with the end goal of process mining: cataloging the deterministic workflows within our enterprise and deploying them as a big part of an "enterprise nervous system." This is particularly valuable in scenarios like customer service, logistics, or manufacturing, where workflows must be executed consistently and predictably.

From Markov to NFA

The method I chose to cover for converting an MM to NFA involves LLMs. Code 79 is a sample of a prompt to ChatGPT along with Figure 96, a graphic snapshot of the *restaurantguest* MM we're now familiar with.

```
Please study the attached Markov model that is based on events serving customers in a
restaurant. Please create an NFA based on the events shown in the Markov model. The nodes
of the Markov model become the edges of the NFA. You must Infer the state that the NFA
nodes represent from the nodes of the Markov model. Create Neo4j Cypher for creating that
NFA.
```

Code 79: Prompt to ChatGPT to convert a Markov model into an NFA.

Figure 96 and Figure 97 illustrate the before and after, respectively, of the transformation from MM to NFA. Each node in the MM (Figure 96) corresponds to an event (arrive, seated, order), and the edges represent the probabilities for the next event.

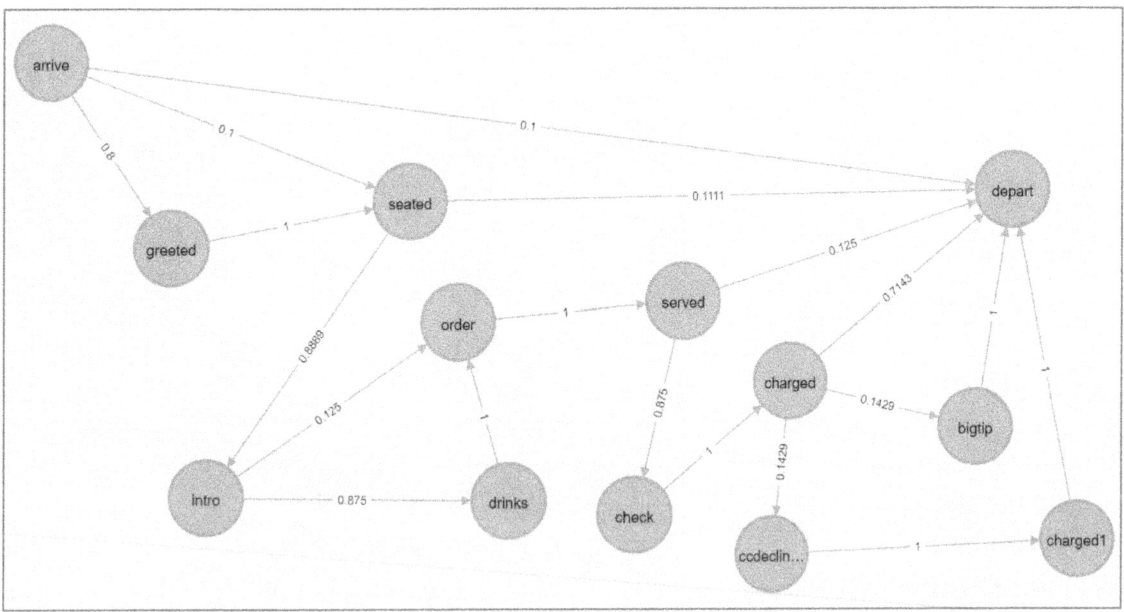

Figure 96: Markov model showing probabilistic transitions between events.

ChatGPT responded with an explanation of what it did along with the Cypher code for importing it into Neo4j (*Markov_to_NFA.cql* on the GitHub repository). Figure 97 pulls all that together into an NFA. The most obvious contrast between the MM (Figure 96) and the NFA (Figure 97) is that the nodes of the MM are now the edges of the NFA.

When converting the MM into an NFA (Figure 97):

1. **Nodes of the MM become edges of the NFA**: Each event in the MM (arrive, order, depart) becomes a relationship (or transition) in the NFA.

2. **States (the nodes) in the NFA are inferred from the MM by ChatGPT**: ChatGPT inferred the NFA states (nodes text in Figure 97) as the conditions that exist after each event. For instance, the seated event from the MM became a transition (relationship) and points to the node, "After Seated" in the NFA—the state of being seated and waiting for your server to come to the table.

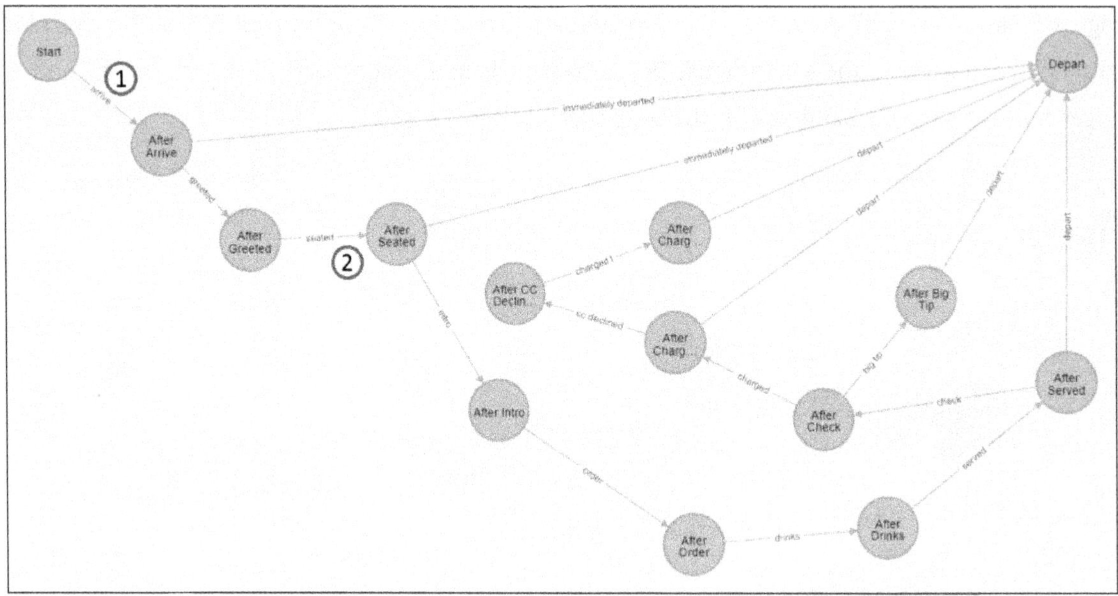

Figure 97: NFA demonstrating inferred states and deterministic transitions.

NFAs in Event Processing

NFAs are a natural fit for real-time event processing, where vast streams of data need to be evaluated against numerous rules simultaneously. Imagine monitoring customer interactions—tracking events like when a customer places an order, if the order exceeds $1000, or if it happens shortly after visiting particular pages on the website. In such a scenario, thousands of rules might need to evaluate the same incoming event. NFAs make this process remarkably efficient as they are very conducive to parallel evaluation.

NFAs excel because they inherently support multiple possible transitions for a single event, allowing them to evaluate many patterns or rules at the same time. When a customer places an order, for instance, the event triggers transitions across all relevant states simultaneously. Instead of evaluating rules one at a time, the system processes everything concurrently. This parallelism ensures that the system remains scalable and performs efficiently, even when dealing with large event streams and complex rule sets.

This concept was taken to the next level by the Automata Processor (AP),[6] a now-defunct hardware device, specifically a kind of chip, developed by Micron Technology. The AP was specifically designed to process NFAs in a hardware implementation, enabling unmatched parallelism for applications like event processing, pattern recognition, and real-time fraud detection. By mapping states and transitions directly onto this specialized chip, it could evaluate thousands of paths simultaneously, something traditional software implementations of NFAs struggle to achieve. Although the AP is no longer commercially available, it demonstrated the potential of NFAs in real-time, high-throughput environments.

Even without specialized chips like the Automata Processor, NFAs remain highly relevant. In fields like fraud detection, NFAs can identify suspicious sequences of events—such as multiple failed logins followed by a large transfer—in real time. Similarly, IoT systems use NFAs to process streams of sensor data, identifying conditions like temperature spikes or unusual patterns. They're also effective for validating workflows, ensuring the proper sequence of steps in a process.

---

[6] Micron Technology, Inc. (2014). Micron Automata Processor: A New Computing Paradigm for High-Speed Pattern Matching and Parallel Processing. Micron Technology. https://www.micron.com.

CHAPTER 15

The Artificial Consultant to a Consultant

In today's complex world—global in scope and now hyper-accelerated by AI improving at a "hockey stick curve" rate—businesses grapple with challenges that are anything but straightforward. These aren't the kinds of problems you can Google your way out of or solve with off-the-shelf analytics. They are complex, multi-faceted, unstructured, and require strategies and tactics that balance competing goals such as profitability, customer satisfaction, and operational efficiency—all while managing risk. This is the domain of a strategic consultant, whose role is to bring deep wisdom and original creativity towards systematically solving complex problems. This is beyond expertise and experience.

However, even such rare consultants can benefit from AI, as do consultants of other levels—just as traditional BI systems raised the value of analysts a level or two. The LLMs of today are like that know-it-all friend who knows a whole lot about most things—only turbo-charged. But this isn't just about building an AI know-it-all. It's about creating an *artificial consultant to the consultant*—a system that empowers human consultants, augmenting their ability to analyze, strategize, and validate solutions for problems that are beyond the reach of existing tools.

This chapter explores how *Time Molecules* lays another layer on the foundation of such a system, along with what I describe in *Enterprise Intelligence*. By integrating process mining, Markov models, and probabilistic reasoning with the context-rich insights of traditional BI augmented with the EKG, *Time Molecules* doesn't just analyze—it facilitates strategic decision-making rooted from an understanding of how an enterprise's processes evolved over time.

The goal of the EKG and TimeSolution is a framework that supports the needs of a consultant in all phases of strategic original thinking: identify the problem, inventory all the pieces lying about, notice things others don't notice, figure out what we still need, and piece together the story out of that big bag of disparate things. We finally test the hell out of it and deliver a plan that solves the problem while seeing ahead through the complexities of real-world trade-offs and contradictions.

This is what I think of in regard to *abductive* reasoning, as I mentioned a few times. The highest form of reasoning beyond so many that the best examples I can think of that are capable of this level of reasoning are fictional—as I mentioned, Sherlock Holmes and House, the TV character—although Dr. Lisa Sanders, a real person, is often cited as the inspiration for the diagnostic prowess of the House character.

As hard as we may try, the world we live in is one of imperfect information—which is why our evolved cognitive abilities have catapulted us far beyond other creatures. Yet the decisions and plans we make are still riddled with blind spots, shaped by missing context, unforeseen variables, and adversarial thwarts from other sentient beings. As a result, outcomes frequently carry unintended consequences—sometimes real doozies—or turn out vastly different from what we intended. In hindsight, we reconstruct these moments as stories of genius, layered with dramatic framing that smooths over the messier truth.

Abductive reasoning is beyond inductive and deductive reasoning. It is about transformative creativity. It requires the true partnership of machine and human intelligence. LLMs and their surrounding innovations (e.g., RAG, chain of thought, agents, etc.) have come a long way. But although it's trained on a wide breadth of the human-generated and/or automatically-generated corpus of knowledge, it's incomplete—LLMs of today have incorporated just a fraction of how most of the billions of people think and what they've experienced.

Pick Two

In the real world, solving complex problems usually comes down to creatively managing trade-offs. Henry Ford famously said (at least it's usually attributed to him), "You can have it good, cheap, or fast—pick two." This idea holds true across industries, from manufacturing to healthcare to AI strategy. True ingenuity isn't just about maximizing one goal—it's about finding a solution that best balances and maximizes multiple competing priorities.

It's a surprisingly elusive ideal. Consider the recent emergence of Magnacut™, used to make knife blades—a rare instance of solving for three competing goals—a blade steel designed to be tough, hold an edge, and resist corrosion. Rather than excelling in just one category while compromising the others, it strikes an ingenious equilibrium across all three at high levels of quality, making it one of the most versatile materials available.

Similarly, as mentioned before, there is the Triple Aim of the healthcare domain—simultaneously improving population health, enhancing individual outcomes, and reducing costs—was the guiding principle before the COVID-19 pandemic. For better or worse, innovations such as HMO/PPOs and preventive healthcare helped raise all three competing metrics to appreciable extents. When the crisis hit, the balance collapsed, and population health became the dominant concern, sidelining cost and individual outcomes in ways that would have been unthinkable just days before.

These trade-offs define the hardest problems in business and strategy. Unlike routine optimizations, where the best answer is rife with "best practices," strategic decisions related to novel problems require navigating contradictions, balancing constraints, and thinking beyond conventional models. This is my intent for the EKG and TimeSolution—not just to analyze data, but to map what we know, identify unseen connections, and reframe problems in ways that reveal novel solutions.

To solve these challenges, we need more than just predictive analytics. We need systems that *encourage* us to think outside the box of possibilities, discovering new ways to align competing objectives with what we have or can create. Time Molecules enables this shifting to a systems thinking mindset—by modeling how processes evolve, uncovering transition patterns, revealing where interventions can have the greatest impact, and linking to rich semantics via knowledge graphs and LLMs. Combined with the EKG's structured reasoning, this framework provides a way to approach strategic trade-offs with the same kind of ingenuity that made Magnacut™ possible, that balanced the Triple Aim before the pandemic, and that drives every real-world decision where trade-offs are inevitable and unintended consequences are dire.

In the end, success doesn't come from just picking two—it comes from redefining the problem so ingenious solutions emerge.

Situation, Background, Analysis, Recommendation - SBAR

Systems and processes, cause and effect, evolving rules, and abductive reasoning matter only when we're concerned with strategic, original, and outside-the-box thinking. In this topic, I'll walk through a framework for approaching novel solutions to novel problems. This discussion is organized using the SBAR framework—a concise method for communicating strategy and problem-solving that stands for *Situation, Background, Analysis, Recommendation.* While its structure was inspired by military and aviation communication protocols, SBAR was formalized and popularized by the healthcare industry, where it became a widely used tool for structuring decisions and communicating clearly under uncertainty—particularly in clinical and consulting contexts. Here, I offer an SBAR approach in an enterprise analytics context:

1. **Situation** – What's the problem? Define the problem in terms of a *strategy map*, a web of competing goals and objectives, and highlight the goals that are suffering.
2. **Background** – How did we get here? What has changed? Investigate what has changed by identifying trends, shifts in processes, and evolving relationships across time and dimensions.
3. **Analysis** – What does the data say? Use tools like MMs and conditional probabilities to map cause-and-effect relationships, inefficiencies, and bottlenecks.
4. **Recommendation** – What should we do? Develop a balanced strategy that aligns goals, mitigates risks, and supports organizational objectives.

This chapter isn't just about how AI can be strategic—it's about how Time Molecules enables this by creating a system that connects data to strategy, transforms insights into action, and empowers consultants to tackle challenges that are beyond Google or the AI capabilities of today.

A strategy map is a graph-based visualization, born out of the Performance Management discipline, that illustrates an organization's objectives, priorities, and causal relationships. It provides a structured way to align strategic goals across key perspectives, often including financial, customer, internal processes, and learning and growth, showing how actions in one area impact outcomes in another.

Because a strategy map is a directed graph, it can be integrated into a KG, enhancing it with the intent of each KPI relationship of the strategy in a semantic format. This makes it particularly useful in abductive thinking, where decision-makers need to map known information, uncover hidden connections, and infer possible solutions. A strategy map linking objectives to real-world constraints and trade-offs helps structure complex problem-solving, making it a powerful tool for strategic planning and decision-making.

Let's now explore how this SBAR approach might work towards resolving very difficult problems within an enterprise, both big and small.

Situation: Defining the Problem

For a doctor, a high-end consultant, the situation is the chief complaint. But there is often more than one problem facing a patient at the same time. How are they related?

A consultant's first task is to define the problem, and the best way to do this is through a strategy map. A strategy map doesn't just present the problem as a linear checklist of tasks—it captures the chains of intents within the complexity of the challenge as a web of competing goals, objectives, and metrics. For example, a business trying to increase revenue may need to balance objectives like optimizing pricing, improving customer retention, reducing operational costs, and staying compliant with regulations. These goals often pull in different directions, and understanding their relationships is critical to framing the problem.

Figure 98 is an example of a simple strategy map. It's a graph of the intended cause and effect of a private medical practice.

In *Time Molecules*, the strategy map becomes the lens through which these competing objectives are visualized. Goals are represented as nodes in the map, connected by relationships that reflect our intent, interdependencies, trade-offs, and/or correlations.

The Effect Correlation Score (ECS)[7] plays a pivotal role in this map by quantifying the correlation between the status scores over a time period of two KPIs (often a Pearson correlation). For example:

[7] Effect Correlation Score: https://eugeneasahara.com/2013/12/02/the-effect-correlation-score-for-kpis/.

- A high ECS between "on-time delivery" and "customer retention" (both statuses go up and down together over time periods) may imply a real relationship. For example, delays significantly impact loyalty, suggesting on-time delivery should be a priority focus area.
- A high inverse ECS between "cost savings" and "product quality" (one status goes up, the other goes down) might highlight the risks of overly aggressive cost-cutting strategies.

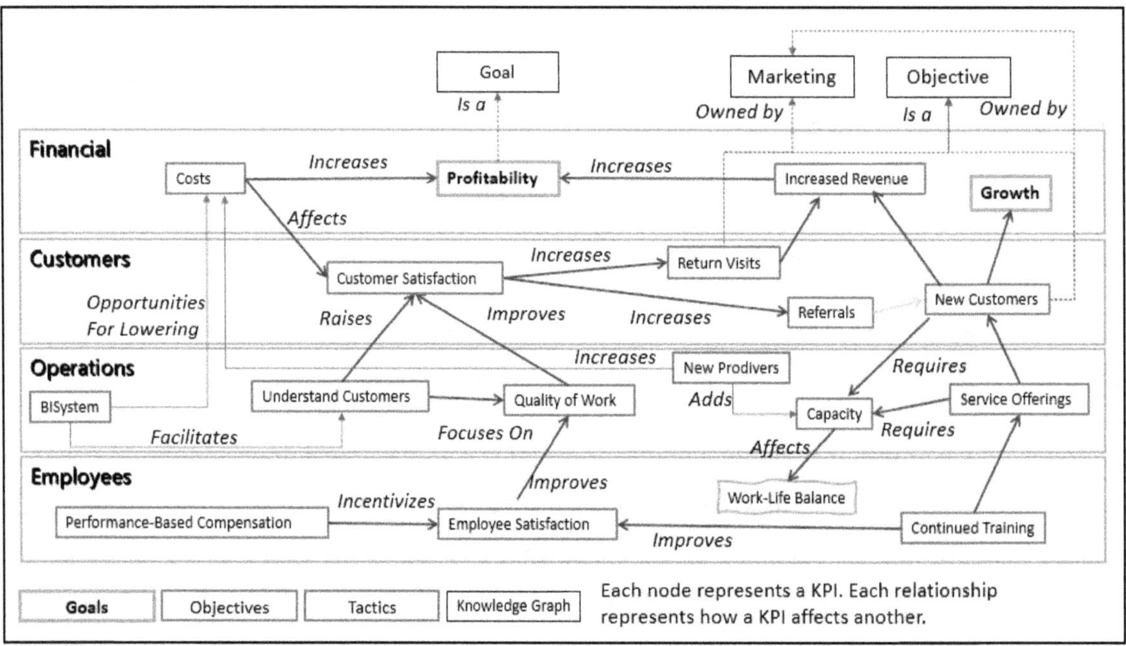

Figure 98: Sample of a generic small business strategy map.

MMs complement the strategy map by abstracting entire processes into probabilities, transitions, and outcomes. While the strategy map explains how competing goals and metrics interact, MMs provide predictive insights into the dynamics of the process itself:

- An MM for a sales funnel might show the probabilities of customers progressing through stages like "browsing," "add to cart," and "purchase."
- Combined with ECS insights, this helps consultants pinpoint where friction in the process is affecting KPI statuses, such as why "customer satisfaction" is trending toward "minor pain." See Appendix C for an exploration of events triggered by KPI statuses—usually exceeding thresholds.

This combination of the strategy map, the EKG, and MMs enables the AI consultant to go beyond merely identifying the symptoms of the problem. Strategy maps are a framework for expressing how we intend to handle competing goals, while the EKG and MMs provide the means to validate each intended cause and effect. Just as a doctor draws on vital signs, symptoms, and patient history—layered onto a mental model of cause and effect built through years of training and clinical experience—the AI consultant uses the strategy map, EKG, and Markov models to form a similarly dynamic and structured understanding of the problem.

The strategy map expressing the relationships of the system from which we can trace the problem is the deliverable of understanding the situation. A modified version of this strategy map will be the deliverable of the final Recommendation.

Background: What Has Changed?

For a doctor, background is about collecting information about the context and what has changed since the patient was last in normal health. What did you notice? Where have you been? Who have you had contact with?

Once the problem is defined, the next step is to understand its context under the stated problem. After obtaining a fair understanding of the system, consultants approach this by asking, "What has changed?"—not just in the environment but in the processes, relationships, and metrics that define the system. In *Time Molecules*, this phase involves uncovering shifts over time, across dimensions (e.g., locations, products, customer segments), or within processes to identify what has led to the current situation.

Traditional BI systems offer a starting point by highlighting trends in KPIs or metrics. For instance, a BI dashboard might show that customer churn rates have risen in the past quarter or that revenue growth is slowing in specific regions. While this information is valuable, it often stops short of explaining why these trends are occurring. *Time Molecules* provides a sharper lens by analyzing changes in processes through event sets, probabilities, and efficiency metrics. Following are key insights from *Time Molecules*:

- **Event Set Changes**: An event set defines the steps in a process. Comparing MMs across time can reveal how these steps have evolved. For example, in a retail setting, the 2023 MM might show a process where customers typically go from "browsing" to "purchase" with minimal steps. By 2024, a new event like "coupon applied" might appear, altering customer behavior and introducing new dynamics that cascade down the process.

- **Probability Shifts Between Events**: Even if the event set remains unchanged, the likelihood of transitioning from one step to the next may shift over time. For instance, the probability of moving from "add to cart" to "checkout" might decrease, suggesting that customers are encountering friction in the checkout process.
- **Variations in Efficiency**: Metrics like the coefficient of variation highlight inconsistencies in process execution. A widening variation in the time between "order placed" and "order shipped" could indicate operational bottlenecks or inefficiencies.
- **Comparing Across Dimensions**: *Time Molecules* enables comparisons across different dimensions, such as locations or customer segments. For example, one region may show a significantly higher probability of customers abandoning their carts after adding items, pointing to localized issues like website performance or shipping costs.

In the Background phase, historical context can be just as important as current observations—it's the comparison between historic and current that holds the answer to "what has changed". Consultants must look for patterns that explain what changed as well as what are the effects. *Time Molecules* facilitates this by enabling a comparison of MMs across time or dimensions, uncovering patterns that might not be as readily visible in traditional aggregated BI data alone. For example:

- A spike in delays might coincide with the introduction of a new compliance step in a manufacturing process.
- A decline in customer retention might align with changes in marketing strategies or pricing policies.

Ideally, the background could be presented as a knowledge graph of how parts relate. In this day of LLMs, textual notes and other artifacts taken during the background stage could be fed to LLMs, requesting it to be expressed as a knowledge graph. That knowledge graph could ultimately be assimilated into the EKG knowledge graph—after all, knowledge is cache.

Lastly, the background phase often reveals that the problem stated during the situation phase isn't actually the root issue. In many cases, the patient—or any customer—describes symptoms or consequences without recognizing the true underlying cause. The situation phase is more about listening: collecting the initial framing of the problem from the customer's point of view. But the background phase is where we begin to validate or challenge that framing—gathering context, uncovering hidden factors, and asking whether we're even solving the right problem.

Analysis: Finding Cause and Effect

For a doctor, analysis is the creation of a theory tracing how background information leads to the problem. And that is our diagnosis.

With the problem defined and the context established, the next step is to trace back to the root causes to understand what happened. This phase requires connecting the dots between clues from the situation and background, forming hypotheses, and testing them iteratively. In *Time Molecules*, this process is powered by the integration of MMs, Bayesian reasoning, and enterprise insights from EKG.

Consultants rely on analysis to answer two critical questions: What caused the problem? And how can it be resolved? *Time Molecules* provides the tools to navigate these questions, identifying inefficiencies, bottlenecks, and patterns that point to the underlying causes of issues.

Leveraging MMs for Process Dynamics

MMs abstract processes into transition probabilities, offering a map of how events flow over a set of process cycles (cases). By comparing MMs segmented across time and/or other dimensions, consultants can identify critical changes in process dynamics. For example:

- **Bottlenecks and Inefficiencies**: A widening coefficient of variation between events (e.g., order_placed→order_shipped) might reveal inconsistent execution or resource shortages.
- **Emerging Risks**: Probability shifts in an MM can signal new risks. For example, if the probability of moving from application_submitted→loan_approved drops significantly, it might indicate unknown stricter compliance checks or changes in customer behavior.
- **Cause-and-Effect Insights**: The sequence aspect of Time Molecules is particularly useful for identifying how changes in one part of the process cascade through the system, highlighting potential root causes.

Bayesian/Conditional Reasoning for Cause and Effect

While MMs focus on transitions and probabilities, Bayesian reasoning adds a layer of causal analysis. By integrating HMMs, *Time Molecules* can uncover hidden states that influence observable events. For example:

- In a customer journey, an HMM might reveal that a hidden state (in a newly developed MM), such as "customer uncertainty," drives increased cart abandonment rates.
- Bayesian reasoning helps consultants explore not just what happened but why it happened—through chains of strong conditional probabilities—connecting observable symptoms to underlying causes.

Iterative Hypothesis Testing

Analysis in *Time Molecules* is not a one-pass process. Consultants must iterate between hypotheses, testing their validity with data:

1. **Form Hypotheses**: Based on MMs, Bayesian reasoning, and EKG insights, consultants form theories about what caused the problem.
2. **Test and Validate Hypotheses**: Data from *Time Molecules and the EKG*—such as probability changes, event set variations, or correlation scores—is used to test these theories.
3. **Refine and Revisit**: As new insights emerge, consultants may circle back to earlier phases to adjust their understanding of the problem or context.

Recommendation: A Diagnosis

For a doctor, the recommendation is the treatment plan—the product of the doctor's vast knowledge and investigative skills. This is the plan of attack to be executed.

The Deliverable: Strategy as a Plan

The culmination of the consultant's work is the recommendation—a clear, actionable strategy that not only addresses the problem but also balances competing goals and mitigates risks (risks to be avoided are often competing goals in themselves). In the context of *Time Molecules*, this phase synthesizes insights from the strategy map, MMs, and the EKG to create a plan that is both dynamic and grounded in data.

Crafting the Solution Strategy

The recommendation phase transforms the diagnosis into a strategy map, showing how specific actions will resolve the problem while considering trade-offs. This is more than a linear to-do list—it's a multi-dimensional plan that accounts for the complexity of real-world decision-making.

For example, a retail business facing increased cart abandonment might need to optimize pricing, improve checkout usability, and address shipping delays. The strategy map would link these actions to the relevant KPIs (e.g., conversion rate, customer satisfaction), showing how they interact and prioritizing them based on their ECS.

Delivering the Plan

The final output of this phase is a comprehensive plan that could be presented as:

1. **Textual Recommendations**: Generated by the consultant and assisted by LLMs, these outline the actions to be taken, the trade-offs considered, and the risks mitigated.
2. **Strategy Map**: A graph representation of the plan, showing how actions align with goals and KPIs. The value of expressing the resolution as a strategy map (a kind of knowledge graph) is to assimilate it into the EKG.
3. **Supporting Data and Simulations**: Evidence-based insights that validate the strategy and provide transparency.

Figure 99 shows an example of the strategy map we created in the situation phase (Figure 98). The area within the dashed outline applies our recommendation to the strategy map. We must add another doctor as well as move into a bigger office, towards the goal of increasing our billable capacity (add a new producer and ensure she has the room to work). In turn, it enables us to take on more new patients, which increases revenue, which increases profitability.

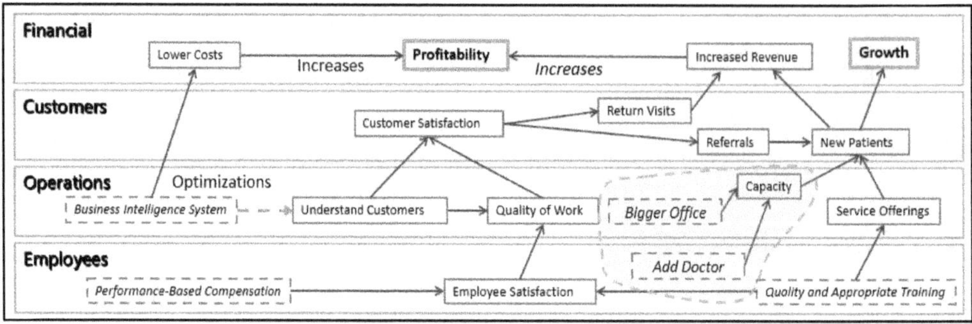

Figure 99: Example of a strategy map after applying recommendation.

Conclusion to the Artificial Consultant to the Consultant

As organizations navigate an increasingly complex world, the ability to reframe data through multiple interpretive facets, uncover hidden relationships, and balance competing objectives becomes the strategic advantage as powerful as human sentience is over other creatures. Traditional analytics provide insights, but true strategic consulting requires abductive reasoning—seeing beyond the data, connecting the dots, and constructing novel solutions.

Time Molecules, in conjunction with the EKG of Enterprise Intelligence, extends this capability by transforming fragmented data into structured, strategic intelligence. Through Markov models, Bayesian reasoning, and strategy maps, this system moves beyond predictive analytics to causal understanding and strategic foresight.

The SBAR framework applied in this chapter demonstrates how AI can augment human consultants, not by replacing them but by enhancing their ability to reason through complex, multi-layered problems. The artificial consultant to the consultant is a partner in discovery, helping decision-makers reframe challenges, explore possibilities, and craft strategies that go beyond "picking two" to redefine the entire problem space.

As AI continues to evolve, the real challenge is not only whether it can generate answers—but whether it can help us ask better questions and process many decks of cards in the air. The future of strategic consulting, in fact, the relevance of our sentience, lies in systems that support, not replace, our original thinking—and that is precisely my intent for Time Molecules and the EKG of *Enterprise Intelligence.*

CHAPTER 16

The Time Side of Business Intelligence

Traditional Business Intelligence has centered on quantifying the world—aggregating facts into cubes composed of tuples that provide measures of what happened. But a system is not a mere value—it's a graph. And as is the theme of this book, the world is made of interacting systems.

While OLAP cubes provide static summaries of co-occurring attributes, Time Molecules aggregate patterns of progression—how things move from one state to another, with all their timing and uncertainty. Where tuples capture presence, Markov models capture flow. Where the cube presents snapshots, Time Molecules presents storylines.

This chapter draws the two sides together, which draws this book to its conclusion. It shows how OLAP and Time Molecules can sit side by side as complementary representations of enterprise behavior—one focused on metric outcomes, the other on process structure. Together, they support a deeper form of intelligence: one that not only measures but reveals the shape and rhythm of change.

Where OLAP cubes organize and aggregate tuples (a qualified "thing" or concept), Time Molecules aggregate massive cases of event sequences over time into hidden Markov models. Instead of just looking at what happened, they focus on how processes/systems unfold—capturing patterns, transitions, and time-based dependencies.

Interestingly, if we think of a memory or observation as the presence of a set of things—all co-occurring at a moment in time—it forms a tuple. This can be visualized as a static snapshot, similar to a Markov model if we disregard the element of time. In this view, each tuple is a cluster of sensed phenomena (sight, smell, emotions, etc.) linked by the "presence of" relationships. While Markov models emphasize sequence and timing, tuples emphasize co-presence, forming a foundation upon which sequential models can later be built.

As mentioned, traditional OLAP cube BI systems serve the fundamental "slice and dice" form of query and provide "descriptive" answers—who, what, when, and where. The answers are scalar and metric-based. But our dynamic world is made up of collections of interacting processes and systems. Rich questions are about how and why. The answer to how and why questions describe a system/process.

By integrating MMs, the TCW, and process mining principles, Time Molecules extend the structured efficiency of OLAP from static values of tuples to dynamic sequences—allowing decision-makers (or AI systems) to analyze patterns of change rather than just snapshots of data.

The result of the partnership between the MMs and TCW (and/or the "Bayesian Probabilities" of TimeSolution) is a massive but structured web of correlations, as illustrated in Figure 100.

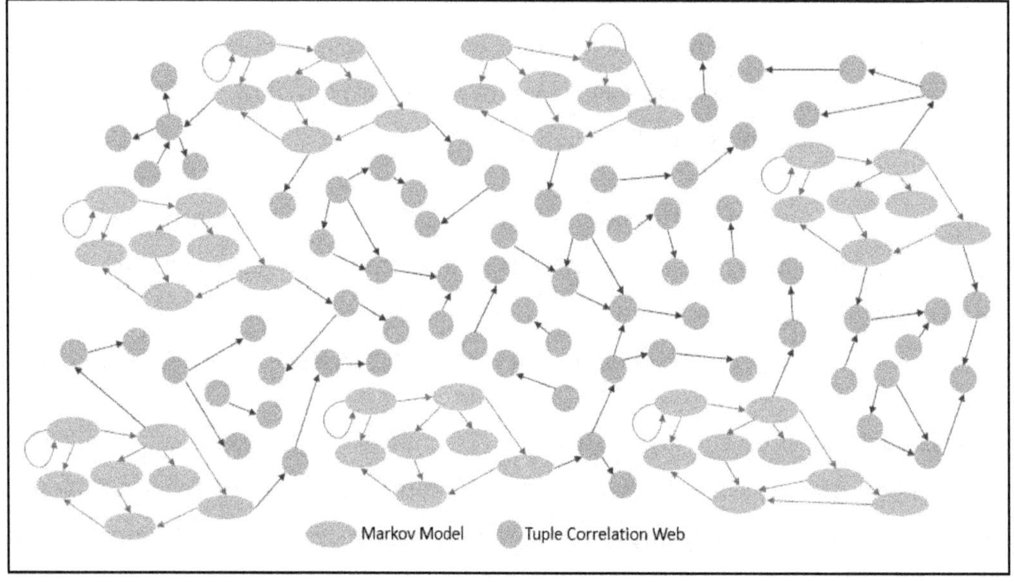

Figure 100: Markov models and the TCW into a web of Hidden Markov Models.

Figure 101 depicts two sides of the same analysis BI coin—process-oriented tuples versus metric-oriented tuples.

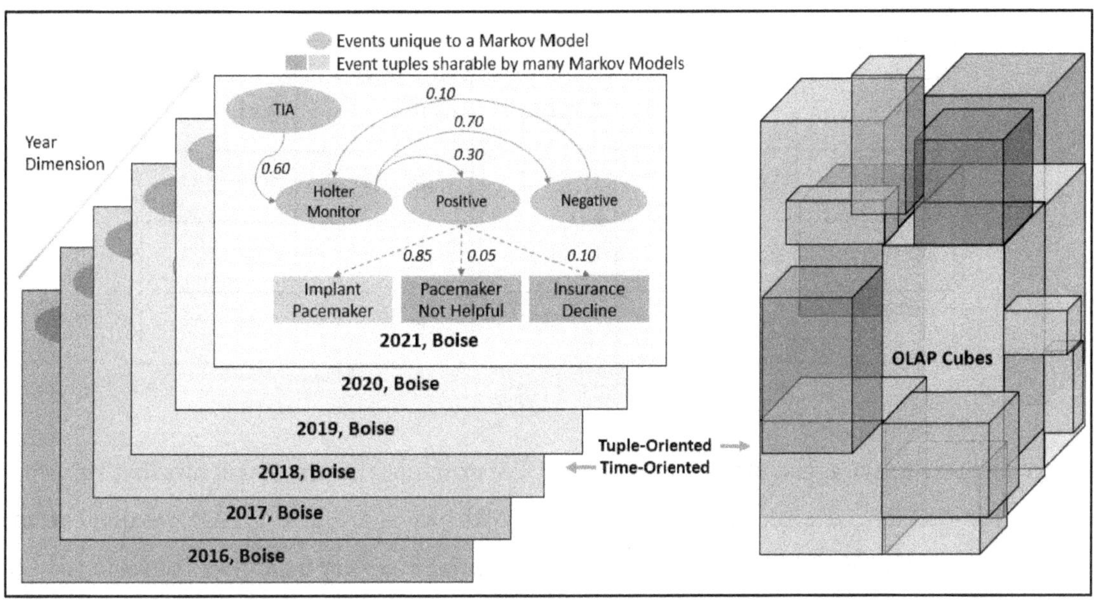

Figure 101 – Depiction of the time-oriented and tuple-oriented data structures of analysis.

On the right is the OLAP cube, composed of a number of sum/count aggregations, each a compression of facts of unique combinations of attributes. Each aggregation is represented by one of the subcubes inside the entire OLAP cube. Each aggregation consists of a *set of tuples*, each element representing a value from each dimension.

Recall the sample tuple from above, *(Laptop, West, Q1 2024,Revenue) = $2.5B*, which is just one tuple amongst many. For example, one of those subcubes could include the set of tuples shown in Table 27.

Product	Region	Date	Revenue	Count
Laptop	West	Q1 2024	2.5B	100M
Laptop	East	Q1 2024	1.3B	50M
Laptop	Northwest	Q1 2024	1.2B	60M
Laptop	Southeast	Q1 2024	5.2B	80M
Laptop	Southwest	Q1 2024	4.2B	45M
Desktop	West	Q1 2024	3.8B	32M

Product	Region	Date	Revenue	Count
Desktop	East	Q1 2024	0.6B	98M
Desktop	Northwest	Q1 2024	1.5B	100M
Desktop	Southeast	Q1 2024	3.1B	50M
Desktop	Southwest	Q1 2024	4.7B	33M

Table 27: Sampling of Tuples in one subcube.

Each row represents the aggregate of some measure. For example, the first row shows that 100 million sales transactions totaled a revenue of $2.5 billion. With pre-aggregated OLAP, we don't need to recompute that value every time it's requested—which preserves very expensive compute costs and wait times—effectively conserving time, Azure/AWS/GCP bills, and the electricity required to compute it.

On the left of Figure 101 is an array of hidden Markov models, an array of the TIA/pacemaker case—diced by year (2016-2021) and filtered to patients in Boise.

Each HMM in the array encapsulates not just an outcome but a graph of transitions leading to that outcome, compressed into probabilities. Unlike metric-based aggregations, which summarize static facts, these models represent aggregated processes, showing how events unfold over time. To reiterate, the structure is similar to an OLAP cube, but instead of each tuple holding a sum or count, each tuple is a *Time Molecule* expressed as a Markov model—a representation of process flow rather than a single numerical measure.

Each frame on the left side of Figure 101 represents a HMM specific to a year and location—in this case, Boise from 2016 to 2021. Each model encapsulates the unique event dynamics for that year, reflecting how probabilities of key events may change over time. For example, if a patient suffers a TIA (transient ischemic attack), the model shows:

- A **60%** chance of being ordered a Holter Monitor.
- A **30%** chance that the Holter Monitor will yield a positive result.
- An **85%** chance that a positive result leads to a pacemaker implant.

The overall probability of receiving a pacemaker after a TIA is calculated by multiplying the transition probabilities along that path: *0.60 * 0.30 * 0.85 = 15.3*

Alternatively, the model captures other outcomes—such as a negative Holter Monitor result leading to no intervention or insurance denial, each with their respective probabilities.

By slicing these models by year, we can observe how medical practice patterns, patient demographics, or insurance policies evolve over time. Each year's HMM reflects subtle shifts in these probabilities—perhaps due to new technologies, regulations, or changing patient profiles.

Where a BI OLAP cube query can quickly retrieve a count of TIAs in a region from millions of cases, Time Molecules retrieves a model that expresses the likelihood of a patient progressing from stroke to pacemaker implantation, with probabilities of intermediate outcomes. The "value" of a tuple is no longer a simple scalar number but a dynamic model of transitions, enabling deeper insight into patterns of change.

By caching these HMMs, Time Molecules achieves computational efficiency analogous to traditional, cube-based OLAP pre-aggregation. This enables decision-makers to not only analyze what has happened but also gain a structured, probabilistic view of how things tend to happen, in a highly-performant and user-friendly manner reminiscent of OLAP cubes. Neither side is replaced—they complement each other.

The two complementary sides reinforce each other. For example, a BI user might slice and dice the OLAP cube and notice, say, a drop in pacemaker implants in a particular region. They can then drill into the corresponding Time Molecules, examining the Markov models related to pacemakers to see which transitions—such as diagnostic steps or approvals—have shifted recently. Or, starting from the Time Molecules side, they may spot an unexpected change in process flow and pivot back to the cube to quantify the business impact. Or a KPI status is unexpectedly poor (KPIs are often calculated from BI data), and we could investigate the problem by studying how Markov models of the business processes related to the KPIs have changed from when the KPI was good to now.

Conclusion

The world is not a static object, memory, or vision—it is dynamic, interconnected, and alive with interacting processes that evolve each other over time. In Time Molecules, we've explored how understanding these processes, rather than just the events they produce, enables us to grasp the complexity of systems in ways that traditional models often fail to capture. By embracing frameworks like Markov models, Bayesian probabilities, and the Tuple Correlation Web, we can build a structure that promotes a richer, more nuanced understanding of how enterprises operate, adapt, and thrive.

Time Molecules expands on the foundation laid in Enterprise Intelligence, where the Enterprise Knowledge Graph provides a way to organize, connect, and navigate the structured relationships within an enterprise—that of the databases, the workers all with unique knowledge, and the agencies outside the enterprise with competing goals. That is, in a way that's reasonably unintrusive to the already over-burdened workers. Here, we've shifted our focus to the fluidity of processes—how events interact and converge to form the lifeblood of business operations. Events are not isolated data points but shadows of deeper workflows, sub-processes, and webs of dependencies. Understanding this interplay is the key to unlocking insights that are not only descriptive but predictive, proscriptive, and transformative.

The value of the concepts laid out in this book is that it not only reveals how systems work but also creates pathways for automating this understanding. The method described involves a combination of human expertise and AI assistance. However, as with most methodologies, eventually, all aspects of this approach can be automated. At the time of writing, AI is already capable of assisting humans to the point of potentially bootstrapping the Time Molecules process itself, automating tasks like ingesting vast streams of events from disparate sources, sorting events into event sets, and leveraging descriptions and object links in a knowledge graph to generate transforms.

At its heart, this book is about shifting perspectives. It's about moving awareness from snapshots to sequences, from isolated events to interconnected systems, and from static data to dynamic processes. This shift is not merely technical; it's a mindset. It asks us to embrace the emergent, the uncertain, and the evolving nature of systems. It's a way of thinking that echoes the natural world, where ecosystems, organisms, and even molecules are defined not by their individual parts but by the relationships and processes that bind them together.

The practical implications of this shift are profound. By recognizing processes as living systems, we can model the flow of events with precision, uncover hidden patterns, and design systems that adapt to change rather than resist it. We can bridge the gap between intuition and analytics, enabling AI systems to operate more like consultants—synthesizing data, reasoning through complexity, and offering strategies that balance competing objectives.

As we move forward, the challenge lies not just in the tools we build but in how we use them to shape the future of enterprise intelligence. The insights captured in Time Molecules are not endpoints; they are stepping stones toward a deeper understanding of how systems evolve and interact. By continuing to refine these ideas and integrate them into our daily practices, we can create enterprises that are not only efficient but resilient, innovative, and capable of thriving in an ever-changing world.

In the end, it's not just about better tools or smarter systems—it's about cultivating a way of seeing beyond our learned constraints. A way of seeing the world, not as a collection of isolated tasks or events, but as a tapestry of interconnected processes. This perspective invites us to rediscover the wonder, complexity, and beauty inherent in the systems we inhabit—and to harness that understanding to shape a better future.

Epilogue

About three-quarters of the way through writing the first draft of *Time Molecules*, life reminded me just how central the concept of time (and its relentless march) is to everything we do. In November 2024, I had a pacemaker implanted, an experience that represents my first major surgery. As disruptive as the experience was, it deepened my connection to the core ideas in this book and provided refreshed perspectives on the importance of transformative events and systems.

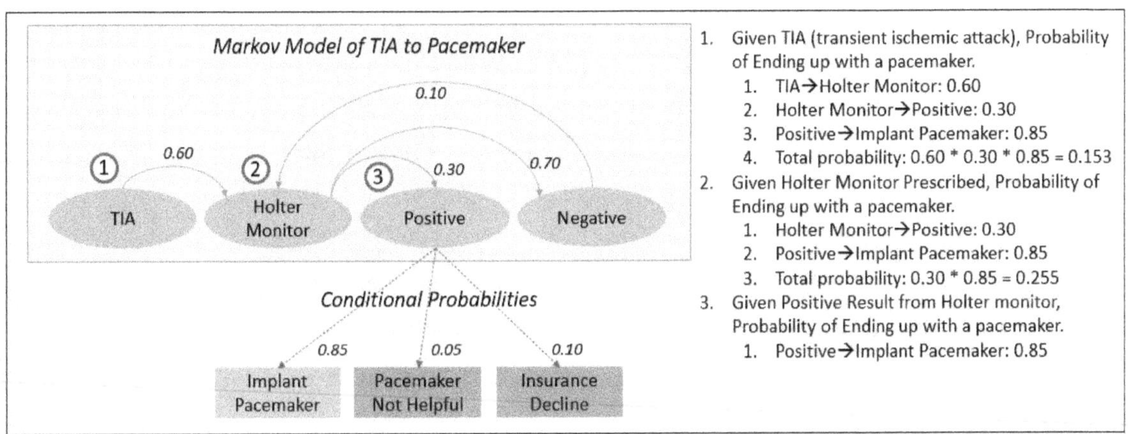

How ironic. Here I was, writing about the interplay of events in time—Markov models, event-driven data, and how systems adapt to the unexpected—and suddenly, my heart became the system at the center of a very personal event stream. Each beat, each irregularity, each test, each test result, and ultimately, the intervention to stabilize it were all part of a process that I saw through the lens of this work.

Immediately after arriving home, I searched YouTube for videos of people sharing their experiences. It comforted me to see so many people sharing stories that were similar to mine in a similar sequence. They spoke of events that I already experienced and events I ultimately did encounter over the next few months.

A pacemaker isn't just a medical device; it's an orchestrator of events. It monitors, measures, senses, and acts—doing its part to ensure that the rhythm of my life continues uninterrupted. It's a machine that interfaces directly with biology, converting signals into action, much like how Time Molecules distill event data into analytical insights. The pacemaker doesn't replace the heart's natural process; it supplements it, stepping in when needed. Similarly, the frameworks in this book are not about dictating decisions—they are tools to guide, support, and optimize the natural flow of processes in an organization.

This experience reinforced a central theme of this book: time, and the events that shape it, are the foundation of every system. Whether it's a heartbeat, a supply chain, or a customer journey, the ability to observe, understand, and adapt to these rhythms is what enables growth, resilience, and innovation.

Writing *Time Molecules* is about connecting the theoretical with the practical, the abstract with the tangible (the Time Solution as a sample system). My pacemaker journey brought that connection home in a way I never expected—not to mention never wanting it. It reminded me that while we often focus on the complexity of systems, their real beauty lies in their ability to keep moving forward—one event, one transition, one heartbeat at a time.

The top joke among my fellow pacemaker recipients is that we became a cyborg. But we've really always been cyborgs—at least since the first hominid used a rock to smash something, whether it was a nut or a head. It's all about extending our capabilities, the ability to reach deeper into the processes in which we are immersed.

My real insight is that after a lifetime of planned events—everything about kindergarten through college, 45 years of project-based work towards planned project goals, all mapped onto calendars—I fostered this subconscious notion that any unplanned events could only be bad and something to proactively mitigate, if not eliminate. That makes for a very unnecessarily stressful life. The world is much bigger than any human-made plans.

Unwanted events are beyond our control. My pacemaker was a serious unplanned event that blew up my holy schedule of deliverables. Sometimes shit just happens. So rather than worrying about them, do what we can, but focus more on learning how to stay calm in the midst of chaos, and how best to pick up the pieces as the starting material from which to pick up your bag and continue down the trail.

Appendices

This is a list of appendices that complement the main content of this book, providing additional context, examples, and technical details to support the concepts discussed. The appendices are in the Github repository in the file:

Time_Molecules_Book_Eugene_Asahara_Appendices.pdf

Each appendix dives deeper into specific aspects of the framework, from comparing AI models to handling event data in real-world systems.

- **Appendix A - The Enterprise Intelligence Prompt**
  Describes the core components of the Enterprise Knowledge Graph (EKG), including the Knowledge Graph, Data Catalog, Insight Space Graph, and Tuple Correlation Web, as well as how they interact within a Retrieval-Augmented Generation (RAG) workflow.
- **Appendix B - Comparing LLMs and Markov Models**
  Explores the strengths and limitations of Large Language Models (LLMs) and Markov models, emphasizing their complementary roles in sequence modeling and process analysis.
- **Appendix C - Key Performance Indicator Status**
  Details the integration of KPI status values into the EKG, showing how they link to data sources, strategy maps, and Markov models to analyze transitions and optimize processes.
- **Appendix D - Azure Event Hub vs Apache Kafka**
  Compares these two event streaming platforms, highlighting their suitability for different organizational infrastructures and their roles in feeding event data into the Time Molecules framework.
- **Appendix E - Markov Models vs Markov Decision Processes**
  Clarifies the differences between Markov models, which are predictive, and Markov Decision Processes (MDPs), which incorporate actions and rewards for decision-making under uncertainty
- **Appendix F - NFA as the Time Crystal Complement to Time Molecules**
  Discusses the complementary roles of Non-Deterministic Finite Automata (NFA) and

Markov models, with NFAs focusing on recognizing sequences in real-time while Markov models predict future events.

- **Appendix G - Handling Events Arriving Out of Order in Streaming Systems**
  Provides best practices for managing late-arriving or out-of-sequence events in streaming and BI systems, ensuring accurate Markov model analysis and insights.
- **Appendix H - State/Event, Cause/Effect, and Event Sourcing**
  Examines the relationships between states, events, and causality, and how these concepts are captured in event-sourcing approaches for business processes.
- **Appendix I - Markov Models in Modern AI: A Complement, Not a Competitor**
  Compares Markov models, RNNs, and Transformers, positioning Markov models as lightweight, interpretable tools that complement more complex AI systems for process analysis.
- **Appendix J - Weighted Standard Deviation** is an approximation method for calculating overall variability across multiple segments without reprocessing all data points. It combines segment-level standard deviations by weighting them based on their row counts. While less precise than full recalculation, this method enables efficient high-level analysis, particularly in distributed systems.

Glossary

Abductive Reasoning: A logical process that starts with an observation and seeks the simplest and most likely explanation, often used to generate hypotheses. Example: "The grass is wet this morning. The simplest explanation is that it rained last night." Application: Used in diagnostics, scientific hypothesis generation, and artificial intelligence for making educated guesses based on incomplete information.

Aggregation (in OLAP context): The process of summarizing or combining data from a detailed level to a higher level within an OLAP cube, typically involving operations like sum, average, or count. Example: Summing daily sales data to produce monthly sales totals in an OLAP cube. Application: Helps reduce data complexity and improve query performance by pre-computing common summaries, enabling faster analysis and reporting.

At-Scale: The ability of a system to efficiently handle large volumes of data or computational tasks, often through distributed architectures and parallel processing. In the context of Time Molecules, "at-scale" refers to processing vast amounts of event data and generating numerous Markov models simultaneously, enabling real-time or near-real-time insights across complex processes.

Azure Cosmos DB: A globally distributed, multi-model NoSQL database service providing turnkey horizontal scale and single-digit-millisecond latencies. CosmosDB supports key/value, document, graph (Gremlin), and column-family data models under a unified APIs framework.

Azure Stream Analytics: A fully managed, real-time analytics service that performs Complex Event Processing on live data streams. You can ingest events directly from Apache Kafka clusters or Azure Event Hubs, then write continuous, SQL-like queries to detect patterns, compute rolling aggregates, and correlate across multiple streams. Outputs can be pushed to Data Lake storage, Azure SQL, PowerBI streaming datasets, CosmosDB, or serverless functions—making it ideal for low-latency alerting, anomaly detection, and pre-aggregation before downstream processing.

Business Intelligence (BI): BI refers to the technologies, applications, and practices used to collect, integrate, analyze, and present business information. The primary goal of BI is to support better business decision-making by providing actionable insights based on data. BI systems enable organizations to gather data from internal and external sources, transform it into meaningful metrics and reports, and distribute this information to decision-makers in a timely and accessible manner. Common components of BI include data warehousing, data mining, online analytical processing (OLAP), and dashboards. BI tools help companies track key performance indicators (KPIs), identify trends, and uncover inefficiencies, ultimately enhancing strategic planning and operational efficiency.

Case: In the context of Markov models, a case refers to a series of events or states associated with a specific instance, such as a particular sale, website visit, or customer service interaction. Each case represents a sequence of transitions that can be analyzed to understand patterns and predict future states.

Complex Event Processing (CEP): A method of analyzing and reacting to streams of events in real time or near real time. CEP identifies meaningful patterns, such as sequences, correlations, or anomalies, from raw event data to generate actionable insights or trigger responses. It is widely used in scenarios like fraud detection, IoT monitoring, and operational intelligence.

Concurrency (Databases) – The ability of a database to handle multiple queries or transactions simultaneously. High query concurrency means the system efficiently processes many user requests at once without significant delays or conflicts.

Data Warehouse (DW): A centralized repository for storing structured data from multiple sources, optimized for querying, reporting, and analytics. It organizes data using schemas like star or snowflake, enabling historical analysis and supporting business intelligence (BI) initiatives.

Deductive Reasoning: A logical process where conclusions are drawn from a set of premises assumed to be true, starting with a general rule and applying it to a specific case. Example: "All humans are mortal. Socrates is a human. Therefore, Socrates is mortal." Application: Common in mathematics, formal logic, and certain machine learning tasks like Hidden Markov Models.

Directed Graph: A type of graph in which edges have a specific direction, connecting one node (vertex) to another. Each edge is represented as an ordered pair of nodes, indicating the direction of the relationship. Directed graphs are commonly used to model systems with dependencies or flows, such as workflows, state transitions, or data relationships. *Unlike directed acyclic graphs (DAGs), directed graphs may contain cycles, allowing the system to revisit nodes.* This entry is especially relevant to Markov models, which are central to Time Molecules and are typically represented as directed graphs where nodes are events and edges denote the probability of transitioning from one event to another.

Effect Correlation Score (ECS): The Effect Correlation Score quantifies the relationship between the status of a KPI ("good," "minor pain," "pain," "major pain," "dead") and other metrics or events. It provides insights into how changes in the underlying processes or conditions influence the status of key performance indicators, helping to map trade-offs or synergies within a strategy map. This score is particularly useful for identifying the downstream effects of actions and for prioritizing competing objectives in a business strategy.

Emission (in HMM context): The observed output in a Hidden Markov Model, which is generated by the hidden states according to certain probabilities. Example: In a speech recognition system, the sound waves produced are the emissions corresponding to phoneme states. Application: Used in HMMs to link hidden states to observable events, enabling predictions or classifications based on these observations.

Event Processing Architecture: A system designed to handle the detection, processing, and response to events. These architectures typically deal with large volumes of events, enabling organizations to analyze and act on the events in a structured and efficient manner. It can include various technologies to ingest, store, and process event data for real-time decision-making.

Event Sourcing: A software pattern where the state of an entity is derived by replaying a sequence of events, rather than storing the current state directly. This approach enables the system to reconstruct historical states, provides an audit trail, and allows for greater flexibility in handling changes over time.

Event Stream Processing Solutions: Technologies that enable real-time processing and analysis of event data as it streams in from sources such as sensors, log files, or applications. These solutions allow for actions such as filtering, aggregating, or correlating events to extract meaningful insights without waiting for all the data to be collected.

Events: Individual occurrences or actions that can be recorded and analyzed, often forming part of a sequence or time series.

Event-Driven Architecture (EDA): A design pattern in which the flow of program execution is determined by the occurrence of events (actions, changes, or conditions in a system). In EDA, systems react to these events in real time, often triggering automated processes or workflows based on the event's attributes.

Heuristic: A practical approach to problem-solving that uses a rule of thumb to produce a solution that is good enough for the given context. Example: Guessing a password by trying the most common ones first. Application: Widely used in artificial intelligence, search algorithms, and decision-making where exact solutions are not feasible.

HMM (Hidden Markov Model): A statistical model that represents systems with hidden states, where transitions between states are governed by probabilities, and each state produces observable outputs called emissions. Example: Predicting the sequence of words in speech recognition based on observed sound patterns. Application: Widely used in speech recognition, bioinformatics, and financial modeling to analyze sequences where the true state is not directly observable.

Hockey Stick Curve: A line graph displaying a sudden, exponential increase following a period of relatively flat or modest growth, resembling the shape of a hockey stick. Commonly used in business, technology, and science, it represents phenomena such as rapid revenue growth, viral product adoption, or accelerated climate change impacts. The "handle" represents the initial slow progress, while the "blade" depicts the sharp uptick.

Inductive Reasoning: A logical process where general conclusions are drawn from specific observations or data points, identifying patterns to form broader conclusions. Example: "The sun has risen in the east every day so far. Therefore, the sun will rise in the east tomorrow." Application: Predominant in machine learning algorithms such as linear regression, decision trees, and clustering.

Inference: The process of drawing conclusions or making predictions based on evidence and reasoning. Example: Predicting tomorrow's weather based on current trends. Application: In machine learning, inference involves applying a trained model to new data to make predictions.

IoT (Internet of Things): A network of physical devices, vehicles, appliances, and other objects embedded with sensors, software, and connectivity that allows them to collect and exchange data over the Internet. IoT enables these "smart" devices to communicate with each other and with centralized systems, facilitating automation, real-time monitoring, and data-driven insights across various industries. Examples include smart home devices, wearable technology, and industrial sensors.

IRI (Internationalized Resource Identifier): A generalization of URI (Uniform Resource Identifier) that allows a wider range of characters, including those beyond ASCII, such as characters from different languages. An IRI can be converted into a URI by encoding non-ASCII characters.

KPI Status: One measure that indicates the current performance level of a KPI relative to its target. It provides a real-time assessment of progress, often categorized using a simple rating system (e.g., on track, at risk, below target) based on a range of 0.0 through 1.0 or -1.0 through 1.0.

Key Performance Indicators (KPIs): Quantifiable metrics used to measure progress toward specific objectives. They help organizations track performance, assess effectiveness, and guide decision-making. KPIs can be financial, operational, or strategic, depending on the goals they are designed to evaluate. The traditional components include:

- **Value** – The current measured result of the KPI.
- **Target/Goal** – The desired benchmark or objective the KPI is aiming for.
- **Status** – The current state of the KPI (e.g., on track, at risk, behind target).
- **Trend** – The direction of movement over time (e.g., improving, declining, stable).

Knowledge Base: A structured, queryable repository of facts and relationships about entities, typically represented in RDF and linked through ontologies and vocabularies (e.g., DBpedia).

Knowledge Graph: A graph-based data structure where entities (nodes) are connected by relationships (edges), typically described using an ontology. Knowledge graphs support reasoning and querying over facts and are foundational to the Semantic Web. Beyond ontologies, they often include other structured metadata to organize meaning.

Large Language Model (LLM): A type of artificial intelligence model, typically based on deep learning, that is trained on vast amounts of text data to understand and generate human-like language. Example: GPT-4, which can generate coherent text based on a given prompt. Application: Used in natural language processing tasks such as text generation, translation, summarization, and conversational agents.

Logic: A systematic method of reasoning that ensures consistent and valid conclusions, forming the foundation for deductive reasoning. Example: Using logical operators to evaluate a mathematical expression. Application: Central to the design of algorithms, programming languages, and automated reasoning systems like Prolog.

Machine Learning (ML): A subset of artificial intelligence that involves training algorithms to recognize patterns and make predictions or decisions based on data. Example: A machine learning algorithm might be trained to identify spam emails by analyzing large datasets of labeled emails. Application: Used across industries for predictive analytics, recommendation systems, image and speech recognition, and more.

Markov Decision Process (MDP): An extension of Markov models that includes decision-making capabilities, where an agent takes actions in states to maximize cumulative rewards, guided by a policy that defines the best action to take in each state.

Markov Model (MM): A mathematical system that undergoes transitions from one state to another within a state space, characterized by the memoryless property where the future state depends only on the current state.

Massively Parallel Processing (MPP): A database architecture that distributes data and workloads across multiple processors or nodes, enabling the simultaneous execution of queries and tasks. MPP systems are designed for scalability and performance, making them ideal for processing massive datasets and supporting complex analytics in real-time or batch environments.

Neo4j: A graph database management system designed to store and query relationships between data. Unlike relational databases, Neo4j models data as nodes, relationships, and properties, making it ideal for use cases where connections between data points are essential, such as social networks, recommendation engines, and fraud detection. Example: Using Neo4j to map customer purchase behaviors and identify patterns in a retail environment.

OLAP (Online Analytical Processing): A type of data processing focused on complex queries and data analysis. OLAP systems enable the analysis of large datasets through multidimensional views, supporting operations like aggregation, slicing, and dicing. It's typically used in business intelligence to extract insights from historical data. Example: Analyzing sales trends across various regions and time periods to optimize marketing efforts.

OLAP Cubes: Multidimensional data structures that allow for the fast retrieval and analysis of data from different perspectives, often used in business intelligence. Example: An OLAP cube might store sales data, allowing users to quickly view totals by region, product, or time period. Application: Used in business intelligence to perform complex queries and data analysis efficiently, supporting decision-making processes.

OLTP (Online Transaction Processing): A class of data processing that handles large volumes of simple, transactional operations. OLTP systems are designed for fast query processing and maintaining data integrity in systems like databases used in banking or e-commerce, where quick insert, update, and delete operations are crucial. Example: A banking system that processes customer transactions, ensuring real-time updates and data consistency.

Ontology: A formal representation of concepts, entities, and their relationships within a domain, often enabling reasoning, interoperability, and semantic integration. Ontologies are typically implemented using RDF/OWL standards and include definitions for classes, properties, and rules (e.g., DBpedia Ontology).

Process Blindness: The inability to recognize or understand the underlying processes within a complex system, leading to a focus on isolated events or outcomes without appreciating how they are interconnected. Process blindness often hinders effective decision-making by obscuring the flow and evolution of events over time. Removing process blindness allows for deeper insights into systems and enables more strategic thinking.

Process Mining: Process mining is a data-driven technique used to analyze and optimize business processes by extracting insights from event logs generated by enterprise systems (ERP, CRM). It automatically maps the real flow of activities within an organization, helping to identify inefficiencies, deviations from intended workflows, and areas for improvement. Key types of process mining include discovery (creating process models), conformance checking (ensuring processes adhere to rules), and enhancement (optimizing processes for efficiency). It bridges the gap between traditional business process management and modern data analytics, enabling continuous process optimization.

Prompt: A *prompt* is the input given to a Large Language Model (LLM) to guide its response. It defines the task or context, ranging from a simple question to detailed instructions, shaping the model's output accordingly.

RAG (Retrieval-Augmented Generation): A hybrid approach in AI that combines retrieval of relevant documents or knowledge with language generation to produce more accurate and contextually relevant responses. Example: A chatbot using RAG might retrieve a relevant article to inform its generated response about a specific topic. Application: Enhances the capabilities of language models by grounding their outputs in factual, up-to-date information, often used in customer support, content generation, and research tools.

Reasoning: The cognitive process of making sense of information, drawing conclusions, and making decisions based on evidence, logic, or intuition. Example: Determining the best route to a destination based on traffic data. Application: Used in decision-making, problem-solving, and analytical processes across various fields.

S-Curve: A graph depicting a process that begins with slow growth, accelerates rapidly during a middle phase, and then tapers off as it approaches a plateau. Commonly used to model innovation adoption, market growth, or learning processes, the "S" shape reflects the natural progression from early struggles to rapid expansion and eventual maturity or saturation.

Scalar Function: A user-defined function (UDF) in T-SQL that returns a single value (a scalar) for each execution. Scalar functions can accept input parameters, perform operations, and return a result based on the logic defined within the function.

Semantic Web: An extension of the current web where data is structured and linked in a way that allows machines to understand, interpret, and reason over it. It uses standards like RDF, OWL, and SPARQL to represent relationships between concepts, enabling more intelligent data integration, search, and automation.

Sequence: An ordered list of events or data points, which may occur at irregular intervals and can include multiple types of events.

Stored Procedure (sproc): A precompiled collection of SQL statements and optional control-of-flow logic that can be executed as a single unit to perform a specific task.

Stream Processing: A computational method that processes data continuously as it arrives. Instead of waiting for a complete data set, stream processing handles data piece by piece in real time, making it ideal for applications like real-time monitoring, analytics, and fraud detection.

System of Processes: A heterogeneous network of interconnected and interdependent processes that collectively contribute to the functioning and evolution of a broader system. In this context, a process refers to a sequence of actions or events that transform inputs into outputs, often interacting with other processes at shared touchpoints. These interactions—whether collaborative, competitive, or incidental—form a dynamic ecosystem where the behavior of one process can influence, constrain, or enable others. Unlike isolated processes, a system of processes emphasizes the relational dynamics and feedback loops that define complex, adaptive systems, such as businesses, biological organisms, or engineered machines.

Systems Thinking: Systems thinking is an approach to problem-solving that views complex systems as interconnected wholes, rather than a collection of isolated parts. It emphasizes understanding the relationships and interactions between different elements within a system, and how changes in one part can affect the entire system. This perspective is used to better understand and manage complex, dynamic processes in fields like business, engineering, and ecology. Systems thinking encourages looking beyond immediate causes to identify patterns, feedback loops, and long-term impacts, fostering holistic decision-making and sustainable solutions.

T-SQL: Transact-SQL, Microsoft's proprietary extension to SQL, used for managing and querying relational databases with added procedural programming features like variables, loops, and error handling.

Table-Valued Function (TVF): A user-defined function in SQL that returns a table data type, allowing the output to be queried like a regular table.

Theory of Computation: A branch of computer science that explores the principles of computation, including the design and analysis of algorithms, the power of abstract machines (like Turing machines and finite automata), and the inherent limitations of what can be computed. It provides the foundation for understanding complexity, computability, and the efficiency of computational processes.

Time Series: A specific type of sequence where data points are collected at regular, evenly spaced intervals, typically involving a single type of measurement.

Tuple: A structured combination of related elements, representing a single, meaningful entity or data point. For example, (coffee, sales, Seattle) combines specific dimensions—product, metric, and location—into one coherent unit. Tuples are used to capture relationships or facts in databases, knowledge graphs, and other data models.

Index